A GENEALOGY OF ITALIAN THOUGHT

Also available from Bloomsbury:

An Introduction to Contemporary Italian Thought, Tim Christiaens, Joost de Bloois, and Stijn De Cauwer

The Bloomsbury Italian Philosophy Reader, edited by Michael Lewis and David Rose

A GENEALOGY OF ITALIAN THOUGHT

From Operaismo to Biopolitics

Dario Gentili
Translated by Clara Pope

BLOOMSBURY ACADEMIC
LONDON • NEW YORK • OXFORD • NEW DELHI • SYDNEY

BLOOMSBURY ACADEMIC
Bloomsbury Publishing Plc, 50 Bedford Square, London, WC1B 3DP, UK
Bloomsbury Publishing Inc, 1359 Broadway, New York, NY 10018, USA
Bloomsbury Publishing Ireland, 29 Earlsfort Terrace, Dublin 2, D02 AY28, Ireland

BLOOMSBURY, BLOOMSBURY ACADEMIC and the Diana logo are trademarks of Bloomsbury Publishing Plc

First published in 2012 in Italy as *Italian Theory: Dall'operaismo alla biopolitica* by il Mulino

First published in Great Britain 2026

Cover design by Jade Barnett

A catalogue record for this book is available from the British Library.

A catalog record for this book is available from the Library of Congress.

ISBN: HB: 978-1-3504-6358-5
PB: 978-1-3504-6357-8
ePDF: 978-1-3504-6360-8
eBook: 978-1-3504-6359-2

Typeset by Deanta Global Publishing Services, Chennai, India
Printed and bound in Great Britain

For product safety related questions contact productsafety@bloomsbury.com.

To find out more about our authors and books visit www.bloomsbury.com and sign up for our newsletters.

CONTENTS

A NOTE ON THE TEXT

This is the English translation of *Italian Theory: Dall'operaismo alla biopolitica* (Bologna: il Mulino, 2012), which contributed significantly to the debate on Italian thought. The opportunity to translate this work, which is now more than a decade old, allowed for a revision of the entire text, an updating of the bibliographical references, and the addition of a final chapter, aiming to bring this genealogy up to the present.

INTRODUCTION
SINISTERITAS

'I live, I am partisan.
This is why I hate those who do not take sides;
I hate those who are indifferent.'

—Antonio Gramsci

1.

In recent years, the terms 'Italian Theory', 'Italian thought' and the 'Italian difference' have all been used to signal the return of Italian philosophy to the international stage.[1] Indeed, after the crisis of various philosophies linked to postmodernism and the 'linguistic turn', Italian philosophy's contribution to the global debate has opened up a new phase in contemporary philosophy. Its current configuration cannot be ascribed to one thinker alone, but ranges from Antonio Gramsci, referenced in numerous cultural spheres,[2] to biopolitics, by way of early and late operaismo.

In this book, I will attempt to reconstruct the genealogy of that Italian philosophical thought referred to as 'Italian Theory' in the international debate, focusing particularly on biopolitics as its most recent outcome. For although first introduced by Michel Foucault, it was Italian philosophers who brought biopolitics to global attention a good thirty years later. The aim of this book is to trace a debate in Italian philosophy that has often been misunderstood or remained implicit, and which, lying at the interface between philosophy and politics, is interwoven with the recent history of the country. This debate was not destined to end in biopolitics, and is not a necessary premise of biopolitics, but can help us to shed new light on our understanding of biopolitics. However, I also want to show that some of the main thinkers in this debate have had a wary or resistant, if not openly polemical, attitude towards biopolitics, particularly those who embraced political theology after the Italian 'long '68' (1968–77). In extreme tension with biopolitics, political theology became prominent in Italian thought as early as the 1980s, through the work of Mario Tronti and Massimo Cacciari, as well as in Giorgio Agamben's and Roberto Esposito's critiques of it. This is only one of many points of tension in Italian Theory, whose peculiarity lies in the very fact that it is traversed by often-irresolvable conflicts and divergences, shaping both its genealogy and content.

2.

The term 'Italian Theory' brings together various philosophical conceptions with an assumed common Italian origin. The first question we need to ask ourselves is whether we can legitimately talk of an 'Italian difference' with respect to the international philosophical debate. Is there something about Italian philosophy that allows it to read and interpret current events in a particular way? Does it really provide, to use the Foucauldian expression often referenced by Italian philosophers, an 'ontology of actuality'? Today more than ever, philosophy is searching for new categories to understand the present. Italian philosophy has contributed to this search with concepts such as biopolitics, Empire, bare life, the commons and economic theology, either created from scratch or found in the conceptual heritage of the twentieth century and developed within the context of globalization. But why has Italian philosophy been particularly adept at producing concepts adequate to the present? And is it in fact possible to speak of an 'Italian philosophy' at all? Can we find a common thread linking its divergent thinkers? In order to try to answer these questions, we should also consider the concept of 'theory', which comes with its own problems and ambiguities.

The term 'Italian Theory' clearly echoes that of 'French Theory' and is used with a dose of irony. François Cusset's book *French Theory* (2008), largely discusses the reception of certain French philosophers (although not just philosophers) within North American humanities departments and their sometimes slightly forced inclusion within a shared post-structuralist framework. Thus, on the one hand, *French Theory* demonstrates the way in which North American academic culture introduces, adopts and re-elaborates thought from Europe, and, on the other, it considers the 'return effect' with which its move to the North American 'outside' has influenced, contaminated and even betrayed the reflections of the thinkers in question. While not wishing to downplay the way in which broadbrush theoretical labels such as French Theory neutralize differences, it is also important to emphasize that these umbrella terms can paradoxically bring to light the 'impure' and 'hybrid' character of the theories they aim to contain (thereby countering simple nationalist readings). With the weakening of continental philosophy in the face of the growing influence of analytical philosophy, a new political and social role has emerged for the former which takes it beyond the classical confines of philosophical knowledge. This begins from a critique of its own metaphysical framework, with the leading exponents of French Theory taking the radical step of pushing philosophy outside of itself, into the arts, literature and other spheres. Thus, the crisis of continental philosophy – which led to the introflexion of philosophical questioning towards the epistemological status of its knowledge and the consequent renunciation of any affirmative, let alone political, position – ended up producing an impure philosophy that crossed over into the humanities. In short, if, on the one hand, philosophy ended up becoming entrenched in a sort of 'jargon of authenticity' (to which we can paradoxically trace both analytical philosophy and that continental philosophy nostalgic for metaphysics), on the other hand, it has contributed to producing so-called theory as an 'inauthentic' philosophical discourse that can be used across a wide range of disciplines.

However, Italian Theory differs from French Theory in one key respect. The 'return effect' produced by international interest helped to elaborate Italian Theory from within, leading to an attempt to emphasize its internal differences and original contributions, and to tie together the threads of a narrative that had been broken, dispersed and neglected in the 'counterrevolution' following the Italian 'long '68' (Virno and Hardt 1997). It is also important to stress that this is not about affirming the original 'Italian-ness' of certain themes; on the contrary, another characteristic of Italian Theory is its impure and non-national character. In short, Italian Theory cannot be dismissed as an American simplification, for it has become a way of reflecting, also from within Italy, on the potential and limits of certain strands of Italian philosophy that have recently emerged in the international debate, at a moment when other previously prominent European philosophies, such as hermeneutics and deconstruction, are losing ground. In short – to adopt the term Alain Badiou (2022) used in relation to French philosophy – it is about considering, both within and outside of Italy, the 'moment' of Italian philosophy within the current historical, political, economic and cultural conjuncture.

3.

Italian thought entered the international debate – for instance, through Antonio Negri and Michael Hardt's *Empire* and Giorgio Agamben's *Homo Sacer* – in the context of the crisis of postmodernism at the end of the 1990s. Although postmodern thought dominated international philosophy for about twenty years, it never became hegemonic in Italy, particularly in philosophy. And although the *pensiero debole* (weak thought) of Gianni Vattimo and Pier Aldo Rovatti, which was completely consistent with postmodernism, was hugely influential (also at an international level), it was met with much resistance in Italy. Rather than following the various 'post-'s in their leap beyond the modern, most Italian philosophy concentrated on excavating, deconstructing and rethinking the categories of modernity, albeit in very different ways. They took the crisis and the collapse of ideologies and 'grand narratives' as an opportunity to address the decisive questions of modern politics. Whereas these approaches had originally been dismissed as backward in relation to the trends of postmodernism, their fortunes changed when the new millennium highlighted the unresolved and interwoven problems of the modern, or at least the shadow they still cast, contradicting the declared 'end of history'.[3] The crisis of the modern led a number of Italian philosophers to seek out another modernity, returning to thinkers who had been 'cursed' (*maledetti*) by the modern philosophical tradition. Above all, they looked to Machiavelli, at the origins of Italian political thought, who had inspired multiple Italian thinkers from Gramsci onwards. However, there are huge differences, at times even contradictions, in the way these thinkers interpreted his conception of politics and the genealogies stemming from it.[4]

Some Italian philosophers also drew on historical events and historicity in order to respond to the global disorientation caused by what we might call the 'return of history'. As Machiavelli teaches, historicizing thought means dropping it into specific 'conjunctures' at different times, thus rendering it immediately political, that is, directly implicated in political struggle. The 'golden age' of globalization had promised a departure from the bipolarity and latent conflict that had marked the period between World War II and the fall of the Berlin Wall in 1989, supposedly signalling a newly pacified and unified world. However, with the collapse of the Soviet Union and so the disappearance of the last real (albeit idealized) alternative to the capitalist-liberal model, new conflicts and divisions arose. Globalization emerged from the integration of the entire world within the capitalist market – a source of further divisions, conflicts and inequalities – as well as from the loss of the 'outside' and of the 'alternative'. It thus arose as a political problem.

The worldwide repercussions of globalization had had an initial gestation period in Italy, although obviously on a limited scale and in a way that was specific to Italy. Given that loyalty to one of the two main parties – either Christian Democracy or the Italian Communist Party (PCI) – was stronger than that to the state or the nation, Italy had reproduced the worldwide division into two foreign policy blocs on a domestic level.[5] However, the roots of the 'Italian case' also went deeper. For while it is true that it was in the second half of the twentieth century that Italian politics became above all about siding with one of the two main 'ethical parties', as Remo Bodei (1998) Hegelianistically defined them, the political primacy of the party and its historical anteriority with respect to the nation state (or any other political form) can already be found in Machiavelli, if not in Dante Alighieri.[6] And so, the sudden disappearance of the two ethical parties at the beginning of the 1990s created extreme disorientation, anticipating a situation found throughout the Western world today. Instead of opening new frontiers, the events of 1989 resulted in a sense of loss in Italy, which it took with it into the era of globalization. And yet, the 'partisan point of view' – which characterized extra-parliamentary political movements during the 1970s – remained the starting point from which to initiate any process of politicization or to seek out new forms of subjectification. In Italy, the global market and the neoliberal model of government were not able to compensate for the loss of the two major parties and their way of doing politics. Already in the 1960s and 1970s, Italian radical thought had discovered that 'politicalness' *(politicità)* was to be found within the Fordist and then post-Fordist modes of production rather than outside of them, in keeping with a certain strain of Marxist thought – including Gramsci – that held that the contradictions and crises of the system were always produced within it. So, if politics is produced within economic apparatuses, then politics as conflict – a politics 'within and against' – would now have to be reproposed as a politics within the global market, rather than as an alternative from outside.

Thus, drawing on a tradition stretching back to Machiavelli, Italian philosophy's political reflections differed from those accompanying the rise of globalization elsewhere, which, by returning political action to a question of ethics, tended to neutralize its conflictual character.[7] Not only, therefore, was Italian philosophy able to respond to a renewed need for politics within the context of neo-globalization, but it also recognized the need for a conception of politics as conflict, that is, for a politics capable of strengthening the constituent potential of conflict.

4.

The concept that I adopt to analyse the philosophical, historical and political peculiarity of Italian thought is that of *sinisteritas*: a Latin word indicating the 'cursed part' which is the etymological root of the Italian word *sinistra* (left), and is associated with error and deviation from the correct line of the 'right' (*destra*), which is the side of rectitude, rightness and the norm. This root is a peculiarity of Italian, not found in any other Western language: for instance, the words 'left', '*Links*', '*gauche*' and '*izquierda*' have no etymological connection with *sinisteritas* and its meaning. An article written in the early 1980s by Tronti entitled 'Sinistra' (1981), and various contributions – including those by Cacciari and Vattimo – from a conference at the time focusing on the Italian peculiarity of the concept of *sinistra*, argue that this was not merely a lexical curiosity, but an important aspect of the 'Italian difference'. These thinkers were thus already questioning the meaning of left-wing politics and sensing the beginning of a new era at a time when the force of attraction of the outside had been weakened but was not yet completely compromised. Again, Italian philosophy was raising questions that would only emerge elsewhere after 1989. As well as the reference to institutional politics and the historical parties of the Italian left, the concept of *sinisteritas* allows us to interpret the category of dualism found in the most important Italian philosophers on a political level. It recalls an original dualism[8] that cannot be reduced simply to the logic of political alignments based on the ideological or party-based right-left opposition – a legacy of modernity that has all but disappeared[9] – but references conflictuality itself. Furthermore, in order to position itself on the parliamentary left (*sinistra*), the *sinisteritas* had to 'right itself' so as not to be maladroit (*maldestra*) in its government – doing incompetently what the right (*destra*) does well. One of the historical anomalies of Italian democracy that the idea of *sinisteritas* helps us to explore is that the PCI, despite being the largest communist party in the Western world and the second largest party in Italy, was never in government, and so never dictated '*la linea retta*' (the 'right' or correct line) to the country, but only to its own side or 'part' outside of parliament. Thus, until its dissolution in 1991, it always maintained an ambivalence between *sinisteritas* – as class conflict – and the parliamentary left (*sinistra*). However, what really prevents the idea of *sinisteritas* from fully corresponding to the parliamentary left is the precedence of conflict over the place in which it occurs. The emergence of an original conflictuality, which is the emergence of politics itself, finds its specific location in each particular case, whether that be the factory, society, the party, the state, life, or somewhere else; parliament is only one of many potential places of conflict, although it does play a specific role in bringing social conflicts into order. Furthermore, *sinisteritas* does not correspond to a particular object or to the content of the thought of this or that thinker, but to the philosophical-political procedure for defining different conceptions or formations of thought through deviations and discontinuities. It indicates a method of reflection that is alternative, even antagonistic, to the line of thought from which it deviates. Each deviation constitutes new forms of alignment and normalization, which in turn give rise to new ruptures and fractures, to further bifurcations. Continuity in discontinuity: this is the common thread that the concept of *sinisteritas* helps us to identify in the various interwoven strands of Italian political philosophy over the last fifty years.

5.

The birth of operaismo and the work of its first theoretician, Mario Tronti, is a clear example of *sinisteritas*: it is a break with the historicist and humanist tradition of Togliatti's PCI – the so-called De Sanctis-Gramsci line – and a re-reading of Marx that favours his 'scientific' approach in *Capital* over the theory of historical materialism, particularly in light of the Fordist industrial revolution taking place in Italy in the early 1960s. But this was only the initial rupture, the first of a long series of breaks and deviations that led to the creation of numerous and diverse – often militant – journals that would help shape the Italian philosophical-political landscape until the 1990s.

This rupture undoubtedly began with Tronti's *Workers and Capital* (2019), which turned the Marxism of his time on its head. It would then provide the premise for further deviations and bifurcations, which gave rise to other philosophies, in particular, that of Antonio Negri. In short, on a philosophical level, *Workers and Capital* broke with dialectical thought and the more Hegelian Marx to instead base itself on the dualism, dichotomy, antagonism and conflict between workers and capital, with no possible synthesis. Tronti would continue to follow this line, although with differing emphases, from the autonomy of the political up until his final works on political theology. This dualistic approach is also shared by various other Italian philosophers, in concepts such as negative thinking, the tragic and the impolitical. Although each developing and deviating from the dominant line in different ways, I will argue that these concepts can all be traced back to the dispositif of crisis.[10] Included in this dispositif are terms such as antagonism, difference and resistance, which Italian philosophy has continuously reproposed, and which have returned to the fore after the hopes generated by the fall of the Berlin Wall began to fade. In short, if today's philosophical lexicon increasingly adheres to that of Italian philosophy, it is because Italy has long been a country in crisis. The crisis shaping the current international debate at every level can be seen not only in the Italian economy, but also and above all in Italian politics.

Workers and Capital also allows us to highlight the other meaning of *sinisteritas*: the definition of a political subjectivity that is no longer constructed on the model of dialectical synthesis, as Gramsci's concept of the people was (unlike Gramsci, Tronti understands 'the people' as the product of a culture of mediation, even compromise). *Workers and Capital* instead explores the crisis of this synthesis and the consequent emergence of an antagonistic subjectivity as a 'cursed part'. The political primacy attributed to conflict thus corresponds to an original and irreducible division into parts, where the curse of one of the parts, which derives from its subjection to or exclusion from the norm, can be converted into transformation and innovation. This is confirmed by Tronti, who, despite having declared at the end of the 1980s the final defeat of the workers' movement and the theory it embodied, saves the cursed part's capacity for subjectification with the idea of the left (*sinistra*): 'The idea of *sinistra* is this original element. We cannot do without it. It can only be developed and translated into the language of a critical and disenchanted subjectivity, into the experience of government by those who have never governed' (Tronti 1981: 146–7). This is a form of subjectification that, as Foucault teaches in relation to the dispositifs of modernity, begins from subjugation. For Cacciari, on the other hand, this curse of the left, its *sinisteritas*, is a sort of contradiction in terms with regard to any aspiration to government, so much so that the left can only have a decisive political function if it is able to renounce its curse and reject at source the dualism that opposes it to a righteous part that is blessed to govern.[11] For Vattimo however, who on this matter is surprisingly close to Tronti, the subjectification of the 'cursed part' seems to be the only strong trait of the idea of the left that should be preserved[12] – the question of subjectivity thus represents the persistence of the modern within the postmodern proposal of weak thought. And so, what emerges from the dissolution of the traditional assumptions of the historical left is its original fact: *sinisteritas*, the 'cursed part' or, put another way, the 'curse of being a part'.

6.

Globalization has now become the condition of parts without a party, by which I mean, without the form that the modern political had assigned to the part. Indeed, today the universals and transcendentals that the modern tradition had used to assimilate and immunize the partiality of the part are losing their authority and effectiveness. But now there is a risk that, rather than entering into political conflict, the part will be abandoned to the curse of exclusion. And it is no longer exclusively workers' subjectivity that embodies this cursed part, but any form of subjectification that is irreducible to the political representation of the modern political. The cursed part has taken on various different subjective forms since the 1970s, including, although not limited to, women, the general intellect, bare life and the multitude.

The traditional left-wing parties not only no longer hold the exclusive right to dictate the political line for the subjectification of the cursed part, but also no longer define themselves as partisan political organizations. They now aspire to the government of the whole people: the era of the partisan party (*partito della parte*) is over. In this context, the thinkers and currents of thought that had in the past been committed to attributing a new subjectivity to the cursed part began to reach different and almost antithetical conclusions: there were those who, although arriving there in different ways, ultimately claimed the capability of this part to 'govern' (Tronti and Cacciari); there were those who, on the contrary, saw the greatest reserve of politicalness in the curse of the part, which should 'self-valorize' as cursed (Negri and the Italian feminism of difference); and there were those who, in order to undo the curse, returned ontologically to the origin of every dualism that implies a decision, which divides life into one part worthy of being lived (*bíos*) and another to be denied (*zoé*). It is through emphasizing the latter division – into *bíos* and *zoé*, biopolitics and biopower, *communitas* and *immunitas* – and the possibility of a new type of relation that Agamben, Negri and Esposito introduce the biopolitical paradigm into Italian theory, demonstrating their 'difference'[13] from Foucault's approach, which had focused mainly on providing a genealogy of neoliberal 'governmentality'. Despite their considerable divergences, they all identify biopolitics as the field in which the cursed part can be released from the 'ban' that binds it to subjection. This introduction of the biopolitical paradigm into Italian thought made it possible to separate the cursed part from the dispositif of crisis that bound it to the 'rectitude' of sovereign power in modernity.

Today, biopolitics identifies life as the fundamental location of conflict and as the place in which there can be an undoing of that curse originating in the division into parts. At a time when the concept of the people is returning to old identitarian categories, and in the face of the crisis of globalization, one of the key challenges for thought is how to prevent the conflict and partiality of the part from being cursed, neutralized and denied.

Chapter 1

THE POSTWAR PERIOD
FROM THE PEOPLE-SUBJECT TO THE ANTAGONISTIC SUBJECT

1. The Gramscian line

Any attempt to grasp the originality of Italian philosophy in the second half of the twentieth century must begin from postwar Italian Marxism. It is widely agreed that Marxism in Italy differed from that in other cultural contexts largely due to its roots in the Italian philosophical tradition. However, we will not find this originality in the Italian Communist Party (PCI) headed by Palmiro Togliatti and its 'Italian road to socialism' (Togliatti 1956), which could be seen as a merely instrumental response to the crisis of Stalinism following Khrushchev's 'secret speech' in 1956 denouncing the cult of personality and the crimes of the dictatorship. Norberto Bobbio gives us a more convincing story of this originality and its philosophical development:[1]

> When, after 1945, and especially after the publication of Gramsci's *Notebooks*, the discourse on Marxism was taken up again in Italy, Gramsci was naturally reunited with Labriola, and the idea that Marxism had developed in an original way in Italy and that one could rightly talk of an Italian Marxism gradually began to take shape. In Italy, in the years between Labriola and Gramsci, the grafting of Marxist thought onto other philosophies bore no fruit: there was no true neo-Kantian Marxism, let alone Bergsonian Marxism. The study of Marx's philosophy always took place under the banner of a 'return to Marx'. (Bobbio 1968: XLVI)

Antonio Gramsci thus represents the culmination of what we might call an 'Italian road to Marxism'. Bobbio also provides a historical-philosophical explanation for the way in which Togliatti shaped the cultural policy of the PCI. Togliatti had supervised the editing of the first edition of the *Prison Notebooks* (between 1948 and 1951), organizing them into topics and themes, and influencing the titles of the various volumes. The first volume was entitled *Il materialismo storico e la filosofia di Benedetto Croce* (Historical materialism and the philosophy of Benedetto Croce),[2] and was intended to encourage readers to see Gramsci's work as an overturning of Benedetto Croce's historicism, and thus to see Gramsci himself as the author of the Anti-Croce he had called for. Based on the role that Friedrich Engels's *Anti-Dühring* had played for the Marxism of its time, Gramsci gave the Anti-Croce the task of destroying the hegemony that the bourgeois capitalist 'intellectual bloc' exercised over national cultural life. It was meant to embrace Croce's legacy insofar as the latter's philosophy was the legitimate heir of German idealism culminating in Hegel – on which Marxian philosophy and Gramsci's own philosophy of praxis stood[3] – but also to go beyond it in order to achieve national cultural hegemony, a fundamental prerequisite for political affirmation:

> We must not only draw up an inventory of what we have inherited from classical German philosophy but bring it back into operative life, to do which we have to come to terms with Crocean philosophy. Putting it in other words, for us as Italians to be the heirs of classical German philosophy means that we must be the heirs to Crocean philosophy, which at the present time represents the world-wide moment of classical German philosophy . . . It would be worth the trouble of a whole group of people dedicating ten years of their life to a work of this type, an *Anti-Croce* that in today's cultural climate could have the same significance that *Anti-Dühring* had for the pre-war generation. (Gramsci 1995: 356)

However, two decades passed before Gramsci's notebooks were published, and these were crucial years: while they had been written in the prisons of the fascist dictatorship between 1929 and 1935, they were published in the very different political and cultural context of the early Italian Republic.

In 1957, Togliatti left no doubt as to who he saw as the true author of the Anti-Croce: 'Even today, Gramsci scholars raise the issue of the "Anti-Croce" that he hoped would be written. My opinion is that this task had already been carried out by our great comrade, and he did this both with his prison writings and with his entire oeuvre' (Togliatti 1967: 125). Thus, the cultural line of Togliatti's PCI had already been laid down by Gramsci; the struggle for cultural hegemony did not have to wait for some future Anti-Croce. For an entire generation of intellectuals,

Togliatti's cultural line was understood as the Italian version of official Marxism. Lucio Colletti not only attributes this to the national cultural context of the time, but also highlights Togliatti's pragmatic and linear translation of the Gramscian programme:

> At that time, official Marxism . . . was Soviet-style dialectical materialism. However, Togliatti was sufficiently cultured and intelligent to realize that the Stalinist synthesis was too blatantly crude and dogmatic to attract the Italian intellectuals whose adherence to the party he hoped for . . . In his cultural policy, Togliatti sought to replace Soviet orthodoxy with an interpretation of Marxism as the national heir to the Italian historicism of Vico and Croce: in other words, a version of Marxism that did not require those intellectuals to make any real break with their previous positions. Most of them had a Crocean background. The party asked them to make only a minimal effort, adopting a historicism that, holding firm to the basic elements of Croce's philosophy, would reject only its most overtly idealistic proposals. This meant that, until 1955–56, Marx's work, and especially *Capital*, had very limited circulation in the Italian left cultural milieu. (Colletti 1975: 12–3)[4]

This succinct passage identifies the premises of that peculiarly Italian return to Marx described by Bobbio, that arrived at Marx via Hegel, which, in Italy, meant via Croce:

> Alongside the polemic against the materialist and deterministic interpretation, there is, if not exactly an idealistic interpretation, a reconnection of Marx to Hegel. Even Croce, who does not assign any importance to Marx as a philosopher, states that to deny Marx's Hegelian inspiration would be 'to deny the evidence'. There are two ways of linking Marx to Hegel: making Hegel a precursor to Marx (Lukács's way) or making Marx a continuation of Hegel. Italian Marxism uses the latter . . . We still need to point out that while it is true that Marx overturns Hegel, the overturning that emerges in the continuous line of development of Italian Marxism does not resolve itself in the opposition between a metaphysical idealism and an equally metaphysical materialism, but in the opposition of a theological historicism and a humanist historicism . . . In the tradition of Italian Marxism, the two interpretations of Marxism as historicism and Marxism as humanism (whose common enemy is naturalism) are connected and interwoven. This is why we speak of a synthetic formulation of humanist historicism. (Bobbio 1968: XLVII)

In this passage, Bobbio summarizes the main elements of official Italian Marxism: the return to Marx has Hegelian philosophy as its theoretical presupposition and thus includes Crocean historicism in its development. For Italian Marxism, the teachings of Croce had to be understood and overcome insofar as they had not been fully liberated from those theological and metaphysical traits that Marx had criticized in Hegel. The synthesis of this is a humanist historicism, which, as Bobbio points out, corresponds to Gramsci's definition of the philosophy of praxis:

> The philosophy of praxis certainly derives from the immanentist conception of reality, but only in so far as the latter is stripped of its speculative halo and reduced to pure history or historicity or to pure humanism ... [T]he philosophy of praxis is the historicist conception of reality, liberated from any residue of transcendence and theology even in their latest speculative incarnation; idealist Crocean historicism is still at the theological-speculative stage. (Gramsci 1995: 347)

Thus, the 'humanist historicism' of the philosophy of praxis not only combined the predominant tendencies in Italian Marxism at the time, but also, and fundamentally, brought together the main philosophical traditions that distinguished Italian thought in general: humanism and historicism.[5]

In fact, the genealogy of the philosophy of praxis that Gramsci lays out in the *Notebooks* does not stop at German idealism, but, as part of his 'immanentist conception of reality', returns to the origins of modernity and the roots of Italian political thought. As well as the more recent influence of Francesco De Sanctis on 'national-popular culture',[6] Gramsci goes all the way back to Giambattista Vico and even to Niccolò Machiavelli. As is well known, Gramsci updates the latter's conception of the political by assigning the role of the modern prince to the party.[7] Bobbio rightly points out the national aspect of this political-cultural operation and of the line of thought that results from it:

> And it is precisely this interpretation of Marxism, going beyond Hegel, that manages to incorporate two fundamental moments of Italian thought, Machiavelli and Vico, into its own tradition . . . Through Machiavelli and Vico, on the one hand, Marx is bound to the history of Italian thought; on the other, Italian thought appropriates Marxism, considering it as the fully developed form of a historicism that is potential or implicit in the immanentist orientation of national philosophy, that is, as absolute historicism. (Bobbio 1968: XLVIII)

Gramsci's return to Marx thus becomes the 'official' version not only because it is promoted by the party leadership, but because it manages to align Marxism with the Italian philosophical tradition without making any major leaps: as 'absolute historicism', Marxism is the necessary and foreseeable outcome of Italian thought, an outcome that was already present as potential in its origins. Gramsci's proposed national genealogy of Marxism might seem provincial, and legitimated only insofar as it was functional to the political strategy of the PCI leadership, and perhaps this is how it was perceived by some of the postwar generation, but it should nevertheless be understood within the cultural conjuncture of the era in which he was educated and wrote, rather than being judged against the era in which he was 'discovered' and read.[8] Bobbio stresses this point:

> one of the reasons for this good fortune [is] the fact that [Gramsci's] thought – beyond the political programme that linked him firmly to the history of the Italian Communist Party and the left in general, not just in Italy – was deeply rooted in our cultural tradition . . . [I]n Gramsci's time, dominated by idealism, [Italian culture] was or was thought to be a strong culture, which rightly or wrongly attributed to itself the merit of having indelibly marked certain fundamental moments in the history of modern thought: Machiavelli and Guicciardini; the philosophy of the Renaissance, with Bruno and Campanella; the theorists of the reason of the state; Vico, the forerunner of no less than Hegel; Rosmini and Gioberti, rediscovered by Gentile as the Italian Kant and Hegel; Mazzini, theorist of nationality who inspired the national revolutions of the nineteenth century . . . The strong national imprint of our culture had been one of the consequences of the restoration of idealistic philosophy against a non-native philosophy such as positivism, which, imported late from France and England, was considered foreign to the Italian tradition. (Bobbio 1990: 81–2)

2. The return to Marx

The idea of a return to Marx is a peculiarity of Italian Marxism. Refusing to embrace or even ignoring re-readings of Marxism in light of other currents of thought, it attempts to interweave the original themes of Marxian philosophy with the most significant moments of Italian national culture. It also helpfully provides a sense of continuity in Italian Marxism over time, legitimizing both the official line and deviations from it. Although Bobbio was right that the return to Marx was a constant in Italian Marxism, there were many different ways of getting there. Indeed, by the end of the 1950s, a new path had opened up by which to return to Marx, this time in opposition to the Gramscian line formalized by Togliatti.

The return to Marx that deviated most radically from the Gramscian-Togliattian line was that of Galvano Della Volpe, whose thought had a huge influence on Italian Marxism, giving rise to numerous deviations that created as many Marxisms.[9] Colletti, one of his students, points out that Della Volpe's first move was to return directly to Marx's texts.[10] In fact, he was the Italian editor and translator of the works of young Marx, including the crucial *Critique of Hegel's Philosophy of Right*. This allowed him to engage in a more philological and rigorous analysis of Marx, freed from the idealist foundation, or at least mediation, which had heavily influenced the previous phase of Italian Marxism. Bobbio points out that Della Volpe made such a radical rupture with the continuous line linking Marx and Hegel that 'only with Della Volpe does a new history start, albeit in the midst of many disagreements' (Bobbio 1968: XLVI–XLVII). Della Volpe argued that Marx's philosophy had been characterized by its critique of Hegel from the start and thus rejected the idea that Marx was the corrector of the Hegelian dialectic, which, once made to walk 'on its feet', instead of its head, could be continued in Marx:[11]

> The exceptional significance of the *Critique of Hegel's Philosophy of Right* – Marx's first philosophical writing after his doctoral thesis, which was posthumously published and dated between the winter of 1841–42 and the summer of 1843 – lies in the fact that it marks the clear detachment even then of (the 24-year-old) Marx from Hegel, in that it is a critique of Hegel's *Logic*, as well as of his *Philosophy of Right*, and is above all a radical critique due to its foundation in motifs that are unfamiliar to the 'left-Hegelian' critique of idealism. (Della Volpe 1949: 19)

The original gesture of Marxian philosophy is thus not that it takes Hegel in a more progressive or revolutionary direction, but that it completely detaches from him. Della Volpe argues that Marx calls into question the entire apparatus of Hegelian logic through challenging its aprioristic and metaphysical approach. Thus, Marx's dialectical-materialist method is not a correction or overturning of the Hegelian dialectic, but is qualitatively different from it, even in conflict with it. In *Logic as a Positive Science*, which marks the culmination of this phase in his thought, Della Volpe writes: 'In sum, in every field, scientific prediction (hypothesis) must replace metaphysical apriorism (hypostatis). We must thus return to the positive gnoseological and logical exigency that arose from Marx's materialist critique of the hypostatizations characteristic of the moral "dialectic" of Hegel: the instance of the "specific logic of a specific object": or, "philosophy as science"' (Della Volpe 1980). Whereas Hegelian philosophy and idealism in general hypostatize reality, transcending it in theoretical and abstract speculation, and so sheltering it from all criticism, the Marxian method returns to concrete reality to test the truth of its hypotheses. Marxian philosophy becomes a science when, like any other empirical science, it uses the 'experimental method':

> The specific logic of a specific object, which we have termed *philosophy as science*, therefore does not and cannot mean anything but the *experimental conception*, the law, wherein lies the solution to philosophical or 'moral' problems no less than the solution to problems of the 'physical' sciences . . . In sum, it is in *practice*, in action, that *theory*, or truth, is confirmed, and thereby affirmed. (Della Volpe 1980)

Della Volpe thus identifies a genealogical line of Marxian philosophy that differs from the Hegelian and idealistic line. This new line is connected to the experimental method of modern science whose philosophical origins stretch back to Aristotle's polemic against Platonic logic. Marx becomes the Galilei of the 'moral sciences':

> the techniques of research do vary, but there is only *one logic* – the materialist logic of modern science. This may be termed the *moral Galileanism* characteristic of Marxism (that is, the proposition that the 'moral sciences', without exception, are 'science' in the most rigorous sense of the word). I say Galileanism so as to underscore the divergence of Marxism as a method not only from idealism, with its hypostases, but also from positivism, with its idolatry of the 'facts' and its consequent repugnance for 'hypotheses'. (Della Volpe 1980)

The most important notion for Della Volpeanism and the lines of thought that, taking Della Volpe as their starting point, diverged even more radically from the official Marxist line, is that of 'determinate abstraction', which Della Volpe finds in the 1857 'Introduction' to the *Foundations of the Critique of Political Economy* (the *Grundrisse*),[12] a book which would then become fundamental to Italian Marxism. According to the experimental method, any theory that abstracts from a given content can only prove its truth by returning to the concrete; to the specific reality of which that theory is the specific conception. Those theories of society that presume to be valid in general, whatever the historical and economic conditions, have no scientific scope: 'What is needed', Marx continues, 'is a "scientifically correct" method. This means above all that we must make abstractions (without which no thought or knowledge is possible) on the basis of the concrete (*das Konkrete*), "the real subject", which in this case is a specific historical society' (Della Volpe 1980). This is the peculiarity of the Marxian method: as it starts from the concrete reality of capitalist society, it can only be applied to that society. Official Italian Marxism had to take note of this, regardless of any theories about the backwardness of Italian capitalism and the proposal for an 'Italian road to socialism' based on faith in progress. However backward it was, Italian society was capitalist and thus was no exception for Marxian theory. Although these conclusions would not be reached by Della Volpe himself,[13] their premise rests on the deviation that began with his return to Marx.

3. The return to the working class

Della Volpe's teaching was also crucial to the formation of Mario Tronti and the rest of the Roman group (Alberto Asor Rosa, Rita Di Leo, Umberto Coldagelli and Gaspare De Caro), who, in 1961, would become part of the *Quaderni rossi* journal led by Renato Panzieri, another student of Della Volpe. Panzieri was also a left-wing heterodox, but unlike the Roman group (which gravitated towards the PCI), came from the Socialist Party. As is often said, *Quaderni rossi* represented operaismo's gestation period. Operaismo was then born in 1964 with the splitting off of the group that founded *classe operaia*, the first truly operaist journal, which was led by Tronti. Della Volpe's teaching, while rejected by official Marxism, was welcomed by Tronti's generation, for, unlike the previous generation, which learned about Marxism in adulthood, grafted onto their previous idealistic education, this generation had direct access to Marx's texts in their youth. In an interview published in 2005, Tronti recalled how important Della

Volpe's return to Marx was in informing his thought and that of the other operaisti, and stressed its theoretical rupture with the cultural politics of the workers' movement at the time:

> We encountered a type of Marxism that differed from official Marxism, from the orthodox Marxism of the time, from the Marxism that, at least in communist circles, revolved around the historicist, idealist, Gramscian-Crocean-Desanctisian tradition: instead, we had the good fortune to encounter Della Volpe's Marxism, which was an anti-historicist, materialist Marxism, theorizing a break between Marx and Hegel, not a continuity. It was a very open Marxism, which gave us direction for research that went beyond what we had acquired in that period. (Borio, Pozzi and Roggero 2005: 289)

A few years before the founding of *Quaderni rossi*, Della Volpe's teaching was still clearly present in Tronti's writing, in which the issues that would later be fully expressed in operaismo were already beginning to emerge. Focusing on the analysis and critique of Gramsci's thought, 'Some questions around Gramsci's Marxism' (1958) and 'Between dialectical materialism and philosophy of praxis: Gramsci and Labriola' (1959) attempt to develop an explicitly Della Volpean-inspired deviation from the dominant line.

In 'Between dialectical materialism and philosophy of praxis: Gramsci and Labriola', Tronti describes the interpretations of Marx lying behind Gramsci's philosophy of praxis, the most important being those of Rodolfo Mondolfo, Giovanni Gentile, Benedetto Croce and Antonio Labriola, revealing a background that is not only idealist, but typically Italian. Picking up on increasing disillusionment amongst Marxist intellectuals, Tronti calls into question the success of the Italianization of Marx, pointing out the limits of a purely national philosophy and politics: 'Gramsci is a typically and, I would say, fundamentally *Italian* thinker. Italy is his natural environment; he sinks his roots into the deepest national fabric' (Tronti 2016a). Tronti thus links Gramsci to Italian idealism, whose thinkers had not directly read Marx, but only Labriola's interpretation of Marx. They took as originally Marxian what in fact was Labriola's contribution to Marx's introduction to Italy:

> But in Labriola there is, additionally, the 'tendency to monism,' which leads him concretely to resolve the science of nature into the science of man; to dissolve the dialectic into the idea of progress; to submerge all the world in history; and to consider all history as the

> development of human praxis. Precisely for this reason, we find him *at the origin* of both Italian Marxism and Italian idealism. (Tronti 2016a)

Tronti understood Labriola's Marx as serving the purposes of Italian idealism, using Marx in its fight against positivism: indeed, despite significant differences, anti-positivism was the common thread linking the various Italian interpretations of Marx up to the 1950s. After his discussion of the Marxism on which Gramsci's work was based, Tronti – in what would become one of the truly original aspects of his thought – engaged in his own overturning by asking what remained of Marx once he was freed from that idealistic, humanist and historicist interpretation that Labriola's Marxism had established:

> Marx is therefore *at the origins* of Italian idealism. And if on the one hand he leaves a visible stamp on the development of this thought, on the other hand he is radically marked by it. In Italy Marx was not only to *flirt* with Hegel; but also Hegel was to *flirt* with Marx. Conclusion: *we have had a tendentially Marxian Hegel and a decisively Hegelian Marx.* Even today, here, those who approach Marx rediscover him through the *filter* of the idealist culture; a filter clearly tendentious and deforming . . . The decisive factor was instead a certain '*interpretation*' of Marxism: because if Marx serves only to resume the discourse on Hegel, once returned to Hegel, Marx is already liquidated . . . First one has all of Marx revolve around Hegel, then one removes Hegel from the center and says: see, Marx fails to rotate on his own. (Tronti 2016a)

Tronti argues that it is at this point that Gramsci and his peculiar return to Marx come into the picture. To make Marxian philosophy stand up on its own without the need for external support, indeed to make it, as absolute historicism and humanism, the philosophy that encompasses and surpasses Hegelianism and idealism, Gramsci searched for a 'current global moment of Marxist philosophy', an Anti-Croce. But Tronti points out that this still falls under the Hegelian dialectic:

> this *antithetical* position preserves in the depths of its nature a hidden Hegelian sense . . . there is a vision of Marxism that contains in itself, uncritically, the *manner* in which idealism has wanted to see Marxism. Yet – for Gramsci – precisely here appears the theoretical nexus by which the philosophy of praxis, while continuing

> Hegelianism, *turns it on its head*; or rather – and this is not the same thing – while turning it on its head, *it continues it.* (Tronti 2016a)

Tronti shows that although Gramsci had the right intentions, wanting to return to the original core of Marxian philosophy through a philosophy of praxis, this goal was never reached, probably as a result of Gramsci's 'cultural Italianism'. Gramsci's return to Marx failed to shake off a Marxism that was shaped at its origins by Hegelianism and idealism:

> [In the idealist interpretation] we have been able to find not only – as Gramsci maintains – the concepts that Marxism has *ceded* to traditional philosophies; but we can and we must also find the reverse: and that is to say the concepts that traditional philosophies have *ceded* to Marxism. In these latter concepts the height of confusion resides; not when they are critically reflected on and re-elaborated, but when they are immediately and unwittingly accepted. Essentially I mean this: that it is not enough to *overthrow* the *praxis* of the idealists in order to make history proceed correctly; just as it is not enough to *overthrow* the *dialectic* of Hegel in order to find the correct path in the movement of reality. It is not enough to *complete praxis* in order to make history *real*; just as it is not enough to make the dialectic *concrete* in order to make reality *historic.* (Tronti 2016a)

At this point, Tronti paraphrases Gramsci:[14] 'It is a matter of understanding that the *pure* act does not exist; that the act is *always impure*. At stake is our ability to envision, within the content of our thoughts, a specific and always determinate *impurity*, a concrete entity . . . within the framework of a particular and determinate objective reality' (Tronti 2016a). Tronti is perhaps excessive in his critique of Gramsci, but his real polemical target is in fact the entire Italian cultural tradition behind the philosophy of praxis, which Gramsci never really managed to break away from, and which Tronti sees as conditioning and invalidating further attempts to return to Marx along that path. Gramsci's 'impure' philosophy of praxis had become the pure philosophy of Italian Marxism. And so the Gramscian route that was meant to culminate in the original 'philosophy' of Marxism was no longer viable, not only because it was uncritically supported by official Marxism, but because it was compromised by an idealist and historicist philosophy. The latter had then become a national philosophy, creating a continuous line connecting the most significant names in Italian thought, from Machiavelli to Vico via Bruno. The philosophical path had reached its end, and so it was better to radically deviate from it, returning to Marx another way, via the Galilean path indicated by Della Volpe: that of Marxism as science.

> And today we find ourselves formulating the same problem: the need for a Marxism that is as far from the *philosophy of praxis* as from *dialectical materialism*; that is not reduced to a purely *technical* methodology of knowledge and of human action, and which does not claim to close within itself a total and definitive *metaphysic*; a Marxism that poses itself, with simplicity, as a *science*. (Tronti 2016a)

In 'Some questions around Gramsci's Marxism', Tronti reaffirms the continuity that Della Volpe identifies between Italian idealism and Gramsci's thought, which was based in the assumption of a filial relationship between Hegel and Marx.[15] We see an explicit debt to Della Volpe in Tronti's interpretation of Marx's rejection of Hegel:[16] 'The Hegelian dialectic's mystification is the overall conclusion of all of idealism, of all of speculative philosophy. Hegel does not need to be concluded; Hegel is already the conclusion. He is precisely the conclusion which Marx refuses' (Tronti 2016b). With Hegel, idealism is completed, and with Marx, a new story begins. Tronti, like Della Volpe, makes clear reference to the young Marx's critique of and detachment from Hegelian philosophy and dialectics. But Tronti goes further, contrasting Della Volpe's 'Marxism as science' with the 'Marxism as philosophy' that preceded it. This not only marked a radical rupture with the Italian Marxist tradition, but also, and above all, highlighted its practical applicability to Italian society in the late 1950s.

> Certainly we must assert the novelty, the originality, the autonomy of Marxism. But the novelty of Marxism against any other philosophy consists in not asking more of it *as a philosophy*; its originality consists in opposing *science* to philosophy, or rather in its conceiving its own philosophy *only* as science, as a 'specific conception of a specific object;' its autonomy consists in its understanding its own method of investigation as *autonomous* in general from all the old speculative philosophy and in particular from Hegelian speculative philosophy which *concluded* and *fulfilled* all the old philosophy. (Tronti 2016b; trans mod)

In short, a Marxism that makes itself the heir to Hegelian philosophy – its continuation and fulfilment – results in a conservative or at best reformist attitude towards that specific form of bourgeois and capitalist society of which idealist philosophy is the abstraction. It is true that this is not so far from Gramsci's own critique of Croce,[17] but Tronti had no qualms in admitting that he had a 'tendentious' interpretation of Gramsci's thought. As we have said, his critique was directed at that line of official Marxism that culminated in Gramsci. The crucial question was not who would write the Anti-Croce, for in fact Togliatti was right, Gramsci had already completed the task he had set for future generations. The problem was that it had not had the desired results: Gramsci's work did not respond to the new tasks of Marxist theory. The latter needed to be the expression – the determinate abstraction – of the determinate society of global capitalism, and not only of Italian capitalist society. And so a radical deviation had to be made from the previous path:

> Therefore the idea of an Anti-Croce is not a chance, contingent task, dictated by particular, cultural, *national* developments; it represents the prevailing *world-wide moment* of Marxism, it is the historic task of Marxism in our time. If today we consider 'the motives for this Anti-Croce to have been for the most part exhausted' . . . we must conclude that its result is 'for the most part' the exhaustion of the Gramscian problematic around Marxism . . . I agree in thinking that Gramsci has *already* written the Anti-Croce (Togliatti). But I believe that precisely this is the limit of Gramsci's thought. (Tronti 2016b)

Using the example of the October Revolution and referencing Leninist theory and practice, Tronti's essay suggests at least two deviations from the line of Italian Marxism represented theoretically by Gramsci and politically by Togliatti's 'Italian road to socialism.' These deviations are based in the idea of taking power through a revolutionary leap rather than through a gradual and progressive process, and in the centrality of the subjective-creative-practical-active element as opposed to a belief in the self-transformation of bourgeois democracy and capitalist society towards socialism:

> Certainly reformism has not *by chance* tended toward a positivistic interpretation of Marxism; it was pushed to this by its very own presuppositions, which saw in capitalism a limitless possibility of development toward socialism, so certain of making superfluous or even inappropriate any attempt at a revolutionary 'leap.' But the failure of reformist politics in *all* countries, the success of revolutionary

> practice in a specific country, represents in that moment the denial of every type of evolutionism, of gradualism, of the objective conflicts' spontaneous solutions; it represents the positive confirmation, the concrete possibility, the immediate fecundity of the revolutionary rupture *in general* . . . [O]ne must study whether this is not a fundamental element which implies, on the theoretical level, the reevaluation of the subjective element, or rather the *creative* element, against the dead objectivity of stratified and inert social conditions; and the revaluation of the *active* side within the historical-social relation, and therefore of the sensuous human activity as practical activity which ultimately also commingles with the object, the real, the sensuous, according to the expression used by Marx in the first of the *Theses on Feuerbach*. (Tronti 2016b)

It is clear that this is not simply a matter of further widening the net of Italian Marxism or adding a new name to its line of continuity. Tronti's theoretical proposal instead implies an overturning of the very paradigm of continuity as the way to return to Marx. Conceiving the revolutionary leap as essential to Marxist politics means breaking with any mediation aimed at re-establishing continuity – in fact, it means attributing positive value to discontinuity. This created a deep crisis in Italian Marxism and, with it, the first signs of Tronti's return to Marx from which operaismo would take its cue: 'Today we can say that any great historical crisis of the workers' movement poses the problem of the "*true*" Marxism' (Tronti 2016b). This rejection of continuity as a truth criterion in favour of a return to the revolutionary leap found in the 'true' Marx, specifically in his critique of the Hegelian dialectic, was Tronti's 'course of action' (*linea di condotta*): 'Of course, major feats are pulled off in sudden leaps. And the discoveries that really count often break the thread of continuity' (Tronti 2019: xvii).

In 'Studi recenti sulla logica del *Capitale*' (Recent studies on the logic of *Capital*), his thought was already beginning to deviate from Della Volpe – and from Colletti, who was also moving away from Della Volpe, although in a different direction.[18] But before elaborating on what would later become the fundamental concepts of operaismo, Tronti identified a further discontinuity. He writes:

> Della Volpe . . . deserves the enormous merit of having been the first to draw attention to these problems and of having begun to find a possible solution which exists today in all its theoretical rigour and practical potential. When we see that from various quarters, and

> through different intellectual experiences, we now arrive at the same understanding of Marx's work, this is already an initial verification of the correctness of this position. But I would say that today this is no longer sufficient. (Tronti 1961: 901)

It was not sufficient, then, to return to Marxian texts while remaining within the logic of *Capital*. Della Volpe had initiated a process that had to be continued on another level, a level that was no longer exclusively theoretical. It was not enough to do a correct reading of Marxian texts, to guide them along the right path:

> This position today is a work in progress – a developing hypothesis – which now needs to be made homogeneous not only in its internal logic, but also in its external projection. This process of development is possible by increasingly refining all aspects of the research *method*. But it will only become a *necessary* process – that is, the new logic will only acquire actual coherence in thought and a real practical hold on things – when this method is completely discharged in concrete investigation; when the *materialist logic of Capital* becomes, *again*, the tool for a *Marxist analysis of capitalism*. (Tronti 1961: 901)

Tronti adopts the Della Volpean notion of determinate abstraction – philosophy as science consisting in 'the specific logic of a specific object' – not only to reiterate that the capitalist system corresponds to, and only corresponds to, a determinate society – bourgeois society – but in order to show that any science that starts from this society is irremediably compromised and functional to the capitalist system and, therefore, must be understood not as a science but as an ideology: 'The process of capitalist development *dictates* the procedure of scientific knowledge, but then *transcribes* this procedure as a *mystified* science. At the same time it produces the *possibility* of scientific knowledge and the *necessity* of its fetishistic mystification. The development of capitalism makes *science* possible, in the same way that it makes *ideology* necessary' (Tronti 1961: 902). So the analysis of capitalism must reach further back than bourgeois ideology to discover the 'workers' science' that had been mystified by that ideology:

> In the analysis of capitalism, as ideology cannot but be *bourgeois*, so science cannot but belong to the *workers*. Capitalism is historically the first *social* organization of production. And this sociality of production serves to make the whole of society live as a function

> of production. 'Society' is the *medium* that allows production to subsist as production. *Society* is the *sociality* of *capitalist* production. Capitalism is truly *bourgeois society*: in the sense that it is forced to position itself simultaneously as the organization of capitalist *social* production and as the system of *bourgeois* private property. (Tronti 1961: 902)

In his critique of the capitalist system and the mystifications that hinder any attempt at a 'scientific' analysis of society, Tronti arrives at the same conclusions that Colletti had reached before him.[19] The originality of his contribution to Italian Marxism instead lies in his identification of the subject of that science. This subject is, of course, the working class. The capitalist system of production creates the conditions for a social relationship, but bourgeois society denies this sociality in the institution of private property. However, this produces subjectification, in the form of the working class, the only truly social subject. The theoretical task was thus to make central what had been left at the margins of the capitalist point of view. Science and society had to belong to the workers, and only the workers: the working class had to be their only subject. For Tronti, identifying the working class as the subject of science and society was equivalent to moving from theory to practice, and so to revolution. As he writes in 'Studi recenti sulla logica del *Capitale*':

> Within capitalism, in fact, the point of view of society can only be the point of view of the working class . . . The social relationship of production coincides with the historical existence of the working class. The social relationship of production is not society in the abstract, it is the working class in the concrete. In order for the contradiction between social production and private property to *actually* exist, the fundamental contradiction between the working class and capitalism must explode in all its revolutionary potential. The *collective worker*, which seems to live as a function of capital, as its negative – is then actually the *real positive fact:* the only one able, therefore, to understand the real process of development, namely the social material relationship . . . And so the scientific understanding of capitalism can remain in the hands of workers' thought only on condition that the working class *separates itself* from the mechanism of capitalism's development, makes itself *independent* of it and *autonomous* in its own organization; it thus presents itself as a class that is antagonistic to the entirety of the

> system of capitalist production, and, in this sense, becomes the living demand of *society* in the face of the infamy of private property. (Tronti 1961: 903)

The fundamental premises of Tronti's operaist approach are already clearly expressed here: the working class is the true subject of science and society, within the capitalist system as labour and against the capitalist system as an autonomous political organisation. This article, which was written the same year that *Quaderni rossi* was founded, clearly departs from Della Volpe, and anticipates *Workers and Capital*:

> Science about capitalism, the science of *Capital*, is *only* possible from the perspective of socialist revolution. *Science* and *history* is a discourse that still completely falls within *science*: it is the logic of theory. But there is the other discourse: science and history that completely fall within *history*, which is the logic of practice. The former presupposes a materialist thought, the latter a subversive praxis. Today, to say theory and practice means little. We must say *scientific* theory and *revolutionary* practice. (Tronti 1961: 903)

4. Workers and Capital: *The antagonistic subject*

A return to Marx means returning to the subject of Marxian theory, thus to the working class: this is Tronti's 'course of action', and the premise of operaismo.[20] Tronti sees the working class as Marx's true discovery, the specific difference of Marxian thought: 'Labour as abstract labour, and thus as labour-power, is present already in Hegel. Labour-power – and not only labour – as a commodity, is present already in Ricardo. As for the commodity labour-power as working class: this is Marx's discovery' (Tronti 2019: 112). François Matheron, in his entry under '*Operaïsme*' in the *Dictionnaire critique du marxisme*, defines operaismo as a 'return to the working class': 'In an era in which the workers' movement, in crisis, is caught up in extremely "ideological" debates, operaismo is essentially characterized by a "return to the working class"' (Matheron 1999: 816).[21]

Della Volpe's return to Marx was insufficient: it risked slipping back into ideology without identifying the concrete subject that demanded that return and which had to draw practical consequences from it. The subject of Marxism could no longer be the people, that national-popular synthesis that Gramsci saw as the 'historical bloc' that the party's cultural politics should strive towards:

> If the relationship between intellectuals and people-nation, between the leaders and the led, the rulers and the ruled, is provided by an organic cohesion in which feeling-passion becomes understanding and thence knowledge (not mechanically but in a way that is alive), then and only then is the relationship one of representation. Only then can there take place an exchange of individual elements between the rulers and ruled, leaders [dirigenti] and led, and can the shared life be realised which alone is a social force with the creation of the 'historical bloc'. (Gramsci 1971: 418)

The new and constructive contribution of *Quaderni rossi* consisted in identifying a subject (through analysing 'class composition'); empirically investigating that subject (through what they called '*conricerca*' (coresearch) in the factories); and politically organising this subject as a class that could not be reduced to any synthesis or be understood as a part of the people. As Tronti writes in 'Studi recenti sulla logica del *Capitale*', 'science cannot but belong to the *workers*', otherwise it is bourgeois ideology. And so, to really become a science, Della Volpe's Marxism needed this subject. The science of the working class adapted to the current stage of capitalist development thus became the programme of *Quaderni rossi* and, as Asor Rosa wrote in the journal's second issue,[22] this meant the end of that form of subjectivity to which Italian Marxism, including that of Della Volpe, had previously referred. Thus the debt to Della Volpe, although acknowledged, had now been settled:

> this demystification is only possible if we agree to look at reality from the point of view of the working class . . . At this point the problem of the relationship between *this* culture and *that* Marxism reemerges, but in a concrete form . . . The *concrete* form of this relationship seems to me to consist precisely in the recognition of the liberating function of the working class. Marxism is indeed the *theory* of this liberation . . . If we accept these indications, the populist, national-popular, Risorgimento, idealist-Marxian and socio-culturalist ideologies and cultural themes will be defeated not so much by theoretical polemics as by the consciousness of a reality that pushes them back into the more or less distant past in which they germinated. (Asor Rosa 1962: 127)

In an interview given in 1978, Antonio Negri also points out the change in the subject of reference from the days of Togliattism, the previous phase of the Italian workers' movement, although he exempts Gramscian historicism from his critique:[23]

> Togliattism was the ideology . . . of synthesis and compromise at all costs. Based on a thought that was essentially Giobertian historicism much more than it was Gramscian historicism. The subject was the popular forces (*forze popolari*); the term 'class' had completely disappeared from circulation, except on ceremonial occasions. Togliattism has popular forces as its referents; these popular forces are the drivers of historical development; in general, the relationship between democracy and socialism is considered in organic terms, as a process of continuity within capitalist development; thus, practically speaking, the antagonisms of the capitalist process of development are not considered specifically, and the dynamics of the forces that develop within capitalism and which enter into contradiction with the most decisive points of that development are never considered. (Negri 2007a: 41–2)

Let us now return to Tronti's *Workers and Capital*, in particular to the initial theoretical hypotheses he made during the *Quaderni rossi* period. In 'Factory and Society' and 'The Plan of Capital' we can begin to see his response to a question that we have so far left unanswered: why was the working class now the subject that could liberate us from the capitalist-bourgeois system? Why, in 1960s' Italian capitalism, could the people no longer be the subject of reference for the workers' movement?

> The concept of the working class comes into being only at this historically concrete level. It is specified in all its particularity, and develops in all the wealth of its determinations. Thus, the simplest social abstraction of a capitalist economic formation, which thus applies to all the successive forms of its development, 'appears as effectively true in this abstraction' only as a category of the most modern capitalism. (Tronti 2019: 57)

The working class is the determinate abstraction of the most advanced phase of capitalist development: it is, we could say, the last possible determinate abstraction within the capitalist system, or at least – and this is the point over which the most significant deviation within operaismo would later take place – within the so-called Fordist phase of capitalism centred on the factory. The more Fordist capitalism extends its domination over society, the clearer the subjectivity of the working class becomes:

> The more that capitalist production attacks and dissolves its external contradictions, the more it is forced to bring its own internal contradiction into the open. The more capital succeeds in organising itself, the more it is forced to organise the working class for its own ends – to the point that the working class no longer has to become the mirror of all social contradictions: it can directly reflect itself as a social contradiction. (Tronti 2019: 57)

Thus, the working class is not simply one among many contradictions in the capitalist system, for, as Marx argued, the essence, vitality and survival of the system consist precisely in positing the contradiction of the working class and dialectically overcoming it. The working class is thus the contradiction par excellence of capitalism and so is only surmountable by overthrowing the capitalist system. The more capitalism pervades society with its internal contradictions and mode of production, the more the working class becomes the subject of reference for all of labour: the part standing for the whole (*pars pro toto*). And it is the 'cursed part' – cursed because it exists only within the capitalist system. Despite its previously limited and sectarian use, Tronti appropriates the term 'operaismo' (literally 'workerism') in an affirmative way. Unlike the people, which, as a synthesis of the contradictions within society, is a form of subjectivity functional to the capitalist dialectic, the working class imposes a new, qualitatively different way of conceiving subjectivity: no longer a subject-synthesis or a universal subject, but an antagonistic subject. The contradiction cannot be resolved dialectically, it cannot be 'mediated'; the separation that the contradiction posits does not foresee a return to unity. It lacks any aspiration to *Aufhebung*: from its place within the system that produced it, the working class must oppose that system. From the point of view of this antagonistic subjectivity, the subjective form of the people is a neutralization of the contradiction:

> Thus, the workers simultaneously free themselves both from any sectarian temptation and from any socialist perspective. The capitalists are well aware of this: the real generalisation of the working-class condition can reassert the image of its formal

> extinction. This is the basis on which specifically working class power is immediately absorbed into the generic concept of popular sovereignty: the political mediation here serves to allow the explosive content of the working class's productive force to function peacefully within the fine forms of the modern capitalist relations of production. So, at this level, when the working class refuses politically to become the people, it in fact opens up the most direct path to the socialist revolution. (Tronti 2019: 57)

As well as identifying a subject that is constituted by virtue of its antagonism rather than its universality, another key trait of Tronti's operaismo is the concept of the modern factory. In the era of the factory, the working class is embodied in the figure of the mass worker: the unprofessional and unskilled assembly-line worker. Tronti's operaismo is thus based on the unbreakable link between the working class – as the antagonistic subject – and the factory. Only in the factory can the revolutionary struggle be generated, and only revolutionary struggle – not reformism – is capable of overthrowing the capitalist system. Thus, based on his original interpretation of Marx, Tronti's theory posits a unity of subject and place (and of time, the era of modernity): just as the working class is the subject of contradiction, so the factory is the place of contradiction. For it is in the factory, at the level of the relations of production, and not in society, at the level of distribution, circulation and consumption, that the contradiction is revealed and manifested in its purest form. As we have explained above, bourgeois thought constructs and exercises its ideology at the level of society, and bourgeois society is the dimension of the people, not of the class. Society is only a 'moment' of the production relationship, a dialectically successive moment in which the contradiction of the factory and the contradiction of the working class is overcome. The latter then becomes part of the mass of consumers and the 'sovereign people' that delegates its power to parliamentary representation, and thus loses its own particular existence along with its partisan curse:

> At the highest level of capitalist development, this social relation becomes a moment of the relation of production, the whole of society becomes an articulation of production, the whole society lives in function of the factory and the factory extends its exclusive dominion over the whole society . . . The process of the unitary composition of capitalist society, imposed by the specific development of its

> production, no longer tolerates the existence of a political terrain even formally independent of the web of social relations. (Tronti 2019: 26–7)

Later, in the journal *classe operaia* (1964) – of which he was also an editor – Tronti completed his operaist theory, laying out what we will call 'early operaismo'. In the first article to be published in the journal, the famous 'Lenin in England' – a title that later became something of an operaist leitmotif – the most original theoretical contributions of Tronti's operaist phase are expressed with his usual force and literary style. The first point raised in this article is the most successful of his 'overturnings':

> We too saw capitalist development first and the workers second. This is a mistake. Now we have to turn the problem on its head, change orientation, and start again from first principles, which means focusing on the struggle of the working class. At the level of socially developed capital, capitalist development is subordinate to working-class struggles; not only does it comes after them, but it must make the political mechanism of capitalist production respond to them. (Tronti 2019: 65)

Thus, not only was the factory working class central to the labouring classes, but, and this is Tronti's so-called Copernican revolution, the class struggle was the driver of capitalist development, becoming its most active and dynamic force. Following this discovery, the fundamental question – which had driven the split from *Quaderni rossi* and the creation of *classe operaia* – becomes how to translate the knowledge and political potential of class struggle into organization. From that point on the key problem for operaismo, which became the source of further ruptures and deviations, would be how to organize the part as a political party. The conclusion of 'Lenin in England' thus opens a new theoretical and practical phase: 'Now let us try to take the opposite path, with the same scientific spirit of adventurous political discovery. 'Lenin in England' is the search for a new Marxist practice of the working-class party; it is the theme of struggle and of organisation at the highest level of the political development of the working class' (Tronti 2019: 72). By raising the question of a working-class party, he further critiques the Gramscian and, above all, Togliattian conception of the party of the whole people. Tronti's proposal once again begins from an overturning: no longer the working class within the people, the whole that incorporates the part, but the people within the working class, the part that becomes not just the majority, but the totality.[24] In the most detailed and elaborate text of *Workers and Capital*, 'Marx, Labour Power, Working Class', Tronti writes:

> How to make 'the people' operate within the working class remains a real problem of the revolution in Italy, specifically in the interest not of winning a democratic majority in the bourgeois parliament, but of constructing a political bloc of social forces and using it as a material lever that will blow up each of the connections internal to the enemy's political power and then all of them at once. This demands a fearsome popular power, deployed, controlled and directed by the working class through its tool, the party. This excludes from the party's tasks something that had hitherto instead seemed to characterise it: namely, the task of mediating the relations that exist between related classes – that is, between the different stratums and all their ideologies, in a system of alliances . . . The Gramscian concept of the historic bloc did nothing but reveal a particular stage, a national moment of capitalist development. Its immediate generalisation, in Gramsci's carceral writings, was a first error. The second error, and a much more serious one, was the Togliattian vulgarisation of Gramsci in the form of the new party: This party's intention was to identify itself more and more with this historic bloc, going as far as to dissolve itself into it, as the history of the nation became identical with the national policy of the party of the whole people. (Tronti 2019: 96–7)

The Gramscian problem of the conquest of political hegemony remains, but the people is not the solution, as it absorbs and neutralizes the working class. Tronti argues that the working class is the only part as such, and the only truly revolutionary contradiction of the capitalist system. Yet, as Gramsci had already pointed out, the antagonism of the working class within and against capital – in the form of trade union struggle in the factory – does not directly translate into a struggle for political power. It would thus be necessary to step outside of capitalist relationships of production, which are exclusively economic in nature and thus controllable and manageable by capital. For there to be politics, the class had to go against itself, against its own economic nature: 'This point is precisely the separation of the working class from itself, from work, and thus from capital. It is the separation of the political force from the economic strategy' (Tronti 2019: 273). For there to be politics, the working class had to make itself autonomous:

> Capital must, that is, counterpose itself to labour-power without leaving the working class autonomous; it must conceive labour-power itself as a working class, but within the capitalist relation of production; it must, therefore, conserve, reproduce and extend the class relation while also controlling it. And this is the thread that links together capital's modern history. Today the strategy of the working-class revolution is to break the thread of this control at some point. To this day, the starting point in the struggle is a separate political autonomy of the two sides' class movements: hence, once more, all the problems of organisation are on the working-class side. Capital strives to shut off the moment of antagonism within the economic relation, incorporating the class relation into the capitalist relation as its social object. Opposite to this, the effort on the working-class side must be to continually try to smash open this economic form of the antagonism. (Tronti 2019: 221)

The political problem becomes decisive when antagonism moves from the factory to society. For Tronti, although the place changes, the subject has to remain the same: there is only one form of subjectivity capable of moving outside of the factory and the capitalist system, and that is the working class, separately and autonomously organized. Although this subjectivity is definitely not the subject-people, we are not that far from Gramsci's party-prince.[25] Tronti's political subject is not the subject-synthesis resulting from the trinitarian Hegelian dialectic, but neither is it any longer that antagonistic subject of workers' science that broke with Hegel's dialectic:

> The existing ambiguity at the outset perhaps lies precisely in the 'trinity formula' – we cannot say, as Marx does, that this holds all the secrets of the social process of production. If the social process of production is capital at the level of its full development, then it cannot be defined by any formula that contains more than two protagonists – that is, capital itself and then the working class facing capital, within capital and against capital. This applies to any definition of this process that counts as 'science'. On the terrain of political practice, a further reduction needs to be made. By its very nature, the trinity ought to be reduced to a singular. When we ask ourselves why the secret of capitalism can be grasped only from the

> working-class point of view, the only possible response is that the working class is the secret of capitalism. (Tronti 2019: 234)

Is it possible to think of the working class outside the factory as an autonomous political subject without compromising with the form of the people and without accepting the democratic and reformist logics that would reduce it to one part among others, having to negotiate its partisan interest in the name of the general interest? Can society, which is dominated by the uniform tendency of bourgeois ideologies, allow for a conflict between two parts? Can the antagonistic subject of workers' science become a political party in society, where it is not directly faced with its enemy? What would become of the working class outside the determinate context of the factory in which antagonism takes place? Can the working class renounce its partisan curse? These are the questions that *Workers and Capital* raises for Italian Marxism and for Marxism in general.[26] Although Tronti had laid out an original workers' science and found his way back to Marx through the theorization of the centrality of the working class in the factory and the identification of the antagonistic subject, he had difficulty trying to translate this to the level of political organization. The working class was the secret of capitalism, a secret that workers' science had revealed. However, the secret of the political remained hidden. He argued that the latter was inaccessible to workers' science, as shown by the failures of workers' political struggles, with the sole exception of the October Revolution. And the secret of Lenin's political success was not to be found in the experiences of workers' struggles, but in the great tradition of political realism, the preserve of the enemy class.[27] In the 'Postscript of Problems' written in 1970 and added to the second edition of *Workers and Capital*, we can see Tronti beginning to deviate from 1960s' operaismo. This deviation in no way implied a disavowal of his theoretical achievements, but only the consciousness that, in order to be able to continue research at the level of politics, it had to be translated onto another plane:

> By counterposing one type of organisation to another, Lenin elaborated the theory of both. He needed to do this because his discourse was truly wholly political. He did not (nor did he want to) start from struggles. His logic was based on a concept of political rationality absolutely independent of everything. It was even independent of class interest . . . We ought not look to the working-

> class struggle before Lenin as the origin of his theory of the party. This does not diminish the immensely insightful significance of the Leninist experience, but, rather, magnifies it. Although not moved by the impulse of the working-class struggle, Lenin completely grasped the laws of its political action. Thus, the classical bourgeois notion of the autonomy of politics is reconstituted from a working-class point of view. (Tronti 2019: 288)

Tronti's operaist phase, and also early operaismo, came to an end with the last issue of *classe operaia* in 1967 (note that this is before 1968).[28] After the last glimmers of 'true' politics, the long 'twilight' had begun,[29] starting with the weakening of the concentration of place, time and antagonistic subjectivity that had created that 'now-time' (*Jetztzeit*) which Walter Benjamin – who became increasingly important to Tronti – had seen as the prerequisite for the revolutionary leap.[30] On a theoretical level, then, early operaismo came to an end with the breaking of the unity between the antagonistic subject and the factory, the place where antagonism had emerged with most intensity. The end of the era of the Fordist mode of production – and, with it, the end of the modern era – had also brought to a close the historical figure of the mass worker. Ultimately, the place of conflict seemed to take precedence over the antagonistic subjectivity, for the latter was possible only while the factory remained the location of subjectification.[31] There was political potential only as long as the factory satisfied Carl Schmitt's criterion of the political: the friend-enemy opposition.[32] And it was satisfied – Leninist practice met Schmitt's politicalCarl Schmitt, the class struggle met political realism – as long as, and only as long as, the factory remained a place of division and, at the same time, social aggregation. Once this was over, the factory lost its potential as a place of conflict.

In the conclusion to the postscript to *Workers and Capital*, although he no longer sees the factory as the place of political conflict, at the same time Tronti criticizes those who try to place the working class after and outside the factory, and in particular critiques the idea of identifying another 'objective definition' of antagonistic subjectivity outside the working class of the mass worker:

> Can one, for instance, abandon an 'objective' definition of the working class? Is it possible to define as 'working class' all those who subjectively struggle in working-class forms against capital, from within the social production process? Is it possible to finally separate

> the concept of the working class from the concept of productive labour? . . . The problem is how to find new definitions of the 'working class' without abandoning the domain of objective analysis and without falling back in ideological traps. To reduce the objective materiality of the working class into purely subjective forms of anticapitalist struggles is another ideological error of the new ultra-leftism. Not only this, but to broaden the sociological boundaries of the working class in order to embrace all those struggling against capitalism from within, such as to reach the quantitative majority of the social workforce or even of the active population, is a grave concession to democratic traditions. (Tronti 2019: 325)

Chapter 2

THE 1970s
CRISIS

1. Red sky at night

Tronti began *Workers and Capital*, the key text of early operaismo, with his proposal for a 'course of action', which also served as the introduction's title. He writes: 'The bosses' science is now condemned to its long twilight, but there will continue to be some flashes of practical thought that still strike us now and then. The quicker the working-class point of view advances, the sooner history's condemnation of bourgeois thought will be complete' (Tronti 2019: xv). More than three decades later, in *The Twilight of Politics*, Tronti admitted that the long twilight of bourgeois science and modern politics had in fact also fallen on the twentieth-century workers' movement, whose destiny in defeat could already be felt in the late 1960s. The red sky they had seen was not the dawn of a new epoch, but the twilight of the West, taking both bourgeois culture and the working class with it:[1]

> From the workers' struggles to the protest movements, it was as if the red proscenium curtain descended and brought the performance of the epoch to an end. To us, to many, it seemed as if an era was opening up. It was a happy delusion, because it helped us – through a process of estrangement – to definitively escape from the representation of the old world . . . At the end of the 60s, the decline [*crepuscolo*] of the West was complete. After, came the small twentieth century. (Tronti 2025: 28–9)

The class struggle was simply the final expression of modern politics, a curtain closing on the great twentieth century and its conflicts. The setting of the sun of modern politics came with the loss of the centrality of the Fordist factory and the end of the working class as the main player in world history. Indeed, Tronti even seems to imply that, with the end of the working class as the antagonistic subject par excellence, the very possibility of antagonistic subjectivity had disappeared.

Antonio Negri, on the other hand, interpreted the red glow of the late 1960s as a new dawn. And so, from 1968, these different interpretations began to diverge, becoming as distinct as day and night, and marking the transition between what we will call early and late operaismo. Negri laid out the fundamentals of late operaismo in an interview entitled *Dall'operaio massa all'operaio sociale* (From the mass worker to the social worker):

> In fact, the situation was completely different: we were at the brink of the rupture of the concept of capital and of the effectiveness of its unified command – the movements of variable capital were revealed as autonomous within and against the organization of constant capital, and so there was no longer only that 'within/against' that operaismo spoke of, there was also the 'against/outside'. A new reality of the labouring class was dawning. (Negri 2007a: 8)

Thus, instead of marking the end of class antagonism, Negri saw the crisis of the Fordist model as creating the possibility for a new antagonistic subject. This subject would no longer be exclusively defined by the factory relationship, 'within and against capital', but would instead be autonomous from it and capable of self-valorization: it would be against capital outside the factory. And so the 'social worker' (*operaio sociale*) would take the place of the mass worker as the key antagonistic subject. Furthermore, Negri not only saw 1968 as leading to the emergence of the social worker as the new antagonistic subject, but as the dawning of a new, longer-term phase. Indeed, a text Negri wrote with Félix Guattari in 1985 claims 'the revolution began in 1968' (Guattari and Negri 2010: 33).

Before looking more closely at this deviation from early operaismo, it is worth noting another interpretation of the late 1960s. Like Tronti, Massimo Cacciari understood this period as the red of the twilight, taking up the Trontian metaphor in an interview many decades later:

> Of course, try to distinguish the dawn from the twilight . . . the colours are the same . . . none of us, above all Tronti, thought that this was the final possible form of Marxism . . . It was really what you managed to scrape out at the end, attempting to react in a positive way to forms that were purely scientistic or movementist or internationalist etc. What you could *ultimately* draw from it was this idea, but there is no doubt that we had thought of it as a new beginning, when in fact

> it was not a new beginning. And that was the fatal error. Fatal for the movement, because if you interpret the end as a beginning you *keep on ending* . . . That discourse was really the ultimate form of communism, not the beyond [*ulteriore*] of communism. (Trotta and Milana 2008: 827)

As we shall see, the attempt to turn the demise of great bourgeois thought – the negative thought of which Marxism was the 'ultimate' form – into an 'ulterior' possibility is a key motif in Cacciari's work. And thus he also moved away from early operaismo, but in a different direction to Negri.

2. Late operaismo

1968 was the watershed of operaismo. And this was also the year of Negri's second and final contribution to *Contropiano*, the third operaist journal, which was edited by Asor Rosa and Cacciari, with Tronti watching 'from the window'.[2] Entitled 'Marx on Cycle and Crisis', the article testifies to the failure of *Contropiano* to hold together the veterans of *classe operaia*,[3] for although they were all against the 'plan' of capital, they no longer had a shared definition of what being within it might mean. The article also laid out some of the key theoretical problems that led to Negri's deviation from Tronti, all centred around the concept of crisis.

He argues that crisis reveals the dualistic and antagonistic nature of capitalist society. The awareness of this dualism, for which there is no dialectical synthesis, had been taken up by bourgeois theory in so-called negative thought:

> Only in the moment of crisis does theoretical understanding keep pace with practice, deciphering the meaning of the social hieroglyphs within which that practice is sublimated. It is as if only the urgency and immediacy of the crisis . . . are able to reduce the margins of mystification within which theoretical awareness is generally confined, forcing it to open up to the process of negative thinking dictated by the raw requirements of practice. (Negri 1988: 48)

Whereas negative thought shows – albeit only on a theoretical level – that the irresolvable and fundamental contradiction of class antagonism is the essence of bourgeois society and the capitalist system, from the 1929 crisis onward political economy had tried to mystify this antagonism through the ideology of development: 'development was, and necessarily had to be, the new form of the capitalist cycle. Now, this theoretical and political line emerged from a deep-rooted change that the crisis had provoked in capitalist thinking. Namely, the realization of the dualistic essence of the economic process, and of the antagonistic forces operating within it' (Negri 1988: 48–9). Therefore, although negative thought reveals the lack of any solution for or alternative to the crisis – and thus the failure of dialectical synthesis – capitalist economics attempted to overcome (*aufheben*) the antagonism inherent in the system: 'the alternative to crisis came to be seen as development, understood as a dynamic system geared to regulating the economic process and as a way of resolving its dual natured movement' (Negri 1988: 49). Development was thus the overcoming of the crisis, re-establishing the capitalist cycle at a more advanced level. However, thirty years of economic growth were brought to an end with the crisis of the 1970s and the dialectic no longer seemed to work. For capitalist economic theory mystifies the fact that the negative emerging in the crisis is not a dialectical moment that can be overcome, it does not create the possibility of a new and perfected equilibrium of the system, but is the antagonism of the working class. As Tronti teaches, the real driver of capitalist development is class struggle. Every capitalist crisis demands a solution from both classes: the working class responds with autonomous power and the capitalist class attempts to negate that power. Negri writes:

> political economy proved incapable of recognizing that the most fundamental characteristic of the new situation was the decisive and autonomous emergence of the working class – and that therefore the whole notion of an economic schema based on equilibrium had to be retranslated into notions based on a relationship between forces in struggle; henceforth any description of the cycle had to be based and grounded in the dynamic of a struggle between classes . . . Once again, bourgeoise thought reacted to the discovery of a negative with an exaggerated determination to eliminate it. (Negri 1988: 50)

Negri leaves it to others to confront the crisis from the point of view of negative thought, preferring instead to focus on political economy and Marx's analysis of capitalist crises, for it is here that he identifies the political potential of a new antagonistic subject.

He argues that despite appearing to be a technical rebalancing of the system, development is in fact capital's political response to the crisis; it is 'capitalism's use of the crisis':

> But what does it mean to say that development has to be, first and foremost, capitalism's use of the crisis? . . . There cannot exist a concept of development which is neutral, or which is sublimated within some formalist perspective of equilibrium. Development is struggle; it is a restructuring of power-relations; and it must necessarily pass via a moment of direct conflict – the crisis – to end with capital's victory over its opposing forces. (Negri 1988: 55)

Contrary to the teachings of classical political economy, the crisis is never resolved through an 'invisible hand', a supposedly natural and spontaneous rebalancing of the system. It is instead always achieved by force and is thus always precarious and provisional. Development represents the victory of the capitalist class in the struggle opened by the crisis, a victory that is first and foremost political.

Before looking at what a workers' use of the crisis might mean for Negri, let us try to more clearly explain the dispositif of crisis. Negri's concept of crisis clearly references Marx and, in particular, the Marx of *Grundrisse* rather than the Marx of *Capital*. For Negri and for a certain operaismo, *Grundrisse* is Marx at his most political: rather than being simply preparatory notes to *Capital*, it is a work in its own right in which Marx develops a political conception that is missing from the later work.[4] For Marx, crises are not fortuitous accidents that the capitalist system occasionally stumbles upon, but are intrinsic to its very functioning and expansion. The crisis is an expression of barriers to development, which it is in the very nature of capital to pose and overcome. But this overcoming does nothing to remove the basic contradiction that triggers these crises. In fact, it only deepens it:

> from the fact that capital posits every such limit as a barrier and hence gets ideally beyond it, it does not by any means follow that it has really overcome it, and, since every such barrier contradicts its character, its production moves in contradictions which are constantly overcome but just as constantly posited. Furthermore. The universality towards which it irresistibly strives encounters barriers in its own nature, which will, at a certain stage of its development, allow it to be recognized as being itself the greatest

> barrier to this tendency, and hence will drive towards its own suspension. (Marx 2015: 410)

Marx understands modern crises as crises of overproduction, which are thus related to both production and circulation, as the latter is meant to absorb overproduction. When this fails, there is a crisis. Marx argues that this is because capitalism's very essence lies in the surplus value derived from unpaid labour, which is what creates profit. Given that capitalism must produce in order to make profit, and its products must always be absorbed by circulation, the crisis of overproduction is endogenous to capitalism. From one crisis to the next, this dynamic becomes increasingly catastrophic, as expressed in the theory of the tendency of the rate of profit to fall: with the increasing use of machinery in production – the constant capital from which no profit can be made – there is a gradual decrease in the capital spent on labour-power (variable capital), that is, in the living labour that is capable of producing profit and thus ensuring the system's survival. And so, in order to survive, the system needs to continuously expand the sphere of circulation, which ends up becoming a moment of production itself. The world market is the intrinsic tendency of capital's expansive dynamic, but it also represents its insuperable limit and its catastrophic destiny:

> The creation by capital of absolute surplus value – more objectified labour – is conditional upon an expansion, specifically a constant expansion, of the sphere of circulation . . . A precondition of production based on capital is therefore the production of a constantly widening sphere of circulation, whether the sphere itself is directly expanded or whether more points within it are created as points of production. While circulation appeared at first as a constant magnitude, it here appears as a moving magnitude, being expanded by production itself. Accordingly, it already appears as a moment of production itself. . . . The tendency to create the *world market* is directly given in the concept of capital itself. (Marx 2015: 407–8)

For Negri (and others), this tendency was now playing out in reality and called for a rethinking and updating of Marxian theory. Firstly, the acceleration of the alternation between crisis and development, and, consequently, of the catastrophic entropy of the system, meant the worker's 'point of view' needed to take Marx 'beyond Marx', and also beyond Tronti. The enlargement of the sphere of production and the resulting subsumption of the sphere of circulation under production had created a new 'political class composition'. Since production had now invaded society – with the sphere of circulation, of consumption, now part of capital's valorization process – the working class could no longer be located exclusively in the Fordist factory. And so Tronti's mass worker left the factory and became a 'social worker'. The second consequence, closely linked to the first, is that crises could no longer be managed by capital exclusively on the economic level but had to be governed politically: this passage was fundamental to the crisis becoming a dispositif for expressing political conflict. On the one hand, each new crisis deepened a class antagonism that no longer found its place and expression in the factory, but instead in the whole of society. On the other hand, in order to govern an increasingly widespread antagonism and a development made increasingly precarious by ever more disruptive crises and tendentially narrower profit margins, capital had to occupy the place par excellence of the modern political: the state. And so the latter lost its dialectical function of neutralizing or mediating social conflict, instead taking the side of capital:

> capitalist use of crisis thus ends up revolutionising social stratification (or, to define it more correctly, the political class composition) and laying the groundwork for a deepening, an extension and a radicalization of the class antagonism. But it has no alternative: capital is irremediably tied to this dialectic of development and crisis, within margins that can never become wide enough to eliminate the fundamental precariousness of the relationship; a dialectic which often results in that relation becoming even more rigid and constricting. In this situation, capital attempts to define a new structure for itself, in order to guarantee the maintenance of its new, precarious conditions of existence. The characteristics of the restructured capitalist state are designed to this end: to guarantee economic development in the presence (in society) of a working-class power that acts as the antagonistic and contradictory force within that development. (Negri 1988: 69–70)

While the world market and politics no longer posed limits to capitalist development, one obstacle still remained that capital needed to dialectically overcome through its integration, but which was in fact insuperable: the fundamental contradiction of the working class. Capital now sought to dominate the development-crisis relationship through a new class composition adapted to 'social capital' and to the politics of the 'planner-state' exemplified by Keynesianism. This is the conclusion of 'Marx on Cycle and Crisis':

> Development is simply the overall process which passes from one stage to the next; crisis is the moment of transition, a transition imposed against the impact of the working class and designed to bring the system back into equilibrium. Precisely this Leninist experience of 'smashing' [working-class intervention] needs to be fully recovered and made part of working-class theory; it is in that experience that working-class struggle becomes entirely political. (Negri 1988: 81)

The new antagonistic subjectivity was born from the crisis. It was under the pressure of crises that production – and with it the most antagonistic relationship between capital and the working class – had abandoned the Fordist factory and spread to the whole of society, meaning the subject of crisis was no longer Tronti's mass worker, but the social worker. Throughout the 1970s, Negri attempted to analyse the figure of the social worker, demonstrating his discontinuity with other exponents of early operaismo, who in turn created their own deviations from the more strictly operaist phase. In 1975, in 'Proletarians and the State', Negri describes the passage from the twilight of the mass worker to the dawn of the social worker:

> An overwhelming hypothesis then begins to take shape: *the category of the 'working class' goes into crisis, but as the proletariat it continues to produce all the effects that are proper to it on the social terrain as a whole* . . . The proletarian once made himself into the worker, but now the process is inverted: the worker makes himself into the tertiary worker, the socialized worker, the proletarian worker . . . We have seen the mass worker (the first massive concretization of the capitalist abstraction of labor) produce the crisis. Now we see restructuring, far from overcoming the crisis, unfolding and lengthening its shadow over the whole of society. (Negri 2005a: 126)

In theorizing this transition from the mass worker to the social worker, Negri clearly made use of the operaist method found in *Workers and Capital*. He fully accepted the precedence of workers' struggles – those of the mass worker of the early 1960s – over capitalist restructuring, and his decision to return to an analysis of class composition following the transformation of the capitalist mode of production was in keeping with operaist teaching. He also grappled with the same problem: the identification of a new antagonistic subject.[5] After all, Tronti himself had been writing for some time about the loss of the centrality of the working class. So what was it in Negri's idea of the social worker that diverged so radically from the previous operaist analysis of class composition, so much so that he wrote twenty years later that he had perhaps been 'too timid' (Negri 2005b: xl) in his description of it? The answer can be found in the term itself: for Tronti, the 'social worker', like the 'social factory', was an oxymoron, as the working class and the factory are radically opposed to any social dimension and any possible absorption into society.

As discussed in the previous chapter, in *Workers and Capital* society is the domain of bourgeois ideology, which neutralizes conflict and antagonism: in society, the working-class point of view is internal to the idea of the people. Perhaps Tronti also recognized the dissolution of the factory into society and the proletarianization of the working class, but unlike Negri, he understood this as the final demise of that subject and not a new political potential. The factory could have been the place where the Schmittian criterion of the political as friend-enemy opposition was realized, but society – like its corresponding political form, liberal democracy – was the complete opposite: a non-place.[6] For Tronti, it was impossible to take a side *(parte)* and form a party *(partito)* in society, because that can only be done in a place. The transition to post-Fordism thus brings about the demise of politics. Indeed, as a movement that was generated within and spread through society, Tronti understood 1968 as the acceleration of capitalist restructuring. In the same period in which Negri theorized an antagonistic subjectivity outside the factory in the figure of the social worker, Tronti continued to search for that workers' politics which he had left suspended in the postscript to *Workers and Capital*. And yet, while the secret of capitalism had been revealed by working-class struggle, the secret of politics remained in the theory and places of the enemy class. The implicit assumption was that true politics could only be found in the methods and places of modern politics and, therefore, the only way for the working class to truly gain political autonomy and break out of the economic relationship of the factory within and against capital – which had ultimately not produced the political rupture that he had hoped for – was to become the state. The Trontian turn of the 1970s, elaborated in 'The Autonomy of the Political', was based on these premises:

> The goal is to recreate an effective duality of power, but on a large scale: no longer in the factory, that is, no longer in the relations of

> production, and no longer even in society, but now *between society and state.* To conclude: the autonomy of the political actually turns out to be a utopia if taken as a directly capitalist political project; it actually becomes the last of the bourgeois ideologies; it becomes feasible, perhaps, only as a working-class demand. *The modern state, at this point, turns out to be nothing less than the modern form of the working class's autonomous organization.* (Tronti 2020)

This could not be further from what Negri was writing at the same time; their conceptions of politics were completely at odds with one another. Although for both thinkers the state is the place of power, for Tronti, politics is essentially a fight for power *(potere)* that takes place at the level of the state – the Political with a capital 'P' – whereas for Negri politics is the *potenza* (power/potential) that is immanent to the social dimension, which opposes itself to the power of the state, whose capitalist function is now evident. And so Negri calls for workers' autonomy from the state, which he sees as a capitalist enterprise and the form of capital's control over society. Meanwhile, this society gradually breeds new antagonisms – it is outside the factory, in society, that new antagonistic subjectivities are formed, and it is always within society that new political potential is created.[7] As Negri writes in 'Proletarians and the State': 'At this point, every transformistic operation, whatever it may be at the level of the "autonomy of the political", runs up against the unreality of this category, its mere adaptation to the mystifying ideology and practice of capital. *Today* the workers' utilization of state institutions is inconceivable: the tendency toward dual power can only result in a class dictatorship' (2005a: 147). And again, in 'Domination and Sabotage', where he explicitly takes leave of Tronti:

> Tronti says it well in his latest work: the modern state is the political form of the autonomy of the working class. But in what sense is he correct? In the sense – for him too, with his revived 'socialism' – of compatibility and convergence? Not at all, my dear comrade: here the methodology of the critique of political economy has to be modified, taking as its starting point proletarian self-valorization, its separateness, and the effects of sabotage that it determines. (Negri 2005c: 241)

In 1978, during his exile in Paris, Negri was invited by Louis Althusser to lead a seminar series on *Grundrisse* at the Ecole Normale Supérieure. This not only allowed him to engage in a systematic reading of this work, but also, away from the demands of political activity, to gather together his ideas and fully develop his interpretation of Marx. It was then that the originality of his thought really began to emerge, resulting in the book *Marx beyond Marx*, which marked a true watershed in his thinking. His focus was still on crisis, but its 'worker's use' was now clearly delineated, allowing the future developments of his thought to start to show through:

> The dynamic of communism rests on the emergence of subjectivity allowed by the crisis of mature capitalist development passively, simply allowing it space – but which also finds in this crisis the possibility to expand and enrich itself. Capitalist production, when it takes over society, renders inextricable the linkage of production and circulation. Circulation and production become, little by little, concepts which imply each other in the manner of production and reproduction. The social antagonism of the capital relation eventually ruptures this compact universe by exploding. The concept and the reality of the working class are displaced and reach the level where this explosion occurs. It is not simply the new antagonism between 'worker' and 'proletarian' which is displaced, but the composition of the proletarian class. Within this space, it is a process of collective constitution of the class which develops. (Negri 1991: 180)

Crisis thus provided an opportunity for an antagonistic subjectivity 'beyond' the working class as defined by early operaismo. When capitalist production moves outside of the factory to every economic sphere, a new class composition comes to the fore. Although this had already been shown in the figure of the social worker, Negri now took a further step beyond the Marx of early operaismo:

> But this sacrosanct insistence of Marx on productive labor as work immediately linked to capital, if it has a *direct political function*, which one can deny (it is probably the most workerist [operaist] of Marx's positions) has as well *ambiguous effects:* the conception of surplus value seems thus to close itself up entirely on the inside of the level of production . . . One can only conclude that the definition of productive labor which we begin to find in these pages of the *Grundrisse* and which we will find in other works is a *heavily reductive definition* in the literal form it assumes . . . Well, but then let us depart from here and see if it is not possible within the general frame of our exposition to apprehend certain terms which would permit us to

> advance and as well to take *the definition of productive labor to that level at once of abstraction and antagonism which seems essential for constructing the theory of surplus value.* (Negri 1991: 64–5)

The task was thus to identify a subjectivity adequate to the new frontier of capitalist production that had extended beyond the factory walls. This would be an antagonistic subjectivity at a higher level of abstraction not only than factory work, but also than a specific national society: an antagonistic subjectivity as the determinate abstraction of the world market:

> the process of circulation has achieved such a broad and powerful expansion that it exposes the circulation of capital not only as an expression of its own collective potency but also as the privileged terrain for the emergence of the power antithetic to it. *The theme of the world market is the most mature exemplification of the revolutionary tendency of the capitalist development.* (Negri 1991: 121)

In line with *Grundrisse*, Negri argues that the world market is the final horizon of capitalist development, and this tendency implies increasingly frequent and violent crises as the class struggle – and the force of antagonism – intensifies. The greater the abstraction of production in order to globalize the market, the greater must be the abstraction of 'productive' labour. It is at this level of abstraction that the new process of antagonistic subjectification must be identified: 'The paradox is completed; and it is no longer a paradox, it is a dialectical development of an exceptional intensity: *the opposition determines subjectivity and this subjectivity of labor is defined as a general abstraction. The abstraction, the abstract collectivity of labor is subjective power (potenza)*' (Negri 1991: 70).

The subjectivity identified by this mode of production no longer corresponds to the factory worker but is instead abstract immaterial labour. At a time when it is mainly machines (fixed capital) that occupy the spatio-temporal place of factory labour, the main productive force of surplus value becomes abstract labour, cognitive labour, whose subject is the general intellect; it is thus no longer reducible to a particular economic class. The notion of general intellect – along with other concepts including social brain, social individual and the collective worker – comes from *Grundrisse* and, in particular, from the so-called 'Fragment on Machines', which was a fundamental reference point for several generations of operaisti:[8]

> Forces of production and social relations – two different sides of the development of the social individual – appear to capital as mere means, and are merely means for it to produce on its limited foundation. In fact, however, they are the material conditions to blow this foundation sky-high . . . The development of fixed capital indicates to what degree general social 'knowledge' has become a *direct force of production*, and to what degree, hence, the conditions of the process of social life itself have come under the control of the 'general intellect' and been transformed in accordance with it. To what degree the powers of social production have been produced, not only in the form of knowledge, but also as immediate organs of social practice, of the real life process. (Marx 2015: 706)

For Negri, the Trontian formula of factory work 'within and against capital' no longer made sense, and even less so as the premise of political subjectivity. The process of subjectification that had taken place in the factory had created a homogeneous and uniform subject: the working class. Negri's new subject was instead politically constituted outside the factory and within capitalist society as a space of production in which cognitive and relational capacities are put to work, meaning that the distinctive trait of this new subjectivity was its 'difference', that plural and multilateral nature that Tronti saw as characterizing the social and not the political. For Negri, the 'criterion' of the modern political had become ineffective; opposition was no longer the condition of working-class political subjectification:

> The social individual is multilaterality. The highest intensity of difference is the highest approach to communism. . . . *Working-class power is not the reversal of capitalist power, not even formally.* It is the negation of the centralized and homogeneous power of the bourgeoisie, of the political classes of capital. It is the dissolution of all homogeneity. This methodological 'plural', this multilaterality triumphs. (Negri 1991: 149–50)

The new antagonistic subject did not need the enemy class to define itself, as it was not politically valorized in opposition: it was self-valorizing, autonomous. The criterion of the modern political no longer served the workers' use of the crisis because it no longer applied to the economic and social reality, which had become post-Fordist and postmodern. It was capital that needed the friend-enemy dialectic, the negation to be removed in the synthesis, the crisis to be overcome by development. Moreover, just as it was not within Fordist capitalism that the antagonistic subject would emerge, neither could antagonistic thought – 'negative thought' – emerge from within bourgeois thought, which, for Negri, was the expression of Fordism. The political-theoretical praxis of new antagonisms was not the overthrow of capitalism from within, but separation from it as the transition to communism:

> We must grasp the progress of capitalist accumulation in a reversed form. But we can not do this if we do not reduce this concept of inversion to that of separation. The relation of capital is a relation of force which tends toward the separate and independent existence of its enemy: the process of workers' self-valorization, the dynamic of communism. Antagonism is no longer a form of the dialectic, it is its negation. There's much talk of 'negative thought' these days. Well, negative thought, ripped from its bourgeois origins, is a fundamental element of the workers' point of view. Let us begin to use it, it will give some fruits! (Negri 1991: 188)

We must ask ourselves, as Negri does in the conclusion of *Marx beyond Marx*, whether the dispositif of the crisis, which reveals and radicalizes capitalism's dualism, must therefore be abandoned when this practice of separation affirms the autonomy and antagonism of the constituent power of a new subjectivity outside of the binary dynamic, delinking it from any constitutive link with the enemy class. Negri's answer is that crisis is the beginning: it provides the opportunity to escape the capitalist-bourgeois system. But if we want to find a way out, we must identify an outside, an elsewhere, here and now. It is in this shift from the logic of within and against to that of outside and against – from the thought of crisis to the autonomy of constituent power – that Negri's theoretical challenge to both Tronti's operaismo and Cacciari's negative thought, which we will now discuss, most clearly emerges: '*In this passage, the constituting process of communism finds its full development.* We must immediately underline that in this light the antagonistic logic ceases to have a binary rhythm, ceases to accept the fantastical reality of the adversary on its horizon. *It refuses the dialectic* even as a simple horizon. *It refuses all binary formulae*' (Negri 1991: 189). However, the question remains as to whether the dispositif of crisis allows us to move from the decision of separation to the decision of autonomy by the antagonistic side. We will return to this later.

3. Negative thought

In the 1977 introduction to *Pensiero negativo e razionalizzazione* (Negative thought and rationalization), Massimo Cacciari almost seems to anticipate the criticism that Negri would make of him in the conclusions of *Marx beyond Marx*. For Cacciari – as Negri himself would go on to claim, albeit in a more limited sense – negative thought, the critique of dialectical synthesis, is not only the theory of the crisis but also its essence. The critique of political economy is thus only possible within negative thought:

> The crisis of the classical synthesis is much more radical than the crisis of *political economy*. Furthermore, it is the crisis of every 'general theory' of the Political. The *critique* of political economy is not fulfilled in the Political, but in the *critique of the Political*. If here we find the most significant 'absences' in Marxian theory, all the more reason to recognize that today that critique is ultimately *the issue*. (Cacciari 1977: 12)

The critique of political economy begins from the same premise as Negri: development in response to the crisis does not result in its dialectical overcoming; on the contrary, dialectical synthesis fails to rebalance the system and the cycle is re-established as disequilibrium. However, unlike for Negri, for Cacciari the crisis is not the explosion of the fundamental contradiction of the capitalist system on which workers' power can impose its own autonomous political use, as the *potenza* (power/potential) of the social against the *potere* (power) of the political system. Cacciari instead understands the dispositif of the crisis as already completely encompassed within the political system: nothing remains outside of it, and so there is no way out. Thus, for him, the decision that leads from antagonism to autonomy remains as crisis within the system; it does not escape it. It is on this point that Cacciari parts ways with Negri. The crisis has indeed transcended the limits of the economic sphere, and in particular that of material production, to permeate the whole system – which capital itself has learnt to make political use of – but precisely for this reason the conflict that is produced within it cannot be activated from outside.[9] Cacciari argues that the critique of the political does not represent one sphere among others, but describes the very condition of conflictuality that is immanent to the system. With Hegel, the modern political reaches its climax in a synthesis of form that overcomes contradictions and removes conflict, but Cacciari's critique of the political points to the impossibility of such a form and the irreducibility of conflict. Indeed, since the idea of the modern political represents the dialectical synthesis par excellence, the critique of the political becomes the critique of every claim to synthesis.

Cacciari explains the primacy of the critique of the political over the critique of political economy in a 1975 article in the journal *aut aut*, 'Lavoro, valorizzazione, "cervello sociale"' (Work, valorization and the 'social brain'). Also beginning from Marx's *Grundrisse*, he partly shares Negri's reading that capitalist command becomes political as soon as it intervenes in the social dimension of the production relationship and identifies the 'social brain' as the main means of production and the source of surplus value.[10] But for Cacciari politicalness *(politicità)* always remains within the crisis; no political autonomy is possible outside of the structural crisis of the system. He argues that because the economic crisis has a political nature, we must move beyond the simple critique of political economy:

> The critique of political economy today must *also* be a critique of the forms and full expression of the political nature *(politicità)* of capitalist command . . . But by fully expressing the *politicità* that capitalist command assumes (its *obligatory autonomy* vis-à-vis original economic 'laws'), we reach an understanding of the structural nature of the crisis, of the ruptures in the process that we have traced, rather than its overcoming, and even less so its negation . . . The *politicità* of the current crisis is . . . a sign of its structural nature: of the fact that it has deeply pervaded the entire fabric and functioning of economic relations and of the social relations of production. The *politicità* of the crisis exists only within the contradictions that are established in these relations. (Cacciari 1975: 37–8)

Contrary to Negri, who argues that antagonistic subjectivity should reject dialectical synthesis or the 'binary form' of dialectics in order to avoid integration within the system and to become autonomous, for Cacciari the system itself, which is structured on the reiteration of crisis and conflict, has already rejected dialectics as ineffective, and has also revealed that no *politicità* exists outside of politics as crisis.

The crisis already represents the system's response to the dialectical Marxian critique of political economy, a response that is formulated within the bourgeois thought contemporary to Marx, in that negative thought that culminates in Friedrich Nietzsche's will to power. Cacciari argues that this is where we must start from if we want to move beyond Marx:

> *At bottom*, life is contradiction and conflict. Not even on the level of the Eternal Return, of the recognition of the equality of the fundamental structure of *Wille zur Macht* [will to power], is life 'reconciled', is there 'synthesis' . . . The conflict is *worthy* of repetition. The Return neither consoles nor concords, it *reiterates* . . . The dialectical system is refused precisely for this reason – because of its *impotence* – and therefore because of its still metaphysical ethical nature (*eticità*). And the dialectical system is *Wille zur Ohnmacht* [will to impotence] precisely because it develops forms for overcoming conflict – because it proposes equlibriums-syntheses . . . [O]nly conflict-contradiction exists – only *crisis* exists. And time develops through these crises – it is an *eternal cycle of crisis*, an Eternal Return of crisis. (Cacciari 1977: 46)

To arrive at Nietzsche and the will to power, we must follow the entire course of negative thought, in which Cacciari includes post-Hegelian philosophical (and other) theories centred on the critique of the dialectic and, in particular, of dialectical synthesis. From *Sulla genesi del pensiero negativo* (On the genesis of negative thought) (1969) onwards, Cacciari gives an Enlightenment-style reading of great bourgeois thought from 1848 to the crucial years of the crisis of the Weimar Republic, a reading that counters the idea that negative thought is irrational,[11] understanding it, on the contrary, to be characterized by rationalization and disenchantment. Cacciari sees negative thought as an attempt by bourgeois thought and the capitalist system to confront the irreversible crisis of the dialectical state in modern politics and of the planner-state in political economy by freeing political organization from all synthesis and from everything transcendental, including labour. However, by integrating and incorporating crisis into the capitalist-bourgeois system, it is not posed as an alternative to it, but as functional to its preservation:

> Negative thought tends to demonstrate the ineffectiveness of dialectics in relation to fundamental oppositions, the illusoriness or mystification of the syntheses it creates. It indicates the elements that remain unmediated, unschematized, irreducible to the level of concrete logic, to the necessity of the system . . . This is not a mechanical transition from the negative to the positive, from refusal

> to acceptance. On the contrary, precisely because of its negativity, precisely because it remains firm in a position of radical refusal of the structure and ideology of the bourgeois system, anti-dialectical thought can appear to be an ideological *function* of this system. It is only its negativity that allows it to have a real, grounded, and therefore functional – structurally functional – critique of the system. It is not a question of 'removing' the negative, but of grasping in it the new relationship that is being established between ideology and bourgeois society, between ideological forms and new needs, the new reality in general that the system's 'dialectical' process irreversibly establishes. It is fairly obvious that this kind of reading no longer has anything to do either with the critique of negative thought as reactionary 'apologetic' 'irrationalism', or with its analysis as pure, 'blocked' contradiction, a total opposition. (Cacciari 1969: 139)

In short, negative thought is that form of rationalization which, in response to the crisis of the dialectical system, does not seek its overcoming, for then it would remain within dialectical thought as the method of *Aufhebung*, turning the negative into a positive. It does not seek a new form of synthesis but instead emphasizes the functionality of crisis as a transformation immanent to the system that is oriented towards the preservation of order, despite the different forms of conflict within it. This is the ideological function of negative thought.

The philosophical triad of negative thought consists of Arthur Schopenhauer, Søren Kierkegaard, and Nietzsche, in that order. And it is Nietzsche that reaches the most radical conclusion:

> In Nietzsche, the historical aspect is taken to its extremes . . . It is the refusal of every *positive* synthesis, which Kierkegaard still sought precisely for its movement-towards-transcendence. For Nietzsche, synthesis became *domination*, the victory of the most 'perfect' will that acts in pure immanence. Therefore, this synthesis would not have any character of 'value', it would not look for any 'justification' in the universal – on the contrary, it would be the refusal of all values, whether aesthetic, ethical or religious. (Cacciari 1969: 172–3)

Unlike for Negri, for whom the Nietzschean will to power represents *potenza* (power/potential), for Cacciari, it represents the refusal of all values and the conscious assumption of *potere* (power).[12] This *potere* is the capacity to dominate, not *over* the world, which would imply the dialectical synthesis of the Hegelian subject, but *in* the world, in 'pure immanence'. Nietzsche goes beyond both Schopenhauer's will as the renunciation of the world and Kierkegaard's Single Individual which transcends the world in the religious (Cacciari 1971). As Cacciari writes in *Krisis*, the book in which he concludes his research on negative thought: 'Power [*potere*] is being integrated into the system' (Cacciari 1976: 66). But to be integrated into the system means leaving nothing outside, nothing can assert itself as 'autonomous': not even the subject. 'Organization' is asserted over autonomy.

For its power to be fully deployed, for the world to completely lose its objectivity and autonomy, the subject itself must lose its privileged position, its own autonomy:

> The subject thus seems to find itself in a paradoxical situation. On the one hand, it rediscovers its active, 'creative' function, which was previously unthinkable, and on the other hand, however, it loses any 'point of view', any gnoseological 'privilege'. It posits the system in its dynamic and contradictory nature – but, at the same time, it is *no longer* distinguishable from it in any way . . . The *Wille zur Macht* is therefore the opposite of all subjectivisms, of any exaltation of late-romantic, genial 'creativity' . . . But by positing such a process, the subject has lost all auratic 'autonomy', it has become part of it, its property. This is the tragedy of the subject. *To have effective power*, it must not only become disenchanted with its own 'a priori forms', with the 'truth' and 'goodness' of the world, with the schematism between forms and the world, with its own capacities to give the world a fully determinate meaning, but it must also reject the extreme Value – that which even the most radical nihilism had preserved, indeed, of which it had been the most fierce defender – of the *autonomy* of subjectivity. (Cacciari 1976: 66)

Nietzsche's negative thought ends in this incomplete deconstruction of modern subjectivity. It is here that the tragedy of his negative thought can be found: every decision demonstrates nothing other than the impossibility of making a final decision that would put an end to the crisis. In *Sulla genesi del pensiero negativo*, Cacciari took Nietzsche's will to power to its extremes, reaching conclusions that Nietzsche had never quite arrived at:

> In Nietzsche, the negativity of the self vis-à-vis the system, reflected in its autonomy, is posited for the last time and completely disappears for the first time . . . Thus the Subject is rather the System itself as the

> will to power, insofar as it had to overcome its 'dialectical form' to ensure the *existence* of its own process. This denotes the historical limits of Nietzschean thought. (Cacciari 1969: 187)

A subjectivity outside the system is no longer conceivable: neither the Nietzschean aristocrat nor operaismo's working class survives. Furthermore, if the system is the subject, the subjective prerogatives of transformation, innovation, production, and creation can no longer be converted into antagonism. However, we mustn't forget that the system is not synthesis, but conflict and crisis: this is the power that we become part of when we integrate into the system. There is no conflict outside the system: within is against. It is no longer the subject that is antagonistic, but the system itself. Negative thought thus leads operaismo into the form of the tragic.[13] Although it has no reconciliation or overcoming, the tragic is still a form of conflict, or, better, it is *the* form of conflict. Affirming the irreducibility of conflict, the tragic forces it into a binary logic without resolution, which, as Negri points out, early operaismo arrived at but did not get beyond. Rather than being one object among others in a conflict, the system is the subject that, by guaranteeing conflictuality within itself, subsumes and dominates that conflictuality as conservation. The system reflects the inevitability of fate in classical tragedy. The problem left open by the tragic outcome of negative thought is whether a revolutionary politics is possible without the possibility of new antagonistic subjectivities to bring it about. Indeed, is even a politics of innovation possible within a political system that converts conflict into conservation? How can a subjectivity that no longer has power over the system make decisions and effective demands? In short, to use Max Weber's terms, since disenchantment as the outcome of rationalization does not transform the system as such, how can the conservative nature of the transformations within it be turned into innovation? This is the problem posed in *Krisis*:

> The problem is: *how* does [the subject] participate in [the system]. Why, with what aim? And what character do its forms of 'participation' have, when every substantivist illusion has collapsed, as well as every simple elementary relation of meaning, and when the relation to the object is 'disenchanted'? To what extent and in what ways are they still effective? Radical nihilism can get as far as that 'disenchantment' – but it cannot address, let alone resolve, these questions. Nietzsche also only intuits and poses them: they constitute the *necessary*

> *[destinata]* conclusion of his work – and would constitute the plot of the Wittgensteinian 'tragedy'. (Cacciari 1976: 63)

It is here that Ludwig Wittgenstein meets and completes Nietzsche: the *Tractatus Logico-Philosophicus* fully formalizes the will to power by translating it into logic. In Wittgenstein, negative thought and the thought of crisis acquire a specific logic, which supplants that of the flourishing bourgeois society to which Hegel had led traditional metaphysics. The world is thus a system of signs that do not refer to any meaning that transcends them – they are pure convention. It is a system of horizontally related equivalent propositions with no hierarchy of meaning. The sign precisely corresponds to the thing, the fact, and language as a system of signs corresponds to what is said and exhausts all that can be said. Thus, for Wittgenstein, power over the form of language is power over the world. But the subject itself is also a sign, performing a function within the system. It is not Wittgenstein, but Weber, who fully integrates the subject into the system, making it a function of the system at the expense of all subjective qualities: the politician becomes an official and the work of the intellectual is a vocation. And yet, for Cacciari, neither Weber nor Wittgenstein succeed in dissolving the last transcendental residue in immanence. That residue comes to the fore when we tackle the fundamental problem of the crisis. For neither thinker does the crisis become fully productive, does it become transformation. Although the crisis is integral to the system, they see it as a cycle and not a transformation: 'however explicitly grounded in the multiplicity of languages [Weber's] system tends to express itself as a *complete phenomenology*: a rigorous science, *without* exceptions. The division of labour, *Rationalisierung*, *Parlamentarisierung*: it is in these 'conflicts', *not* in others, in *these* dynamics, not elsewhere, that the subjects of capitalist development are posited' (Cacciari 1977: 165). This is similar to Cacciari's criticism of Wittgenstein's *Philosophical Investigations* and the latter's theory of linguistic games. Cacciari argues that these games, when applied within the context of the crisis, tend to restabilize, and so confirm the order of the system: 'The ordering appears simply as restoration. The response to the crisis is the exact opposite of identifying new paradigms, of breaking with the normal game played up to that point' (Cacciari 1976: 86–7). Thus, although in both Weber and Wittgenstein the modern poietic and creative subjectivity has abandoned identification with either the sovereign or with economic and social classes, the function of subsumption and domination has been assumed by the system.

And so we are left with a problem: if the perfectly and completely disenchanted and formalized world presents itself as a totality, if no transcendental assures its perfectibility, and if traditional subjects have lost the privileged position that guaranteed them the possibility of decision – if the system itself is now the subject – then how can the transformations that the crisis demands be converted from preservation into innovation? In an attempt to answer this question, Cacciari uses Wittgenstein to introduce the concept of the mystical. In *Krisis*, the mystical transcends the boundaries of the logical-epistemological sphere of the *Tractatus* to get to the heart of the tragedy of negative thought:

> The 'mystical' is not the experience of the transcendent – *but the opposite*. Neither is the 'mystical' the question of *what the world is like*. The 'mystical' is the experience of the world as *completely limited*. The 'mystical' originates in *the fact that the world exists*. Therefore, the conclusion of the *Tractatus* is really the only *logical* conclusion . . . The 'mystical' is radical *worldly* experience . . . *At its root* is the complete formalization of the Schopenhauerian theory of representation-formalization, which, as we know, was also Nietzsche's 'project'. The world-representation relationship can no longer be transcended – thus there can no longer be value propositions *in* the world. The critique of the subject is an integral part of this approach, as in Nietzsche . . . This reality, thus defined, is formalizable. But this process of formalization is the same as that of the 'mystical'. It proceeds only *within these limits*: feeling [these limits] is the 'mystical'. It is not only, then, the awareness of the limits of formalism, but also the awareness of formalism *as a limit*, that characterizes the 'mystical' conclusion of the *Tractatus*. This limit includes the whole 'history' of 'philosophy'. (Cacciari 1976: 94–5)

Thus, the mystical is the destination of negative thought, and, consequently, of Western philosophy itself. It is a twilight that does not herald a new dawn – it is its completion.

Like in Wittgenstein, for Cacciari the effectiveness of the mystical lies in its ambivalence. We have already highlighted one aspect of this ambivalence: the mystical is radical worldly experience, the experience of the world as a 'limited whole',[14] and yet, if this totality encompasses everything that can be experienced, if every expression is included within the limits of language and nothing exists outside of it, if the political is functional to the administration of order, if 'on that which cannot be spoken about – on that which is not integrated into the system – one must be silent', how can there be innovative transformation? In other words, how can we think of crisis as something other than conservation, and thus beyond negative thought? 'The problem of transformation-crisis is not attacked or rejected, it simply lies completely outside this ambit. We can also repeat the *despair of the Tractatus*: what counts is not the *sayable* result – what counts is other, *it is the Other*' (Cacciari 1976: 92). This is the second aspect of the ambivalence of the mystical: the Other does not represent a return to transcendence but is given precisely by virtue of the insuperable limits of language. That which must be kept silent can be 'manifested':[15]

> The 'mystical' has another, complementary and opposite function. Just as it excludes from linguistic expression any reference to an 'ineffable', and therefore founds the possibility of propositions endowed with meaning, so it also *manifests* the ineffable. It manifests it – it knows it cannot say it. This is of fundamental importance. Without the 'mystical', formalism would always tend to become 'everything', to present itself as 'truth', to eliminate every limit from itself. (Cacciari 1976: 96)

Only the complete exhaustion of every meaning that transcends the sign and of every sense that transcends the logical and formal relationship between propositions manifests this totality within the disappointing limits of 'Can this be all?',[16] and manifests this completely disenchanted world in its irredeemable 'misery', in whatever form it takes. The dominant system, the capitalist-bourgeois system, is reduced to misery, one form among others, without any primacy or privilege. If *the* form is not given, neither is the subject: the mystical shows that not even the system is subject. If the fully formalized and disenchanted world is effectively recognized as a totality leaving nothing outside itself, it is only here, in this totality, that it is possible to act. If this totality is not only not the form of synthesis that removes conflict and contradiction but is not even an 'apologia' of the system as the one and only form, then at least an effective trans-formation is possible – a transition from one form to another. Although revolutionary transformation cannot be affirmed, neither can pure conservation, as all forms are equal on the plane of immanence:

> Here, despite everything, the fixed structure of the world and the doctrine of meaning assumes the role of the *theatre* of a radical act

> of *negation* that is the transformation of every relationship. The 'mystical' makes impossible an 'apologia' for the relationship between logic, proposition and the world. It senses and *manifests* the 'misery' that the sciences will never be able to overcome, in fact, they must not, in order to be truly such (and not pose as a false totality) . . . The intuition of the world *sub specie aeternitatis* founds the awareness of the 'misery' of this totality. And so only it becomes formalizable-formulable-feasible. It becomes the space of scientific propositions – and of the variety of games. (Cacciari 1976: 98)

The mystical is the ultimate outcome of Cacciari's attempt in *Krisis* to convert the crisis into transformation-innovation, that crisis which negative thought had understood to be the result of the final dissolution of dialectical synthesis and which, at another level, it integrated into the capitalist-bourgeois system in order to preserve it.

4. The impolitical and the autonomy of the mystical

The mystical on the logical-epistemological level corresponds to the impolitical on the level of the critique of the modern political. In Cacciari's *Dialettica e critica del Politico* (Dialectics and critique of the Political) (1978a) the impolitical is given as the Nietzschean solution to the crisis of the Hegelian dialectical state:

> this critique [of dialectical reason] – in Schopenhauer and in Kierkegaard – concludes in the *Impolitical*, in the utopia of the subject as a Single Individual 'free' from the Political. This 'figure' is still dialectical, it is still Hegelian: it denounces the totality of the Political as *false*, but it does not transform the effective language of *this* Political. The Nietzschean impolitical is instead a *critique* of the Political. That no subject and no Truth are expressed in the State does not entail the utopia of the Single Individual – but the *problem* of great Politics . . . But precisely because the Political no longer appears as *the* Language capable of producing the Truth of the subject in the State, this State is *transformable*, and that Political is the continuous revolution of its forms. (Cacciari 1978a: 73–4)

As Cacciari reiterates in 1978 in 'Nietzsche and the Unpolitical' (2009a), the political was completed in Hegel in the dialectical state. Once its irreversible crisis and the irresolvability of its contradictions (of class, above all) had been ascertained,[17] all that was left was the impolitical as a critique of any return of the political as synthesis and value. As a result, the state became transformable and indeed the only place of transformation.[18] In political terms at least, it seems that Cacciari ends up reaching the same conclusions as Tronti in 'The Autonomy of the Political' (2020). Yet since Cacciari's conception of the autonomy of the political represents a form of the impolitical, it differs from Tronti's, as we can see in this passage from the introduction to *Pensiero negativo e razionalizzazione*:

> The Autonomy of the Political and its redefinition . . . are thus the obligatory theme of any introduction to the historical problem of the Political. The 'autonomy' it 'enjoys' does not give the Political any privileged point of view. It defines the particularity of the functions, the 'value' of the functions, that it is called upon to perform in relation to and because of the limitations inherent in the other elements of the system. Without such limitations, and thus without such elements, there would be no 'autonomy' of the Political. A complex system of 'autonomies', for which differences-conflicts-contradictions are but 'other names', takes over from the homogeneous, centripetal structure of dialectical *Rationalisierung*. The Political *is/in* this universe. (Cacciari 1977: 11)

The political is impolitical: it is within the system of language games, each of which has its own 'autonomy' conflicting with that of others. It does not in any way occupy the privileged position of *the* language capable of translating all other languages into its own terms; on the contrary, the autonomy of other languages limits its own autonomy.[19] In short, the state cannot represent the place par excellence of the struggle for power, because conflict takes place between different 'autonomies' within the system, none of which prevails over the other. Thus, Cacciari's autonomy of the political does not locate the state where it had been found in the modern political. Indeed, it could be argued that the crisis of the modern political split it in two: the state is one of the two parts, the bureaucratic-administrative part, while the other part, that of the revolutionary project, is pure utopia – *ou-topia*, nowhere, a non-place (Cacciari 2009b). Cacciari's state is thus the result of the crisis of the modern political. It is organization that deploys technique as politics: organization as the administration of the limits between the respective forms of the various conflicting autonomies. This organization is not aimed at taking power, but only at ensuring that no form can escape transformation and thus impose itself over others.[20]

Giacomo Marramao takes a similar position to Cacciari, beginning from the Schmittian idea of the impossibility of delineating a specific domain of the political, from which follows the always contingent movement of its centre. In *Il Politico e le trasformazioni* (The political and transformations), Marramao argues that in the crisis of the planner-state the autonomy of the political no longer means identifying the place of conflict but is instead the continuous dislocation of conflict. It is therefore impossible to locate the political and identify its definitive reference subject: 'economic politics is not *planned* on the basis of *a single* interest (even the "common" interest) but is rather the result emerging at different times from the conflict between the different "autonomies" into which the political system is "constitutionally" divided' (Marramao 1979: 62).[21]

In Cacciari, the mystical and the impolitical both seem to affirm radical immanence and, as Negri pointed out in his review of *Krisis*,[22] the illusory nature of any presumed autonomy with respect to the organization of the system. Indeed, autonomies and antagonisms are only given within this organization of the crisis – in both its logical-epistemological and its state form.[23] Thus, Cacciari holds that the autonomy of the revolutionary – the autonomy of the antagonistic subject – would not be *potenza* (power/potential), but the mirror image of the *potere* (power) to which it is opposed, and so also a form of *potere*. It is difficult not to see the following lines in 'Critica della "autonomia" e problema del politico' (Critique of 'autonomy' and the problem of the political) as being addressed to Negri:

> the Autonomy of the Revolutionary is nothing but the reversal (the reversal that leaves everything as it was before, only reversed, so as to make its apperception and analysis even more difficult) of the Autonomy of Power (*Potere*). The Power that represents itself in these terms, as System, State, and the Philosophy of the State, generates the abstract Autonomy of the Other, and vice versa. (Cacciari 1978b: 129)

Both in philosophy and politics, the autonomy of the antagonistic subject has been completely revoked – both have fulfilled their destiny in modernity. Philosophy and politics are finished because they are perfect. The mystical is the end of philosophy: 'Philosophy doesn't "finish" because it is "betrayed" or "forgotten" by the development of science, but because it is completely realized in this development. Philosophy ends once it has achieved its fundamental destiny: to annihilate the Being of the Entity, translating it into subjectivity, without remainders . . . Philosophy finishes because it is *perfect*' (Cacciari 1977: 77). And the impolitical is the end of politics: 'The unpolitical [*impolitico*] is the recognition of the occurred perfection of the political' (Cacciari 2009a). In the following years, however, the mystical and the impolitical, which Cacciari originally understood as complementary and on the same plane of immanence, ended up splitting and diverging in his work, much like modern politics. Whereas he would use the mystical as a starting point for later developments in his philosophy, he would come to see the impolitical as a dead-end. The main reason for their divergence was Cacciari's encounter with Martin Heidegger, which allowed him to find in philosophy potentialities that politics had exhausted.

The philosophical path that Cacciari follows thus leads to a shift in his thought: from Nietzsche to Heidegger, from negative thought to the premise (*presupposto*). The Nietzsche-Weber line of negative thought culminates in the impolitical, which represents a dismissal of modern politics and its fundamental categories. But, in 'Law and Justice' – published in *il Centauro*, one of the most influential journals of the 1980s – Cacciari argues that Heidegger inflicted the final blow to the modern political. Although the article still ends on the question of the impolitical, Cacciari's analysis is in fact already theological-political in character:

> The play of differences and mirrors between the theological and the mystical, and within each of these dimensions, fundamental to understanding the modern problem of the political, is here, rigorously judged as confusion, equivocal, as inner face of the They: in short, as nondecision, which does not mean that up to now we have not succeeded in founding political decision, but that such foundation is impossible, that the desire to find it leads to idle talk. What is the extent of this recognition? That today only the space of the program is sensibly available, or that idle talk is inevitable for the political just as the equivocal is for discourse? That, anyway, the modern political not being able to abandon those terms, is compelled to repeat them as ideological myth, or that one has to be able to radically renounce them, as if words that seemed proper of the political (decision, engagement, responsibility, representation), in their complexity and diversity, were by now justly sayable only in nonpolitical spheres, better, in the unpolitical [*Impolitico*]? (Cacciari 2009c)

The fate of the modern political seems to be sealed, and, far from representing an alternative path, the impolitical is the acceptance of its end. In the crisis of the modern political, the rationalization of negative thought is translated into politicization, technicization, bureaucratization and democratization.[24] This process advances through the destruction of the value of modern political categories and is realized in the chatter of the Heideggerian *Man*, in which these categories become equivalent to every other word, pure signs in search of signification. Having lost its own peculiar domain, the political is realized in the domain of technique. The rationalization of the system, which, only a few years before, Cacciari had thought might still offer potential for transformation, had now become mere administration. The Heideggerian embrace proved fatal for Marx. This could already be seen in *Pensiero negativo e razionalizzazione*, in which Cacciari had reread Marxism in the light of Heidegger:[25]

> Marxism, as it is *essentially* conceived by Heidegger . . . concerns the problem of the indissoluble relationship between subjectivity and Technology, of the 'non-technological' essence of Technology: of its being, that is, a complete and *complex* expression, not reducible to neutral instrumentality, of a cultural-historical destiny – [Marxism] concerns this fundamental problem of the non-neutrality of Technology, which opens up to the *political* dimension of Technology, to its being-existence of determinate 'wills to power', of instruments, functions and organizations of the Political. (Cacciari 1977: 79–80)

It is worth noting that in 'Law and Justice' Cacciari also distances himself from Weber, the most significant thinker in the application of negative thought to political theory. He opposes the mystical to Weberian 'innerworldly asceticism' as the origin of capitalist ethics and modern politics:

> It is necessary to withdraw mysticism from this progressive scheme in order to evaluate, at the same time, both the radical opposition to innerworldly asceticism (which in the evolutionary character of that scheme ended up as dialectic overcoming of asceticism itself) and its actuality in the formation of the modern political, or, better, in the definition of the problem of the modern political. To grasp the irreducibility of mysticism does not mean, however, devaluing its importance for political form. On the contrary, it means analyzing it in its structure. This both deepens and complicates the concept

> of rationalization, since it has to be redefined in the presence of an autonomous mystical dimension with respect to that simply innerworldly of the ascetic. (Cacciari 2009c; trans mod)

It is as if the 'innerworldly' and immanent aspect of the mystical in *Krisis* can be attributed to Weberian asceticism, while another aspect related to Heidegger's thought – the mystical – became autonomous. As if Marxism and Heideggerianism, initially understood by Cacciari – albeit problematically – as having a common horizon, had finally parted ways:

> Heideggerian thought interrogates (and challenges) Marxism here: is Marxism still an ideology, *one* ideology [among others], however historically decisive, however totally different from other contemporary ideologies, from the 'isms' that ravage language? Or *can* it currently exist as a presence, a 'will', a completely original historical force vis-à-vis Technique *as politics*? . . . Without *demonstrating* an affirmative answer to the Heideggerian question there is nothing but research into the origins of the meaning of metaphysics either as the *memory* of Being (which is the Heideggerian 'solution') or as Marxist 'tradition'. (Cacciari 1977: 82)

According to Heidegger's 'Letter on Humanism', Marxism is still a humanism – it is still completely internal to that tradition. And so, to engage in a radical critique of humanism – the same critique that had led others to return to Marx – Cacciari reaches for Heidegger.[26] Only a few years later, Cacciari would describe Marxism as the 'ultimate' form of the metaphysical tradition and the 'Heideggerian solution' as an 'ulterior' possibility that was still open to philosophy – its unrealized and unrealizable possibility. However, he would find no other effective outcome for politics than fully – democratically and administratively – deployed technique. The impolitical, being still *in* the political, remains trapped in the rationalization of the political as the democratization of political language, while the autonomy of the mystical becomes thinkable.

A year before 'Law and Justice', Cacciari had already discussed the autonomy of the mystical in *Dallo Steinhof* (Posthumous People), responding in particular to Giorgio Agamben's interpretation of the Wittgensteinian mystical. The debate with Agamben raised some problems for Cacciari. For instance, in *Infancy & History* Agamben writes:

> What Wittgenstein posits, at the end of the *Tractatus*, as the 'mystical' limit of language is not a psychic reality located outside or beyond language in some nebulous so-called 'mystical experience', it is the very transcendental origin of language, nothing other than infancy. *The ineffable is, in reality, infancy*. Experience is the *mysterion* which every individual intuits from the fact of having an infancy. This mystery is not an oath of silence or mystical ineffability; on the contrary, it is the vow that commits the individual to speech and to truth . . . Truth is not thereby something that can be defined within language, nor even outside it, as a given fact or as an 'equation' [*adequatio*] between this and language. (Agamben 1993: 51)

The mystical of *Krisis* seems to share the immanence in language of Agamben's mystical. Cacciari writes: 'The "mystical" denotes the tragedy of the unity and coherence of language in and for its being-silence . . . The "mystical" manifests silence as the fundamental *agent* of the general organization of the system of language' (Cacciari 1976: 134). In *Krisis*, therefore, the mystical is the silence that belongs to the totality of language as its limit. For Agamben, too, infancy as mystical is manifested in language itself; truth – as non-linguistic and not as linguistic, hence as *aletheia* and not as *adequatio* – is the in-difference of language, a difference that appears within language, that is immanent to it. Yet – and this is where Agamben departs from Cacciari – this difference does not belong to language. On the contrary, it prevents human experience from being entirely reducible to language: infancy is the difference between the human and the linguistic. And like infancy for the human being, the non-linguistic is not the negative of the linguistic, although it is manifested in it. The mystical as infancy can be manifested within language because it is different from it:

> *In terms of human infancy, experience is the simple difference between the human and the linguistic. The individual as not already speaking, as having been and still being an infant – this is experience* . . . For the very fact that infancy exists as such – that it is, in other words, experience as the transcendental limit of language – rules out language as being in itself totality and truth. (Agamben 1993: 50–1)

For Agamben, as for Cacciari, Wittgenstein's mystical is a fundamental resource for questioning language, contesting the ontological primacy that the emergence of hermeneutics attributed to it at the time. However, it is precisely on the difference between the mystical and language that their interpretations, and ultimately their thought, diverge.

Cacciari, too, ends up claiming the difference of the mystical with respect to language, but for him this difference is possible because the mystical is manifested not as non-linguistic, but as other, as transcending language, whose truth consists in *adaequatio rei atque cogitationis*. Responding to Agamben, in the chapter 'On the Mystical Again' from *Posthumous People*, Cacciari ultimately conceives the mystical as a dimension other even than that silence which, in *Krisis*, is immanent to language and constitutes it:

> The ineffable cannot be understood simply as the silence that accompanies and transcendentally limits every proposition, the silence that binds speechlessness, truth, and language in a 'founding relationship' (Agamben). This reading, if it cancels all 'mysticism', does not capture the autonomy of Wittgenstein's dimension of the ineffable or the problematic possibility that it can exceed the limits of that relationship . . . Agamben is right. The mystical inexorably accompanies the utterable. But it does so in a dimension other than that of the utterable itself, in contrast with it: as manifestation. That which manifests itself is not spoken, is not produced by saying. It is the premise of speech. As speakers, we are ever mere in-fants. We exist prior to the dimension of manifestation, before that which manifests itself, before the premise, the presupposed . . . Not by accident does this self-manifestation remind us so much of *aletheia* [unconcealment]. (Cacciari 1996: 99)

In his confrontation with Agamben, Cacciari renders the mystical autonomous from the system of signs of language, identifying it as the 'premise' (*presupposto*).[27] This concept was key to his philosophy in the following years, and provides the starting point of the diptych of *Dell'Inizio* (On the beginning) and *Della cosa ultima* (On the ultimate thing).[28] The reference to the Heideggerian conception of *aletheia* – which is absolutely other to the Western notion of truth as *adequatio* ultimately realized in technique – suggests that Cacciari had bent the mystical of *Krisis*, the fulfilment of negative thought, towards the 'Heideggerian solution'. Heidegger offered the possibility of a philosophy prior to any rationalization and delinked from the idea of an end, in other words, philosophy as premise. Cacciari ends 'On the Mystical Again' with a reference to this premise, taking his thought beyond *Krisis*: 'But in the manifestation of the mystical there lives the near-memory of the premise, and the intensity of its recognition for a moment seems truly to interrupt the nihilism of the logos' (Cacciari 1996: 101). A few years later, in 'Sul presupposto' (On the premise), he interrogates the possibility of an 'ulterior' with respect to the 'ultimate', thus with respect to that silence which had concluded the path of negative thought in the mystical of *Krisis*:

> Critical philosophy, which claims to 'transform' everything in the immanence of thought, arrives at the idea of the absolutely transcendent – and here it becomes pure silence. This ultimate silence 'makes true' its constitutive negativity. But the transcendence of the simply existing is overturned into a new beginning . . . Now, only by beginning from the actual experience of the forms of this revelation is it possible for us to prove that the necessarily existent is not simply an idea, it does not 'conclude' in the Ultimate of negative philosophy, but is, indeed, free creative action. (Cacciari 1986: 48–9)

But this new beginning is not available to Marxism. For Cacciari, Marxism shares the fate of negative thought as the last, most extreme form of critical philosophy. And so, like Tronti, by the end of the 1970s, Cacciari interpreted the red glow they had seen at the beginning of that decade as the twilight of antagonistic political subjectivity.

Chapter 3

THE 'CONSTELLATION' OF THE 1980s

1. *The crisis of the party and its intellectuals*

Following Italy's 'long '68' (1968–77), Italian philosophy gradually moved away from the dualism and antagonistic conflict connected with the *sinisteritas*. Previous attempts to identify the 'line' and deviations from it – which, in turn, became new lines, provoking yet further deviations – seemed to have exhausted their heuristic capacity. In the 1980s, the link between the antagonism of the cursed part and the official line of the Italian Communist Party (PCI) began to come apart. The 'historic compromise' of Enrico Berlinguer's PCI, which proposed an alliance with the Christian Democrats in order to form a government – which failed due to the 1978 kidnapping and murder of the Christian Democrat leader Aldo Moro by the Red Brigades – proved that the PCI had abandoned all ambiguity, placing itself wholly within the reformist logic of liberal democracy. This was part of a long crisis in the PCI, stretching from the 1970s right up to its dissolution in 1991, a little over a year after the fall of the Berlin Wall. There had also been a change in the subjectivity the party referred to, with the working class gradually abandoning its partial and partisan character. The latter was no longer the fundamental antagonistic part, nor the only part which the party attempted to represent. Meanwhile, outside parliament, a space opened up for extra-parliamentary social movements, expressing a plurality of parts without a political party. Applying the idea of *sinisteritas* to this context, when its traditional subjectivity and political organization had been lost, brings to light the subjectification of other 'cursed parts'. From that point on, the parliamentary left could potentially become the party of government, while other cursed parts demanding political recognition and affirmation remained outside.

The debate emerging in the 1970s still strongly emphasized the dichotomy between the inside and outside of the party: those within it included the so-called entrists, like Tronti and Cacciari, who saw the PCI as the only potentially effective organization and returned to it with the intention of transforming it from within;[1] and those outside, like Negri, who understood organization as arising from workers' autonomy rather than vice versa. Although one group privileged organization and the other autonomy, they both assumed a close link between theory and practice: theoretical work meant taking a side and was valid precisely to the extent that it could be realized politically. From this point on, however, as we see particularly clearly in Cacciari's work, philosophical theory and politics began to diverge, ultimately becoming completely autonomous from each other.[2] As Cacciari's thought showed, any philosophy that located politics outside of forms of political organization ended up dislocating it into the sphere of the impolitical. This was the final blow to the Gramscian concept of the organic intellectual,[3] the idea of the party intellectual embodying the unity of theory and praxis that had previously been embraced by the PCI. Although, on the one hand, this meant Italian intellectuals lost their influence on state institutions and public opinion – exacerbated by accusations that some of them had been the '*cattivi maestri*' (bad teachers) of the generation that had embraced armed struggle – on the other hand, it allowed them to develop their thought without worrying about the ins and outs of Italian politics. Indeed, from the 1980s onwards, Italian philosophy began to transcend national borders, taking on a more international character.

Their withdrawal from the public sphere in the 1980s, in contrast to the previous decade of political commitment and struggle, led some Italian philosophers to return to the fundamental questions of modern political philosophy, and others to respond to stimuli in the international debate. In both cases, the detachment from politics – whether desired or not – led to a deepening of their theoretical positions.[4] Emblematic in this regard were two journals founded in the first half of the 1980s: *Laboratorio Politico*, headed by Tronti, which did not have a directly 'militant' perspective,[5] marking a break with previous operaist journals; and *il Centauro*, headed by Biagio de Giovanni, who later argued in an interview that it emerged from a fundamental shift in the history of Italian intellectualism:

> For me, *il Centauro* was essentially the end of a certain interpretation of organic intellectuality . . . there was clearly . . . a desire to take the 'organic' character of intellectual work – that of being both theorists and political leaders – in a different direction . . . *il Centauro* was a philosophical journal that wanted to make its detachment clear; of course, behind it there was a reading of current events, but that

> was reinforced through a real attempt to rethink the categories of theoretical-philosophical thought. (Gentili 2007: 420–1)

A similar trajectory was followed by *aut aut*, one of the most long-standing and important philosophy journals in Italy, founded in 1951 by Enzo Paci. After closely following the 1970s' social movements and the debates arising in them, in the 1980s it began to shift its focus to international currents of thought. In fact, at this point it introduced much international thought to Italy, much like it had with phenomenology in the 1950s. In short, as there was no official line to follow or diverge from, and no political efficacy to be tested in specific times and places, the various lines of thought within 1980s' Italian philosophy became increasingly autonomous from each other, ending up intertwining with, if not actually aligning with, emerging international issues.

The fall of the Berlin Wall in 1989 marked the end of an era. While Italian philosophy made important contributions to the analysis of globalization, which on a geopolitical level was the most disruptive phenomenon to arise from this transition, it also responded to another fundamental change: a new political role for Europe. The latter had begun to be seen as a new horizon onto which the thought of crisis could be projected and developed. At least starting from the fall of the Berlin Wall, the crisis of the party form – which in Italy had coincided with the crisis of the state form – led various thinkers, some of whom had previously been the 'organic intellectuals' of the party, to seek in Europe the possibility of a political form adapted to the crisis of modern politics and to the various other transformations underway at the time.[6]

And so, rather than gathering (and clashing) around a few specific nuclei – which after 1989 would be indiscriminately dismissed as ideologies – the philosophies of the 1980s formed a 'constellation'. While previously the so-called crisis of Marxism had hegemonized the debate on the Italian left[7] – which, although expressing different Marxisms, had remained within Marxian thought – this crisis was now seen as only one of many expressions of a broader and more complex crisis of modernity and its fundamental paradigms.

2. Weak thought and postmodernism

'Today, the philosophical debate has at least one point of agreement: there is no single, ultimate, normative foundation' (Vattimo and Rovatti 2010: 7): thus begins Gianni Vattimo and Pier Aldo Rovatti's foreword to the Italian edition of their 1983 essay collection *Il pensiero debole* (Weak Thought), a book that immediately sparked debate beyond Italy, where it joined other philosophies analyzing the emergence of a post-ideological society of global communication.[8]

First arising in the economic and political spheres, the crisis had ended up undermining the very foundations of modern rationality. Vattimo and Rovatti argued that the theory of crisis formed in the previous decades was always destined to end in tragedy, as it remained conditioned by the very form of rationality whose crisis it decreed:

> In the 1960s, *another* foundation was being sought. While one sense of knowledge now appeared to have crystallized, philosophy took it upon itself to confront this 'crisis', mobilizing in an attempt at a scene-change . . . The most striking example of this was the discussion around the foundations of Marxism . . . The next scene, that of the 1970s, appears to be marked by much less optimism. The merciless eye of a thought without redemption enters the stage – a 'negative' thought – with which, however, many still active and hidden metaphysical residues can be discerned . . . At this point, the 'crisis' of the foundations can no longer be treated as a bad truth that can be overthrown by a new one: the crisis shifts to the very idea of truth. The tone of the debate changes: even if unwelcome, a tragic element steadily breaks into it, and in the end, whether they know it or not, all positions are ways of elaborating this element or keeping it at bay, an element which a language rendered opaque by old customs continues to call 'irrational'. (Vattimo and Rovatti 2010: 7–8)

While the various currents of 1960s and 1970s philosophy had revolved around the question of the foundation – whether an alternative foundation could be found or whether a foundation existed at all – the 'weak thought' of the 1980s aimed for a shift in perspective. As we have seen, the critique of dialectical synthesis by negative thought, far from being irrational, had created a more advanced form of rationalization: the absence of a metaphysical foundation in fact strengthened the power of reason, reinforcing reason as power. Although this opened up a debate on the crisis of reason, Vattimo and Rovatti argued that this debate had failed to free itself from the essential traits of rationality, including its capacity for synthesis:

> In Italy, meanwhile, the debate was around the 'crisis of reason': rather than making it work, there was an attempt to 'save' reason

> from the irrationalist phantom that had still been barely exorcised. The Italian case is typical. Nietzsche, Benjamin, Heidegger and Wittgenstein himself first surreptitiously and then overtly entered the debate, producing all sorts of mixtures and medleys . . . but which almost never overcame the resistance of a theoretical attitude that could perhaps be called 'political': a theory, that is, understood as power, the capacity for control, absorption and totalization. The explicit renunciation of any metaphysical foundation was always balanced by an attempt to safeguard the capacity for synthesis, the still generalizing power of reason. (Vattimo and Rovatti 2010: 8)

For Vattimo and Rovatti, then, we should not be legitimizing irrationalist tendencies by recognizing their rationality, or proposing another form of rationality, but instead should aim to 'lighten' and weaken the very rationality that modernity had aligned with power. This was weak thought's specific attempt at a shift in perspective, towards an 'overcoming' of modernity and the political:

> rationality must weaken itself internally, give ground, not be afraid to retreat towards the supposed shadow zone, not remain paralyzed by the loss of the luminous, unique, stable, Cartesian reference . . . It begins, perhaps, with a loss or, if you like, a renunciation. But right from the start we find that it is also a movement away from an obligation, the removal of an obstacle. (Vattimo and Rovatti 2010: 10)

From the beginning of his essay 'Dialectics, Difference, Weak thought', published in *Weak Thought*, Vattimo lays out the terms needed to understand the conception of overcoming proposed by weak thought. These terms, which include 'dialectics' and 'difference', are of course fundamental to the traditional philosophical lexicon, but precisely for this reason indicate that it is within this tradition that the overcoming or, more correctly, the Heideggerian process of *Verwindung*, takes place. In fact, weak thought primarily begins from the explication and interpretation of the concept of *Verwindung*:

> I will try to sketch the main tenets of weak thought, *il pensiero debole*, and how it is related to dialectics and difference. This connection is not to be understood mainly or solely as an 'overcoming' but, rather, it is to be defined primarily in terms of the Heideggerian notion of *Verwindung*, a term whose sense also must be understood

within the horizon of a 'weak' notion of what it means to think. (Vattimo 2012: 39)

As we shall see, Vattimo attributes different meanings to this Heideggerian notion, including decline (in the sense of decrease, turn down and in the grammatical sense of listing various forms), distortion and recovery. For Vattimo, remaining on the level of a simple overcoming means remaining within dialectical thinking, which is true also of those philosophies aimed at liberation or redemption. He claims that it is wrong to understand the work of Benjamin, Adorno, and Bloch as mere attempts to rethink the Hegelian dialectic for the benefit of those excluded from the dominant power, for this would fail to recognize the innovative potential of their philosophies: 'The importance and suggestiveness of thinkers like Benjamin, Adorno, and Bloch consists less in their having rethought dialectics in such a way as to incorporate the critical exigencies of micrology, than in their having reassessed such exigencies even to the detriment of dialectics . . . They are not dialectical thinkers. They are thinkers of the dissolution of dialectics' (Vattimo 2012: 42). Benjamin, Adorno and Bloch[9] – and, Vattimo adds, also Sartre and the young Lukács, who at the time were being discovered in Italy as exponents of a heterodox or heretical Marxism – were not a deviation from the fundamentally dialectical line of orthodox Marxism but instead represented its exhaustion. Likewise, weak thought was not a critique of the dialectic, but a different way of thinking, which Vattimo called 'micrology'. Inspired by Foucault's 'microphysics of power'[10] and other tendencies in contemporary French thought, the idea of micrology was elaborated in particular by Rovatti, first in his essay 'Transformations in the Course of Experience', also published in *Weak Thought*, and then in other essays published shortly afterwards in *Elogio del pudore* (In praise of modesty).[11] In the following decades, Rovatti would further develop this line of thought based on a weak conception of subjectivity, understanding it as a narrative philosophy of the everyday and the marginal. Vattimo, on the other hand, used Nietzsche and Heidegger to set out a weak ontology or an 'ontology of decline' (*Verwindung*) as the recall and transmission of the past. Unlike those thinkers that we associated with *sinisteritas*, he did not attempt to identify a cursed part as an alternative to the dominant part, but instead completely rejected the logic of the part and the party, as well as the logic of conflict deriving from it. The dissolution of the dialectic, which Vattimo reformulates as the 'thought of difference', thus aims to free itself from the idea of the liberation or redemption of the cursed part:[12]

> Having assimilated the Marxist overthrow of idealism, twentieth-century dialectical thought presents itself as a philosophy of totality and reappropriation, for it redeems as materialism what the culture of the masters has excluded. Yet that 'cursed part' excluded by the masters refuses to be reabsorbed in a totality so easily. Those who are excluded feel that the very notion of totality is a 'lordly' notion, one belonging to the masters. (Vattimo 2012: 43)

Weak thought describes itself as a thought of difference but does not posit difference as the new foundation of thought and reality, which would mean simply replacing, and, indeed, dialectically overcoming, dialectical thinking. The concept of difference in weak thought does not refer to the tradition of dialectical thought but rather to Heidegger's ontological difference:

> The issue of the difference between Being and beings, called the ontological difference, ultimately leads much further than even Heidegger expected . . . We truly distinguish Being from beings only when we conceive of it as historical-cultural happening . . . The world plays itself out in horizons constructed by a series of echoes, linguistic resonances, and messages coming from the past and from others (others alongside us as well as other cultures). (Vattimo 2012: 44–5)

No state of affairs can claim ontological supremacy or represent a truth justifying its dominance either in the present or in some future in which history guarantees the liberation of the oppressed. As Nietzsche claimed, 'God is dead', and he is dead both for the dominated and for the dominators. Protecting the difference between being and entities – between truth and opinions, between substance and appearances – does not imply the Platonic separation and hypostatization of two spheres, but means that only entities, opinions and appearances exist. And they exist only as such and not as the copy or shadow of the being to which they refer. And, Vattimo adds, they are such – that is, they are entities, opinions, and appearances – because their being is linguistic. As the German philosopher and Heidegger's student Hans-Georg Gadamer, whom Vattimo introduced to Italy, wrote in *Truth and Method*: 'Being that can be understood is language'. This hermeneutics that 'declines' truth as interpretation is the clearest heir to Nietzschean nihilism, understood not in a negative but in a constructive sense, as the possibility of a post-metaphysical, plural form of rationality based in solidarity.[13] Without the absolute truth of reason, the different forms of reason of each individual and each civilization – including those that in the past had been (dialectically) imposed on others – cannot be presupposed, but must all be re-expressed and re-elaborated. They must be 'declined' in each specific case within ever-changing and multiple horizons of meaning, and 'recovered' in transience, contingency and fallibility. The constellation of these concepts – decline, recovery and so on – composes *Verwindung*:

> The dialectical heritage through which difference is declined (*verwindet sich*) into weak thought is condensed in the notion of *Verwindung*, and with good reason, for *Verwindung*, as we know, is the term Heidegger adopts in place of *Überwindung*, the overcoming or sublimation proper to dialectics. *Verwindung* (declination/distortion) and recovery . . . mark the attitude which characterize post-metaphysical thought in relation to the tradition handed down by metaphysics. More than that, in the Heideggerian concept and 'practice' of *Verwindung* we find a concentration of the dialectical (and thus metaphysical) heritage that still lives on in the thinking of difference. (Vattimo 2012: 46)

The practice of *Verwindung* is possible only if we think being in the sense of the Nietzschean eternal return: all of the past returns, but this return takes place within the context of the present that declines and distorts what is passed down, thereby weakening it. Following the debate triggered by the publication of *Weak Thought*, Vattimo returned to the notion of *Verwindung* in 'La filosofia del mattino' (The philosophy of the morning), published in a special issue of *aut aut* dedicated to weak thought. There he emphasized the Nietzschean basis of Heidegger's concept of *Verwindung*: 'The tension towards a thought that is totally other can lead to mystical outcomes, whereas the interest in going back not so much beyond but through the wanderings of metaphysics leads us in the direction of a Nietzschean 'philosophy of the morning' and emphasizes a 'nihilist' tone in Heidegger's thought' (Vattimo 1984: 12). Vattimo was trying to clarify his position both with respect to Gilles Deleuze's interpretation of Nietzsche at the time – which Vattimo describes as the 'glorification of simulacra' (Vattimo 1988a: 161), since it attributed the strong aspects of being to the cursed parts of metaphysical thought, such as appearance, drives, desires and creativity – and with respect to Cacciari's interpretation of Nietzsche and Heidegger and the relationship between them.

Cacciari identifies a discontinuity between Nietzsche and Heidegger, from which the two increasingly divergent lines of his thought emerge: the first, that of negative thought, which culminates in Nietzsche's work, which – more or less in line with Heidegger's interpretation of Nietzsche – corresponds to the end of metaphysics and the emergence of the will to power as technique; and the second finds in Heidegger the possibility of a thought of the *beginning* beyond metaphysics, which he calls *Andenken* or 'recall'.

Vattimo instead sees a substantial continuity between Nietzsche and Heidegger, thus contesting the interpretation advanced by Heidegger himself in his book on Nietzsche.[14] Indeed, we could argue – as with Vattimo's definition of *Verwindung* – that Vattimo constructs his own categories from his weakening of both philosophies. Thus, the end of metaphysics does not make possible a thinking beyond metaphysics, a new beginning as *Andenken*, but entails 'taking leave' from metaphysics, resulting in a 'recall' of its own tradition in the sense of a repetition-distortion – *Andenken* thus becomes synonymous with *Verwindung*:

> Heidegger's *Verwindung* is the most radical effort to think Being in terms of a 'taking account of' [*presa d'atto*] which is at once a 'taking leave of', for it neither conceives Being as a stable structure nor registers and accepts it as the logical outcome of a process . . . [I]t is synonymous with *An-denken*, the other more current term with which the later Heidegger designates postmetaphysical thought. This is thought which recalls Being. (Vattimo 2012: 47)

We are not interested here in establishing which of the two interpretations of Heidegger is philologically more accurate – after all, Vattimo himself considers both to be legitimate – but rather in determining the extent of their divergence. In Cacciari's deepening of the difference between *adequatio* and *aletheia* – the two conceptions of truth he borrows from Heidegger, from which negative thought and *Andenken* respectively derive – he ultimately maintains a political thought of conflict that would be inconceivable for an ultra-metaphysical philosophy of recall. And this leads him to reproduce, on another level, in the form of the organization of the political and the autonomy of the mystical, that dualism that his immanent conception of the crisis had rejected in principle. Vattimo, on the other hand, by conceiving of overcoming as *Verwindung* and *Andenken*, dissolving the dialectic in a thought of difference, ends up also dissolving conflict. This is the way that the postmodern and philosophy as hermeneutics should be understood, rather than as *novum*, totally other, or as a critique of the modern:

> It is in this way that ontology becomes *effectively* hermeneutic, and the metaphysical notions of subject and object, indeed of reality and truth as foundation, lose their force. In my opinion, in this situation we must talk of a 'weak ontology' as the only way out of metaphysics – by way of an acceptance-convalescence-distortion that no longer contains anything of the critical overcoming characteristic of modernity. It may be that therein lies, for postmodern thought, the chance of a new, weakly new, beginning. (Vattimo 1984: 14)

Herein lies the peculiarity of Vattimo's hermeneutics: it is not only a philosophy of language – in line with the linguistic turn of the 1920s and 1930s stressed by postmodernism[15] – but is also a weak ontology. Conflict thus arises between different interpretations, styles and rhetorics, but always within the context of dialogue. Thus, as Vattimo seems to suggest in the chapter 'The Adventure of Difference', Gadamerian dialogue, which allows for the fusion of different and possibly conflicting horizons, is the postmodern 'declination/distortion' of dialectical synthesis:

> Although in *Truth and Method* Gadamer does not say much about ontological difference (a fact which is in itself worth pondering), the centrality for Gadamerian hermeneutics of dialogue testifies to the persistence there of this fundamental element of Heidegger's thought. It is the presence of a plurality of *Daseins* that makes it impossible to conceive of the hermeneutical integration of the horizon of presence as a dialectical *Aufhebung* . . . [T]he fusion of horizons takes place to the extent to which each of the interlocutors 'renounces' his *own* horizon, not by renouncing the fact of having a horizon, but by renouncing the fact of managing it as his own or disposing of it as he pleases. (Vattimo 1993b: 152–3)

In dialogue, the interlocutor's renouncement of any claim to a certain horizon of meaning as their own entails the dissolution of conflict, but at the same time also the dissolution of that subjectivity whose subjectification is determined by the logic of belonging:

> For it is perhaps precisely at the point where the forgetting of difference appears to be most complete, in the experience of metropolitan man, that Being speaks afresh; and it does so in its 'weak' modality, which involves a dissolution of the subject with all the violent characteristics (those of master and slave, for example) attributed to him by the metaphysical tradition. It is *this* weakened subject who lives being-towards-death . . . The weakened subject should thus also be open to a less melodramatic relation with his own mortality. (Vattimo 1993c: 6)

But although dissolving the Hegelian master-slave dialectic might make mortality less dramatic and reduce the fear of death, surely the dialectic remains the form of the subjugation-subjectification process. This raises the question as to whether a weakened subject can still be called a subject. Can the renunciation of conflict represent a form of subjectification, albeit a weak one? Does the weakened subject – post-humanist but not post-human, dislocated from the centre of the cosmos but not without *ethos* – correspond to a new form of subjectivity? Certainly not, Vattimo would reply, as affirming novelty is an aspect of the critical overcoming that characterizes modernity:

> Modernity is defined as the era of overcoming and of the new which rapidly grows old and it is immediately replaced by something still newer, in an unstoppable movement that discourages all creativity even as it demands creativity and defines the latter as the sole form of life . . . [T]hen no way out of modernity can possibly be found in terms of an *overcoming* of it . . . Modernity is not only constituted by the category of temporal overcoming . . . but also by the category of critical overcoming. (Vattimo 1988b: 166)

One of the many contributions to the debate on weak thought[16] was de Giovanni's 'Apologia del moderno contro il pensiero debole' (Apologia of the modern against weak thought), published in *il Centauro*, which pointed out the ambiguity of the weak subject and argued that the critique of the modern had to be made from within the modern, recognizing its complexity:

> The *weak subject*, thinned out, is nothing but the extreme and in some respects also irreducible form of that same subject that, with quite different ambitions, is posed at the origins of the modern. It is the same subject that has declared its ambition defeated . . . Why

> does weak thought not choose the more decisive path of the *death of the subject*? Or better: why does it waver symptomatically between the two metaphors of weakening and death? An outline of an answer might look something like this: the death of the subject implies an excessively strong, tragic break; the death of the subject implies the unsettling question of a *new* beginning. (de Giovanni 1986: 58)

To avoid the dialectical overcoming that the question of a new beginning implies, Vattimo and Rovatti propose not the death of the subject but a weakened subject. However, there is the risk that this subject is more easily captured by dispositifs of subjugation, which despite the opacity, indeterminability and elusiveness of phenomena in the postmodern world, are in fact not weak at all.

Rovatti proposes a subjectivity adequate to a constantly changing reality: a weak subjectivity that abandons the central place which the subject had held in modernity and finds other places, converting its subjectification into a permanent becoming. This is what Rovatti proposes using the Foucauldian lexicon – the lexicon which I am also using here – in *Trasformazioni del soggetto* (Transformations of the subject):

> A restlessness of the subject, whose fragility not only makes it versatile, but also renders it a real excess with respect to any possible individualization. And which, at the same time, exposes it to risk. Not, therefore, a simple absence, an empty space, something that can only play at power by means of a resistance-withdrawal, removing the ground it could stand on. The movement that we can try to read is not one of subtraction (as opposed to 'subjectification' as a process of the micro-physical constitution of power) but rather of risk-taking, gathering from this versatility (of a subject that can do what it wants) the character of an unsubjugatable 'presence' (the subject always escapes one's grasp, and it is this risking of its identity that makes it a subject). (Rovatti 1992: 100)[17]

Rovatti's weak subjectivity – paradoxical in its oscillation between death and versatility – is thus active. The fact that this is one of the main characteristics of the modern definition of the subject explains why he still uses the term 'subject'. And yet, can being unsubjugatable really be a form of subjectification? Although Rovatti aims to explore practices of subjectification as an alternative to subjugation, if the abandonment of the central place of the metaphysical subject means its dislocation to other places,[18] it would seem that what distinguishes the weak subject is the renunciation of conflict – the renunciation of that essentially political place which, although now more dispersed and dislocated than it had been in modernity, remains the only space where subjugation and subjectification are reciprocally implied. And so, if we do not want to renounce the political subjectification produced by conflict, we must think up forms of antagonistic subjectification, or, at least, new subjectivities, that are adequate to new processes of subjugation. Alternatively, we could abandon the category of subject, which is inextricably linked to modern thought and its sites of power, in order to confront those new forms of the 'government of life' that Foucault identified through the biopolitical paradigm. In other words, we must explore whether it is possible to think conflict beyond dialectics and also beyond the negative dialectics that criticizes its synthesis.

3. *The thought of sexual difference*

Carla Lonzi's manifesto *Sputiamo su Hegel* (Let's spit on Hegel) concludes with the announcement of a new subject whose novelty does not result from a dialectical overcoming. This text, written in 1970, represents the beginning of the thought (and practice) of Italian feminism:

> We say to the man, to the genius, to the rational visionary, that the destiny of the world is not in continuously moving forward as foreseen in his longing to overcome. The world's unforeseen destiny lies in beginning the journey again with woman as the subject. We recognize in ourselves the ability to turn this moment into a total transformation of life. Those who are not in the master-slave dialectic become conscious and introduce the Unforeseen Subject into the world. (Lonzi 1970: 37)

Deviating from the Hegelian-Marxist line, she argues that the subjectification of women as such does not take place within the conflict formalized by the master-slave dialectic: 'The Hegelian master-slave relation is internal to the male human world, and the dialectic is adapted to it in terms deduced precisely from the premises of the seizure of power' (Lonzi 1970: 6). For Lonzi, unlike class struggle, the gender question does not arise within the struggle for power, which is always a male dynamic involving a succession of slaves and masters within the same order. Indeed, from the beginning of the 1970s, the

Italian feminist movement separated from the workers' movement, taking its own autonomous path.[19] It argued that women's collective consciousness (*autocoscienza)* would not be achieved through liberation from an oppressive power, for in this essentially dialectical logic, the power of a particular class is simply replaced by that of a new class in which the subject and power remain male: 'Standing up as women does not imply participation in male power but calling into question the concept of power' (Lonzi 1970: 4).

The philosophical challenge is clear: to think of a form of subjectification outside the logic of power, thus outside of the subjugation-subjectification nexus. This can be done by moving onto another plane: 'Woman is not dialectically related to the male world. The demands she makes do not imply an antithesis, but *a shift onto another plane*' (Lonzi 1970: 32). Women are oppressed on the basis of their sex, and this sexual difference is the 'unforeseen' that allows women to recognize themselves as subjects. This is not the *novum* of modern thought, but the 'never before seen' that has in fact always been there – the original and perpetual presence of an absence: 'Woman's difference is thousands of years of absence from history' (Lonzi 1970: 4). And not only is sexual difference the unforeseen of the patriarchal order, which, although shaken by transformations and revolutions, has shaped history in its own image and likeness, but it is also its 'unthought'.[20]

It is the thinking of this unthought that gives Italian feminist philosophy its peculiarity, also at an international level, especially with respect to later Anglo-American feminism that attributes the same cultural – and therefore non-biological, non-constitutive – origin to sexual difference as to gender, effectively doing away with the distinction between sex and gender.[21] While pointing out the complexity of all feminist theories, in *Il pensiero femminista* (Feminist thought), Adriana Cavarero stresses the specific originality of the Italian thought of sexual difference. Its idea of the primacy of practices, which went back to the 1970s, meant that, like other strands of Italian philosophy at the time – with the sole and significant exception of weak thought – it was impervious to postmodernism and the linguistic turn of the 1980s and 1990s:

> [Postmodernism] finds significant correspondences almost everywhere in international feminism, but is one of the respects in which the Italian thought of sexual difference develops in an original and, in some ways, anomalous manner. This essentially has to do with the rooting of theory in *practices*, among which the so-called

> practice of collective consciousness *(pratica di autocoscienza)* has a founding role. (Cavarero 2002: 97)[22]

The theory of sexual difference thus arises from the practices of Italian feminism: experience becomes thought, and only on this condition can a 'thought of experience' be elaborated. The fact that this thought originates in experience and practice means that it is impossible to define a fundamental theory of sexual difference. And precisely because they originate in practices, the constellation of theories in the thought of sexual difference are configured through misalignments and disjunctions rather than oppositions.[23]

The founding practice of Italian feminism is that of collective consciousness *(autocoscienza)*, as elaborated by Lonzi. In order to think of themselves as subjects, women must begin from themselves, otherwise they remain bound to a form of subjectivity in which difference is a mere accident. Traditional philosophy begins from an identity whose rationality and universality either excludes sex or implies masculinity. Thus, woman has at most been understood by it as different from a given self, but not in herself. So the difference that must be thought is not that passed down by the philosophical tradition, conceived within the universal-neutral One which was constructed through abstracting from the body. And sexual difference is also not included in the multiple differences into which the postmodern fragments the metaphysical One. It is neither one nor many, but is originally 'a two'. This is how Cavarero summarizes the specificity of sexual difference in *In Spite of Plato*:

> This is a radical revolution in perspective with respect to the existing philosophical context that began with Parmenides and has come down to our postmodern mode of thought. Here, in the new philosophical horizon of sexual difference, the basic element of philosophy is a *two*, not a *one*. Here, the original speakability of difference is inscribed as the *two*, not the *many*. And this *two* brings into language living and embodied humans, in all the splendor of their finitude. (Cavarero 1995: 6)

Sexual difference does not therefore mean that woman is the other of man as the universal One, but neither can she speak of herself as the Other-One of the original Two: the woman-essence. As history has shown, the experience of speaking of herself as the Other-One is tantamount to staying silent, because the language of the philosophical tradition emanates from the One, the product of the patriarchal symbolic order, within which the feminine part has not only been cursed (*maledetta*) but has also been expressed wrongly (*detta-male*). Thus, for a woman to speak of herself without having to repeat what man has *detta-male* or to avoid being reduced to silence in order to escape this repetition, she must be able to begin from herself. In the 1970s, against what they saw as a logic that denied sexual difference in left-wing movements' claims for equal rights,[24] the most radical feminist groups introduced the practice of separatism. They understood the possibility of subjectification in sexual difference as arising from making oneself a 'part', but in a completely different sense to that of the part created in the conflict for the seizure of power.[25] In her contribution to the first book published by the community of women philosophers 'Diotima', Cavarero outlines the theory arising from the experience of separateness: 'The essence we seek is thus the historical essence of a real subject that wants to understand herself by beginning from herself. The essence found in thinking of herself is therefore the experience of separateness . . . the experience of a separateness that is no longer mute but coming to the word [*venuta alla parola*]' (Cavarero 1987: 60). In this experience, woman is recognized as separate in herself, different to herself: separateness is not dialectically removed – or overcome – she does not constitute herself as a female identity, as 'Woman' or as the 'Other-One'. The thought arising from the experience of separateness must abandon this identity, for, in the removal of the difference between individual women, the universal woman ends up as the double of the universal man. And so, in order not to fall into the identitarian logic it wanted to escape, the theory of sexual difference comes to think of woman – as a subjectivity in which individual women are similar to each other but not identical – as a difference of Difference, part of the Part or, to use the formula which Luce Irigaray used to describe the irreducibility of sexual difference, the other of the Other.[26] Woman is both the Other of the human subject within language, and the other as such, who cannot speak of herself in that language. It is this constantly active difference, which happens whenever a woman speaks of herself as a subject, that challenges the linguistic reductionism found in so many postmodern philosophies. And yet, as Cavarero points out, although she was not foreseen in theory and language, woman had begun to find words to speak of herself through the experience of separateness: 'In speaking of herself as the experience of separateness, the other can now appear in a representation that includes her' (Cavarero 1987: 63).

Women are constitutively and voluntarily 'indifferent' to the seizure of power, in the sense that it makes no difference to them. Given that women speaking of themselves as subjects is neither translated into the language of the liberation of her 'part', nor expressed in the weakening of metaphysical language into one of the various dialects of postmodernism, she now needs to locate herself within a symbolic order in which she can recognize herself and find a language of her own. Cavarero argues that the experience of separateness allows this need to be expressed:

> The experience of separateness, which we have defined as the essence of female sexual difference, is thus a first step towards the construction of a symbolic that can give representation to the foundation of our being similar . . . A first word for a discourse that contemplates woman as subject, the first step across the threshold of *her* word. This discourse, the home of woman's language, has no obligatory paths, or, at least, has paths that we cannot yet perfectly trace from here, from this poor beginning, but we can already foresee that sooner or later it will have to tackle the question of maternity, despite our frequent desire for reticence. (Cavarero 1987: 72–3)

The experience of separateness is thus only the beginning of a theoretical journey that uses the thought of sexual difference to rethink the world in its entirety or, to use the title of a book by Diotima, to '*Mettere al mondo il mondo*' (Bring the world into the world, also in the sense of giving birth to it).[27] The becoming-part of women revealed the primacy of the relationship, ensuring that female difference would not be reduced to identity. The political choice to escape the patriarchal order also demonstrates the partiality of the latter's presumed totality and so the untenability of its assumed autonomy and self-subsistence. As Cavarero points out, the construction of a symbolic order of the mother would from then on guide Italian research on sexual difference.

In *In Spite of Plato*, Cavarero reworks the categories of Hannah Arendt's philosophy in the light of the thought of sexual difference and through a female reappropriation of the figure of Demeter, the mother-goddess of Greek mythology, with the aim of identifying a symbolic maternal order. This meant a radical reversal of the predominant line of Western philosophy. A philosophical thought that privileges birth opens up a world separate from the *polis*, which reduces the differences – above all of sex – of each person's unique experience to the unity of the abstract and universal political body.[28] These differences, which determine the irreducible finitude of every living being, instead find expression in an order that resists standardization and normalization, that of the mother:

> A recuperation of the sense of human engendering from the mother, a philosophy of birth has thus the main purpose of disinvesting the concrete individuality of each human from societal totalization . . . But turning the gaze toward the mother, one can acknowledge that these [experiences of birth, love and death] are separate from the site of negotiable common living, and not subject to social regulation. They are *physis* rather than *polis*. (Cavarero 1995: 81–2)

That the origin is the mother – and not nothingness as understood by the conception of creation corresponding to the Heideggerian being-towards-death, which also ends in nothingness – means giving a name to 'the two'. At the origin, there is the relationship, that between the mother and child. The child carries within itself this relationship as finitude, as an unfulfillable desire – as the impossibility of a complete and perfect autonomy. This relationship penetrates the public space of the *polis* but finds its meaning and expression in the symbolic order of the mother. Thus, Cavarero identifies a newness that does not arise from an overcoming: birth is a beginning that, in its relation to the uniqueness of maternal generation, eludes both overcoming and repetition. Novelty comes into the world embodied in each and every one of us and is expressed in the unrepeatability of the history we begin:

> Here *physis* means birth, as befits its etymological origin . . . [C]ontrary to death, in birth one is not alone but in a duo: the mother and the one who is born . . . Certainly, the newborn is unrepeatably 'new', it is a re-present-ation (a making eternally present) of the 'beginning' . . . However, in its singularity the newborn is a 'beginning' found already 'started' inside the mother. (Cavarero 1995: 82)

Luisa Muraro's *The Symbolic Order of the Mother*, a classic of the Italian thought of sexual difference, was published around the same time as *In Spite of Plato*. Having previously identified the deficiency in the symbolic dimension, experienced above all at the level of language,[29] Muraro took a different theoretical path, largely informed by metaphysics, psychoanalysis and the philosophy of language. She too comes to recognize in the mother, and in particular in the daughter's relationship with the mother, the principle of the symbolic order. Like

Cavarero, Muraro attributes a higher symbolic authority to the mother than to other political, social or cultural symbolic orders, since these derive their authority from having replaced and 'usurped' the maternal position, and for this reason are often manifested as authoritarianism:

> But I place [the maternal principle] above authorities and powers whose codes make up both the symbolic and social order, any historical order in which one happens to live, we might say by chance if it were not for the history of our birth. This discourse has two distinct but inseparable levels. At a more accessible level, which is not evident yet (although the politics of women is emphasizing it more and more), there is an alternative and there is a choice to be made. We must choose whether we want to identify symbolic authority with established power, since it assures (or in the case of the established opposition it promises to assure) some kind of social synthesis, or whether we want to acknowledge the authority of the woman who brought us into the world and taught us to speak. It is because of our relationship with her that the mother is entitled to authority that, instead, established powers usurp from her. (Muraro 2018: 96)

A clear distinction between authority and power begins to form in Muraro's discourse, which is far stronger – rooted as it is in sexual difference – than the distinction Arendt makes in *The Human Condition*.[30] In line with the etymological derivation of *auctoritas* from *augeo* (to grow), Ida Dominijanni argues that the mother's authority arises from the 'act of producing from her own breast' and from the 'gift of raising something and bringing it into existence' (Dominijanni 2001: 73). Power, on the other hand, is incapable of generating anything from itself, and thus cannot do anything but repeat the maternal creation. But this repetition is not really creative: Cavarero argues that it cannot begin something new, for it does not give birth. Power, whether political or social, establishes an artificial body through a synthesis that does not take account of certain human experiences (including, but not limited to, women's experiences) and does not recognize a higher authority that can renew and open this body to those who are excluded or who exceed the given social order. Muraro calls this 'unforeseen' part of the order of power the 'wild body', which can only find words and forms of subjectification within the symbolic order of the mother:

> There is the social body, which finds some kind of synthesis, and there is the wild body. I give this name to that part of human experience that

> goes beyond what a given symbolic-social order can mediate and that, consequently, remains outside of the social synthesis or enters into it as object of interpretation and of other people's interventions. Before the politics of women, female experience was this wild body. I believe that for the type of human experience that is outside the social order, or is unhappily within it, there is only one possible symbolic order. This is the symbolic order that can refer experience to the authority of the mother . . . We must give a social translation to maternal power in order to prevent social synthesis from closing up. We must fight to keep social synthesis open to anything we want to say, however distant or abnormal that may be. For me, keeping the social synthesis open is the condition of freedom. (Muraro 2018: 97–8)

Female freedom, disconnected as it is from any claim to power, is on a completely different plane to liberation, which is wholly included in the logic of patriarchal power: 'Female freedom is therefore not suited to the dialectical movement of liberation, but rather, at the outset, to a shift in the symbolic order' (Dominijanni 2001: 59). It thus calls for another symbolic order, that of the mother, which makes female freedom possible, and, more generally, the freedom of that wild body that power does not 'foresee'. For, as Ida Dominijanni suggests, only a part that is already included in the social body, whose subjectivity – albeit oppressed and subjugated – is already foreseen in it, can liberate itself: 'the paradigm of liberation proves inadequate for generating freedom: it nurtures consciousness of oppression but does not translate this into free social forms . . . In essence, the oppression-liberation paradigm fails to focus on female desire and reproduces the subaltern condition of women, rather than smashing it' (Dominijanni 2001: 57). Since the Italian thought of sexual difference has always understood practices as primary and has thus always moved within the context of a 'politics of women', the questions we have raised in relation to the other philosophical positions in this book also apply here: what is the location of this surplus of female freedom and its symbolic order? Inside or outside of the *polis*? In order to escape the normative power of the *polis*, Cavarero proposes a politicization of the 'home of Penelope', in order to make it the birthplace of another, new *polis*:

> the symbolic effectiveness of the figure of Penelope lies in this absolute 'separatism'. In fact, when we *begin* from the space of the vital sign of female subjectivity, we draw a boundary that restricts the patriarchal political order through a process of reappropriation.

> Penelope does not redefine the *polis*, she simply allows the *polis* to be elsewhere and not to touch, not to invade, her home. In this sense Penelope's act is crucial to constructing a female space and indicating its primacy, despite, against and separate from the patriarchal *polis*. And nevertheless starting from this home of the living where meaning is returned to being born of woman, nothing prevents the imagining of another *polis*. (Cavarero 1995: 84–5)[31]

However, Muraro takes a different position to Cavarero, arguing that 'standing against is a declaration of trust that constrains us and pushes us into the gravitational field of power' (Muraro 2009a: 12). She thus repeats Cacciari's claim that being within the system of power is the only way to be against it: standing against means entering the logic of power. However, this logic, as we have seen, does not allow for the freedom of women and the wild body, but only the eventual liberation of those parts already included and recognized within it. And so she turns the system on its head, assuming the point of view of the part that is excluded from it and so is outside, arguing that although doing politics requires us to remain within the *polis*, we must place ourselves on a radically different plane from that of power. More recently she has begun to develop the idea of the symbolic independence of politics from power, which further addresses that difference between authority and power that she had explored in *The Symbolic Order of the Mother*. Unlike other feminist theories that had attempted to move politics into the private sphere, the aim is not to find a different location for politics, but to shift it onto a different symbolic plane: 'politics untangles itself from power thanks to its symbolic independence with regard to power itself. Or better, politics is the name for our slipping away or untying ourselves from the tangle of the relations of force by which we are molded and restrained, in order to shift to another level, in a move whose character is distinctively symbolic' (Muraro 2009b: 93–4).[32] This politics cannot be asserted against the dominant power, which would make it indistinguishable from that power, but neither can it weaken power from within, for this would mean remaining in relation to power, and thus being impotent. It must instead dodge power while formally obeying it. Power only sees those who oppose it, while the wild body acts unforeseen within the *polis*, because it is made subject by another authority and another symbolic order.[33] There thus arises the possibility of a form of political subjectification not bound to subjugation within the logic of power, a subject capable of conflict without having to be in opposition as a part.[34]

4. Secularization and hypermodernity

A conflictuality that is manifested and measured through its degree of integration within the system – the state – leaves increasing numbers of unforeseen subjectivities outside. These are conflictual figures that, as the Italian thought of sexual difference argued, cannot be identified and represented according to the logic of the modern political, as they cannot be organized into a party – their conflictuality cannot be reduced to the class antagonism of 'the Part'. These parts without a party emerge in the social sphere or at least outside of the traditional places of politics. Marramao argues that they do not converge in an ethics that is tolerant of difference as understood in certain postmodern thought, but, rather, the expression of their specific difference is in itself a politics.

This is a politics that is neither directed by the dialectical logic of liberation nor weakened in the hermeneutics of dialogue or communication. For Marramao holds that the crisis of the modern political not only cannot be overcome, as it is inherent to the political, but also cannot be declined-distorted and weakened in the sense of the *Verwindung* of weak thought. The traditional sphere of the political, that of the state and party, can no longer provide representation either to certain subjectivities – because they are unforeseen – or to those experiences that increasingly define the existence of each and every one of us in post-industrial societies. In short, the modern political gives form and representation to an increasingly standardized, simplified and limited subjectivity, while the space outside of it expands disproportionately, eventually accommodating that conflictuality generated by the unanswered demand for the symbolic. Although this conflictuality can no longer be resolved in the synthesis of the state, and in fact expresses the irreversible crisis of the modern political, it is nevertheless a political expression, albeit still a formless one: it is thus not 'post-political' (Marramao 1984: 185). In an essay that appeared in the same period in *Laboratorio Politico*, Marramao argues that the present condition is in fact 'metapolitical':

> instead of the category of the post-political I preferred . . . another interpretation that we summarize in the concept of the *metapolitical.* By this term we do not so much mean a neo-synthesis of the political – a sort of 'superpolitics' – but rather the need to conceptualize a semantic field that is double-edged, which accentuates and translates the 'duality' inherent to the modern concept of the 'political' at a level of greater complexity. The problematic underlying the category of

> the metapolitical implies: *firstly*, that the hermeneutic apparatus for capturing the current conditions of practicability for politics must be directed towards *oblique data*, towards areas that, according to classical topology, are presented as remote or eccentric with respect to traditional political nomenclatures; and *secondly*, that in order to decipher the potential political relevance of these areas, one must attempt to give form to the *symbolic networks* produced by new conflictual interrelations. (Marramao 1983: 98–9)

In *Potere e secolarizzazione* (Power and secularization), Marramao challenges weak thought's basis in the idea of the equivalence between post-metaphysical thought (Nietzsche-Heidegger) and postmodernity. As emerges from Marramao's genealogy of secularization,[35] the dissolution of the theological-metaphysical hypostasis is still an entirely modern dispositif, as it is characterized by the 'consummation' of all transcendental order and authority. This consummation is guided by that specifically modern temporalization of history that has taken the form of an irreversible process: 'progress'. He writes: 'It is within this *irrepressible* tension that the "typically constructive" idea of Progress comes to light . . . as cumulative-irreversible temporality (albeit internally differentiated and "complex") representing the dimension proper to the modern process of secularization. Time as constant change and transformation – that is, as the original *experience of acceleration* – thus becomes the Form par excellence of modernity' (Marramao 1984: LI).

Following Karl Löwith,[36] Marramao understands the temporality peculiar to the modern as arising from the secularization of the *eschaton* in the Judeo-Christian idea of redemption. The 'time that draws to an end' is historicized in progress, which, proceeding through stages aimed at perfection, accelerates towards liberation. The pace and direction of this process are dictated by the revolutionary project. Rather than emphasizing the moment of overcoming or novelty, progressive modernization entails the absorption of revolution and liberation into the increasingly intensive temporalization of planning: the endless repetition of the *novum* of the modern is thus transformed into the eternal return of the identical. Given the disenchantment with the ultimate end produced, according to Weber, by increasing rationalization, all that is left of the progress entrusted with the liberation of the cursed part is the contentless form of 'development' (of which capitalist development is the prototype). This process has become tendentially entropic and, through broadening the horizon of expectations and accelerating time in order to satisfy these expectations, consumes and reduces the space of experience in which the conflicts that traditionally determined processes of political subjectification took place. Marramao uses the notion of 'futures past' coined by Reinhart Koselleck[37] to describe the temporality typical of modernization:

> The Modern, from being an exciting adventure of marginality, is transformed into a geometric progression perpetually threatened by the abyss of the present. The Future is no longer intended and envisaged as finality, but as a phase to be passed over: it exists only to be consumed as quicky as possible and deposited behind the dangerously small margin left to experience. The age of modernization is the age of the definitive narrowing of the hiatus between past and future, of the future that passes with imperceptible speed into the past: it is the age of the *vergangene Zukunft*, of futures past. (Marramao 1984: 48)

The crisis of the revolutionary project or of liberation necessarily entails the crisis of the subjectivity it creates. And yet, having lost its symbolic content and its orientation in meaning, the modernization project does not fall apart, but, on the contrary, is strengthened and accelerates. This not only, as Cacciari had argued, relegates the revolutionary project to a *ou-topia* (non-place/utopia) irremediably separated from the state and institutions, but also contracts the time of the present in the futures past, so that the present loses any possibility of antagonistic subjectivity or of rupture and discontinuity with the past. The increasing spatial and temporal decentralization from the modern project demonstrates the irreversible crisis of modern subjectivity but can also open up the possibility of an experience and practice of 'eccentricity'. Intervening in Cacciari and Agamben's discussion of the mystical, Marramao identifies the peculiar excess produced by the modern project with the 'eccentricity' of everyday existence in the 'time of misery' of *Dasein* (Marramao 1984: 86), which is what remains after the crisis of the modern subject:

> The *Dasein* that has become the starting point of interrogation cannot be conceived of as something topologically determined (such as a place of in-fancy that accompanies all the developments of language) or as a Before of unbroken innocence. But nor is it conceivable as a mystical Beyond of language. The Mystical is *Dasein*, not as the location of transparency, but as a remainder that escapes the web of the project and poses the radical question of liberation. (Marramao 1984: 86–7)

It is therefore neither a matter of overcoming the modern in a critical-dialectical sense, nor of a 'recovery' of the consummation of metaphysics, as in Vattimo's positive nihilism. The opening in the 'iron cage' produced by the rationalization of the political must instead be found within modernity. This is the philosophical and political outcome of Marramao's genealogy of secularization. It is a sort of 'genealogy of genealogy', aiming to demonstrate that every process of secularization, including that of modernization, always has a remainder. Completely renouncing the modern project would mean losing its remnants and residues, which are still present today. We must instead valorize and re-enchant our own time and our own space of experience on a symbolic level, both despite and because of its 'misery'. Following Benjamin's theses in *On the Concept of History*,[38] valorizing the present could mean counterposing to the myth of a blind and unstoppable progress the idea of the unrepeatability of the present, whose chances of liberation we can only grasp if we experience time in a kairological sense, that is, as a 'gift', a debt, for which we are responsible, to which we must 'respond'. This is what Marramao explicitly argues in *Kairós*: '*Due*: what is due, the gift, the inclusive and binding responsibility of time. Of a time that is not "appropriate", authentic, because it can never be truly and only "mine": because, paradoxically, it is always the Other that makes it possible for me' (Marramao 2024: 110). The idea of kairological temporality, which Marramao elaborates on in later works (Marramao 2012), makes it possible to see opportunity in the decentralization of the processes of (male, Western) subjectification brought about by modernization. Much like in a lot of feminist thought, eccentricity, difference and marginality become key places for the encounter and (also conflictual) confrontation of diverse individual and cultural experiences. In order to stress that it is still within the modern that these opportunities arise, Marramao defines the present era as 'hypermodernity'.[39] This distinguishes his position from the postmodern,[40] which, in understanding the thought of modernity exclusively in a metaphysical sense and in proposing itself as its consummation and dissolution, ultimately remains within modernization, and in fact becomes it's paradigmatic expression:

> The 'dromomania' which afflicts the institutional and normative structures of hypermodernity (a term we much prefer to 'postmodern') is a symptom of the difficulty of keeping social symbolism alive: a consequence of the compulsion to reproduce the programme of futurization without any longer having symbolically effective recourse to the myths of progress and revolution. In this

> regard, the 'postmodern condition' is not in the least in a relationship of rupture, but rather of intimate continuity (albeit that of an illegitimate child), with the Modern: it is simply derived from its premises, the heterogenesis of its planned ends. (Marramao 1984: 81)

Twenty years later, in *The Passage West*, Marramao again stresses the significance of the category of hypermodernity, finding in globalization further reasons to challenge the theoretical assumptions of postmodernism:

> I am still convinced of the greater heuristic efficacy of this expression [hypermodernity]. It is important, nonetheless, to be free of the artificial antithesis, modernity/postmodernity . . . To pretend to tie the modern project to a substantially monistic and self-referential paradigmatic framework and, in contrast, to mechanically attribute to postmodernity only the thaumaturgical virtues of plurality, dissemination and eccentricity, is to close one's eyes or ignore the multiple (and conflicting) conceptions that are habitually assembled under the rubric of 'the Modern'. (Marramao 2012)

In the same book, Marramao not only stresses the importance of the category of hypermodernity, but also that of secularization and points to the emergence of a new global (dis)order characterized by a conflict primarily concerning cultural values and identities.

The apparent contradiction between techno-economic globalization and the so-called return of religion leads Vattimo to more closely analyse the idea of secularization, a subject that he had first explored in the 1980s. Taking a position that is completely consistent with weak thought, he argues that 'the *Verwindung* of metaphysics is nothing other than secularization' (Vattimo 1988c: 61) in the form of the dissolution of the theological hypostatization of being: the death of the God of the Old Testament. In the years that followed, beginning from his largely philosophical interpretation of secularization, Vattimo developed his own conception of Christianity: the death of the theological-metaphysical God announced by Nietzsche actually corresponded to the incarnation of Jesus Christ. Secularization begins with God becoming man; this is a desacralization of the divine attributes of omnipotence and transcendence, the correlate of the sacrifice in natural religion.[41] Secularization thus coincides with the salvation story, as the dissolution of original violence and the 'weakening' (with which Vattimo translates the Christological term *kenosis*) of the power of the God of the Old

Testament.[42] Leaving aside the issues raised by this conception of a post-religious Christianity – without dogmas, rules, and the Church – and returning instead to the context of globalization, Vattimo argues that this is the era in which the Christian message is finally realized and the process of secularization is completed. He writes in *Belief*:

> Thus we return to secularisation as the essence of modernity and of Christianity itself. From the religious point of view, the threat presented to the subject by techno-scientific society lies in the dissolution of sacral values in an increasingly materialistic, consumerist and Babel-like world . . . the character of kenosis in which the history of salvation is realized must be attributed to this whole experience of 'dissolution', or of the weakening of strong structures. (Vattimo 1999: 52)

Before exploring their differences, it is important to stress a fundamental point of agreement between Marramao and Vattimo: both focus on the present, engaging in what Foucault called an ontology of actuality[43] – something that they share with a number of other Italian philosophers, including Agamben, Negri and Esposito – and both premise their respective ontologies of the present on Karl Löwith's interpretation of modernity as a secularization of Judeo-Christian eschatology. However, their conceptions diverge radically. For Vattimo, secularization moves towards the dissolution and consummation of the strong structures of modernity. In this, he makes reference to the Heideggerian approach to the history of nihilism, which sees the latter as the fulfilment of metaphysics, that is, the fulfilment of the oblivion both of being and of ontological difference. Vattimo thus ended up identifying the postmodern with the post-metaphysical. For Marramao, on the other hand, and also for many of the other founders of *il Centauro*, modernity is constitutively and originally defined by crisis – by an ambivalence, splitting and conflict that are irreducible to synthesis and reconciliation.

Thus, for Marramao, secularization is an exemplary modern dispositif because it is able to reactivate ambivalences and dualisms, allowing them to produce conflict and subjectification. It allows power and the dominant line to emerge, but also its remnants and misalignments. The application of the idea of secularization to globalization in *The Passage West* implies that the movement of all cultures towards modernity – dislocating these cultures from their centres – deconstructs every presupposed identity, including that of the West (and, for Vattimo, that of Christianity). In the context of a modernity that is now beginning to move outside of the ambit of the project of rationalization – whose process of global integration if anything produces localisms and identitarian tendencies – there is no longer a single straight line in the passage towards the West, the part is no longer identified with the whole. Instead, each part is allowed its own unique passage by virtue of its partiality. A theoretical-practical programme such as that of the 'universalism of difference', supported by the binary logic of a 'disjunctive synthesis' that does not remove conflict,[44] implies a concept of modernity-world that is not based in either metaphysical or dialectical traditions, but instead provides an alternative to them. The dialectical tradition created the modernity-nation and its peculiar political form of *reductio ad Unum*, the synthesis constituted by the state form. The 'universalism of difference' is instead the form of modernity in the age of globalization:

> Unification and differentiation, expansion and contamination, order and conflict. Keeping to the descriptive focus, these are the two inextricable sides of the same coin of the global era. In shifting the focus from the descriptive to the prescriptive terrain, the two-pronged optic underlying the thesis of the passage to the Occident will be translated, through the theoretical programme of a *universalism of difference*, into a revival and 'transvaluation' of the cosmopolitan paradigm of the Modern. (Marramao 2012)

5. *The thought of the impolitical*

As we have seen, the interpretation of modernity as crisis, splitting, conflict, contraposition and contradiction has been a distinguishing characteristic of Italian philosophy at least since the 1970s. But from this shared critique of dialectical synthesis, different conceptions of politics have emerged. As we have seen, the concept of modernity as a pluriverse playing out in the present allows Marramao to elaborate a metapolitics that moves 'eccentrically' with respect to the traditional subjects and places of the modern political, finding new political opportunities in this decentralization. Esposito's exploration of the impolitical, on the other hand, sees the widening and fragmentation of space beyond the places of power as the result of an excess of politics, which reproduces the same philosophical-political logic that governs the modern political. The depoliticization that has permeated every sphere of individual and collective life – and which Carl Schmitt argued was an expression of the modern as the ever-increasing neutralization of conflict – has led to a blurring of the distinction between the public and private spheres and between the political and the social. Esposito argues that this is not an anti-political drift, but rather an enhancement of the political, despite the fact that it can no longer be reduced solely to the sphere delineated by the state form and its politico-legal categories. It is from this political interpretation of the modern that *Categories of the Impolitical* begins:

> any account of the modern must be understood within the register of conflict. The modern is constitutively contradictory, in the sense that its extremes remain permanently opposed rather than being resolved dialectically. That is certainly true, and it is perhaps most true, where the modern problem of the political is concerned. Where there is talk of modern depoliticization, or rather of modernity *as* depoliticization or neutralization, these processes takes [*sic*] the form of an *excess* of politics (see for example the works of the young Schmitt . . .). To put this differently, the ever-increasing neutralization of the political is the result of the acquisition by politics of every ambit of life . . . It is referred to as a neutralization because its aim is the exclusion of conflict from the 'civil' order. (Esposito 2015a: 2)

If even depoliticization is understood as a political phenomenon, then the contradictory nature of the modern is fully manifested in its political configuration. For this reason, the political and its contradictions can be understood only from the perspective of the im-political, in its double meaning of being 'in' the political and being non-political. As it is within the order of the political, it offers no possibility for points of view external to the political in which antagonism could be located. And being within it means not being against it. It can at most be non-political, the negative of the political and not its negation, for if it were its negation it would fall into a dialectical logic, positively representing the overcoming of the political – which, however, having nothing outside itself, would not initiate a post-politics, but would make the impolitical another, perhaps superior, category of the political. Thus, it is a negative which, being within the political, does not affirm an antagonistic exteriority or otherness, another form of power, but is instead the impossibility of another form of power. The impolitical precludes the possibility of thinking or identifying new subjects outside this political and its logic of power: 'There exists no real alternative to power, no subject of antipower, for the simple reason that the subject is already constituted by power. In other words, power inheres naturally in the dimension of the subject, in the sense that its only language is that of power' (Esposito 2015a: 13–4).

In *Reflections of a Nonpolitical Man*, Thomas Mann understood the impolitical as the custodian of those values that had been rejected by a politics that had become disvalue. Like Cacciari's impolitical, Esposito essentially turns this meaning on its head, making it instead the immanent critique of any return of value to politics, of any further theological-political *reductio ad Unum* in reaction to depoliticization. The impolitical instead becomes the critique of political representation as 'good' and of that recovery of transcendence pursued by the Catholic-political conceptions of the young Schmitt and Romano Guardini. For this recovery only *appears to* be an alternative to the process of the neutralization of conflict, and therefore of depoliticization, inaugurated by the 'Hobbesian paradigm of order' (Esposito 2015a: 3). Both Schmitt and Guardini share the theological-political assumption of reducing multiplicity and plurality – that *complexio oppositorum* at the origin of the political as conflict – to political representation:[45]

> The impolitical attempts to rebel against this combination of depoliticization and theology, technology and value, and nihilism and justification. The impolitical, we have said, is something 'other' than representation. Or better, it is the other of representation and remains obstinately outside of it. But its specific unrepresentability is very different from that imagined by modern depoliticization, because it in no way opposes the political. In this sense, the impolitical is far removed from Mann's term 'nonpolitical'. It is not an alternative good to be posed in opposition to the political. Quite the opposite: It is the making good of the existing failure of the political and the 'theological' revalorization that attends it. The impolitical is a critique of enchantment, even if this does not mean that it can be reduced to a simple disenchantment, or the carefree polytheism of being 'post'. It disavows any connection with the great modern deracination, but without any utopian attempt at securing a new ground – which on the contrary it condemns. (Esposito 2015a: 8)

The unrepresentability of the political is not against the political, because it remains within the political, creating a space for its deconstruction. As the limit of representation, it reveals the political's determinacy and finitude. The impolitical thus also resists any gnostic interpretation, eschewing the possibility of reactivating that 'gnostic pearl' which, in

Potere e secolarizzazione, Marramao had considered as the possible source of an alternative temporality capable of interrupting the entropic and depoliticizing temporality of secularization as modernization.[46] Yet, when discussing *Categories of the Impolitical*, Cacciari argues that Esposito's impolitical risks falling into this gnostic attitude:

> It is certainly difficult to think of the *impolitical* outside of the gnostic attitude. We can, however, try to think of it in terms of an absolute *indifference*; *indifference* towards politics, of which a true image cannot be given, but also *indifference* towards the impolitical as you understand it, that is, as the limit of the space of politics . . . It must be thought of in non-oppositional terms, freed from any gnostic aura. (Cacciari and Esposito 1988: 18–9)

Esposito does not deny that the impolitical risks falling into gnosticism – indeed, he argues that this is exactly what happens to the mysticism of Simone Weil[47] – but he stresses that the impolitical must still be understood as 'inherent to the political'. He argues that it is from within the political that the impolitical differentiates itself from the political, without opposing it, as that would mean moving outside of it. And this is the problem, if not the contradiction, that the impolitical runs into: if it wants to be a critique of the present, its immanence to the political cannot produce 'indifference'. The idea of the impolitical critique of the political indicates that the impolitical is included within the thought of crisis: it is not the negation of the political – for this would hypostasize dualism in a gnostic sense – but it is within the political as its internal difference. In short, because the deconstruction by the impolitical presupposes a *complexio oppositorum* without a theological-political synthesis, this very deconstruction is inscribed in the thought of crisis and shares its tragic outcome. Returning several decades later to the impolitical in *Living Thought*,[48] Esposito emphasizes this point:

> In order for the negation of the impolitical to make itself positive, it should first negate – or deny – itself, establishing itself as another reality alongside, or against, what it declares to be unique. It would thus adopt the Gnostic perspective, with a dualistic framework that pits the realm of good against that of evil. But in so doing, it would contradict the principle of immanence outside of which the entire argument loses its force of impact. The impolitical – if it wants to avoid being reduced to an apolitical or antipolitical attitude – can only be conceived as inherent to the political. (Esposito 2012a: 227)

The aporia or contradiction between within and against, between immanence and antagonism, was already present in Cacciari's impolitical: he saw in this contradiction the condition of democratization as the deconstruction and critique of every universal and singular value to which the political is reduced.[49] But this is not the fundamental distinction between Cacciari's and Esposito's understandings of the impolitical. Cacciari's impolitical claims equivalence between being within and being against. As he says when challenging Esposito, it is only within political representation that the unrepresentable of the impolitical can be represented. The conflict arises within that political order that the impolitical makes precarious and contingent by disenchanting its value. Indeed, the more the *techne* organizes the space of the political, the more centrifugal and deconstructive forces are released. This is the 'dia-bolic' soul of the political, which has no 'symbolic' synthesis: conflict is immanent to it because so too is its principle of order. Cacciari also reiterates this in his discussion with Esposito in *Pensiero e politica* (Thought and politics):

> The principle of all praxis is thus this *two*, a *complexio oppositorum*, the opposition between *mania*, which is impulse and appetite, and *techne*, which is strategic capacity . . . Aristotle knows the 'diabolic' nature of the political, and not in the vulgar sense of manipulation, but as something that is internal to the political soul. Thus, for Aristotle, conflict is irreducible precisely because it is immanent to the soul. (Cacciari and Esposito 1988: 16)

Esposito, on the other hand, thinks of conflict not within order, but as an absolute alternative to it. He holds that if it were thought within it, conflict would be inexorably functional to the preservation of order. We must therefore consider its difference from the political. And so, in his own way, Esposito also adopts the theme of difference that characterized various Italian philosophies at the time.

Order is the dispositif with which political philosophy represents, and thereby neutralizes, the conflict in which the very reality of politics lies. Thus, for political philosophy, conflict is unrepresentable outside of order, but that in no way means that it is unthinkable *tout court*. It simply shows that philosophical representation is not capable of thinking it as such, of thinking conflict as conflict. Political philosophy can only represent order and, therefore, has to neutralize conflict, reducing all politics to the political as the organization of state and party. But this means that it is politics itself that is unrepresentable.

The impolitical is the difference, in a positive sense, of politics within the modern political; it is the non-representational thinking of politics within the representative order of the state. Thinking explicitly of the impolitical not only as a margin of the political, but as at the very heart of the political and its fundamental categories, is the main proposal of *Nove pensieri sulla politica* (Nine thoughts on the political), the second book that Esposito dedicates to the theme of the impolitical, a few years after *Categories of the Impolitical*.[50] It is no surprise that it is under the heading of 'The Political' that he most clearly sets out the question posed by the impolitical:

> [Political philosophy] can only think [politics] in the form of *representation*. And, more precisely, as the representation of *order*. There is a close and binding link between order and representation, in the sense that representation – in all its possible forms – is always *of* order. Even when it encounters conflict, it does so beginning from and within the presupposition of order, which is possible if not actual. Conflict *for* order. (Esposito 1993: 16)

Only a thought of conflict such as that of Machiavelli[51] – which cannot be ascribed to political philosophy, and which in fact political philosophy opposes as diabolic or cursed due to its unrepresentability for the order – can truly think of the part as such, that is, freed from any belonging to a whole. Only politics as conflict can think of a part that does not have to be reduced to the unity of the party in order to exist:

> There is no *philosophy* of conflict that does not reduce it to its own categorical order, and therefore ultimately negates it precisely while it represents it and through that representation, as witnessed in political philosophy by the traditional primacy of the *reductio ad unum* of what by definition is particular: the 'part' remains, but as an organ (either natural or artificial, it does not matter for now) of the whole. Philosophy does not say, it *cannot* say, that there is no whole without a part. But still always says there is no part without the whole. (Esposito 1993: 17)

The figure of the unrepresentable that the impolitical affirms without falling into gnostic-type dualism is what Bataille understood as the 'community of death', as '*partage*' (sharing/a sharing of parts). Bataille – and later other French philosophers of the community[52] – uses the word *partager* to mean 'to put into relation by differentiating' (Esposito

2015a: 15), to share a difference that is not hypostatized in identity, but is common to all of us, the difference of death. Death is the part that belongs neither to me nor to the other; it is the difference that is shared: it is that part that, insofar as it is irreducible to unity, is impossible to identify and represent.

The part is such because what is shared *(partagé)* is its difference from every unitary principle of subjectification, including that of the antagonistic subject, which, in order to have power, must be *represented* as a *counter*-part. The part can therefore only be unsubjugatable if it is not subjectifiable as a counter-part. And yet, within the political of the state, the difference of politics – which, as conflict, is always an expression of the part – is only affirmed as negative, as death. The community of death is thus the extreme outcome of the impolitical, and perhaps the only one that is consistent with critical and deconstructive thinking:

> Death belongs only to the individual (or perhaps the individual belongs only to death), in the sense that it is a part of him that cannot be divided up among others. And yet, community is precisely this dividing up. It is a kind of dividing up, though, that does not identify parts or draw them together; rather, it infinitely distances them . . . Community is therefore the sharing of the impossibility of dying one's own death. This is why community is, in a specific sense, impossible. It is thus always an impossible community – the community of impossible commonality . . . In this sense, community is truly the extreme figure of the impolitical. (Esposito 2015a: 197)

And yet, for Esposito the community of death – which is in fact the impossibility of community – is not the only possible way of thinking of a community without foundation and without subjectivity.[53] And neither is it the 'extreme', in the sense of a final liberation from the yoke of the political. The idea of a politics as conflict, which the deconstruction of the impolitical has revealed to exceed every order of representation, can now be delineated in a different way, and not just as a divergence remaining within the modern political, not only, that is, as crisis thinking.

Chapter 4

BIOPOLITICS

Since the 1990s, biopolitics has become a major issue in the global philosophical debate, which has led to increasingly widespread interest in Italian thinkers who have confronted this subject and in 'Italian thought' as a whole. But is the convergence of Italian thinkers around biopolitics simply a coincidence? Or is it the result of a specific trajectory of 'Italian thought' – perhaps not its only result, nor the only possible result, but at least that which has resonated most internationally?

Foucault was the first to introduce the idea of biopolitics, in the first volume of *The History of Sexuality* in 1978: 'For millennia, man remained what he was for Aristotle: a living animal with the additional capacity for a political existence; modern man is an animal whose politics places his existence as a living being in question' (Foucault 1978: 143). Although Agamben, Negri and Esposito all began from Foucault when developing their own conceptions of biopolitics, this chapter will not be based on their shared Foucauldian origin.[1] For while Foucault introduced the field of inquiry within which Italian thought moved, his own reflections on biopolitics, at least in the 1990s, were little more than suggestions.

And in fact, the later publication of other Foucauldian works added little in either depth or breadth to his conception of biopolitics. For although Foucault's courses at the Collège de France, in particular from the late 1970s onwards, were meant to provide a history of governmentality, their posthumous publication revealed that biopolitics had lost its centrality in favour of a return to the subject. We can thus speak of an 'Italian difference' with respect to biopolitics, and not only because Italian philosophers developed Foucault's thought in an original way, but because their biopolitics brought together the themes and motifs of the broken line of the *sinisteritas*, while also making further deviations from it.

1. *The curse of the* zoe

In the 1980s, various attempts were made to start from negative thought and the thought of crisis in order to go beyond them, creating a philosophy that began from the exhaustion of the categories of metaphysics and the modern political. This resulted in Cacciari's autonomy of the mystical, and its conversion into the 'premise', and Esposito's 'community of death', which took the impolitical to its extreme. Giorgio Agamben also confronted negative thought and the thought of crisis in the same period, as seen in his debate with Cacciari on the concept of the mystical. However, unlike Cacciari and Esposito, he did not attempt to overturn negative thought from within, but to demonstrate that it was the fullest expression of that metaphysics from which it was meant to have been freed. In *Language and Death*, a seminar published in 1982, Agamben points out that the 'post-metaphysical' critical thought of the time had the same problem: it had understood the negative within the foundation of metaphysics as a presupposition for going beyond it, without realizing that this 'ungroundedness' was the 'fundamental problem' of metaphysics itself. Various different forms of critical thought, including the philosophy of difference, negative thinking and Derrida's grammatology, remained within metaphysics: 'the limitations of any critiques of metaphysics are made evident; they hope to surpass the horizon of metaphysics by radicalizing the problem of negativity and ungroundedness, as if a pure and simple repetition of its *fundamental* problem could lead to a surpassing of metaphysics' (Agamben 2006: 85). And thus, in *Language and Death*, he returns to Wittgenstein's mystical, and also discusses Cacciari's interpretation of it:

> Inasmuch as the experience of the language of metaphysics has its final, negative foundation in a Voice, this experience is always already divided into two distinct planes. The first, which can only be *shown*, corresponds to the very taking place of language disclosed by the Voice; the second is, on the other hand, the plane of meaningful discourse. It corresponds to what is said within this taking place. The scission of language into two irreducible planes permeates all of Western thought. (Agamben 2006: 85)

The voice is the mystical unattainable foundation of language; language takes place due to its removal. The unspeakable of the voice is the presupposition of the sayable, its transcendental negative foundation. But Agamben argues that this is the very essence of metaphysics. A post-metaphysical thought would not think of the foundation as negative – as if by denying every value, every positive, metaphysics would cease to exist – but would instead place itself beyond this dualism, thus beyond the presupposition of the crisis and the 'critique' of metaphysics. For the negative cannot be conceived independently of the language to which it gives rise; only within language is the negative thinkable as the unsayable of the sayable. Although Heidegger's conception of truth as *aletheia* had called this dualism into question, he had continued to think of the voice – as being-towards-death – as *Dasein*'s most authentic destination. Likewise, Derrida's grammatology,[2] which identified *gramma* as a trace of the removal of the voice, still remained entangled in metaphysics insofar as this trace was the presence of the absence of the voice. The mystical, whose difference from language can only be thought from within it, is in fact the dispositif of metaphysics, which can only be escaped through its 'liquidation' rather than its radicalization:

> If this Voice is the mystical foundation for our entire culture (its logic as well as its ethics, its theology as well as its politics, its wisdom as well as its madness) then the mystical is not something that can provide the foundation for another thought – attempting to think beyond the horizon of metaphysics, at the extreme confine of which, at the point of nihilism, we are still moving. The mystical is nothing but the unspeakable foundation; that is, the negative foundation of onto-theology. Only a liquidation of the mystical can open up the field to a thought (or language) that thinks (speaks) beyond the Voice . . . that dwells, that is, not on an unspeakable foundation, but in the infancy (*in-fari*) of man. (Agamben 2006: 91)

As we saw in the second chapter of this book, in *Infancy and History* Agamben argues that infancy is not the negative foundation of language. And in *Language and Death* infancy is clearly distinguished from the mystical that he had referred to in the previous book. Instead of indicating the possibility of overcoming metaphysics, the mystical 'shows' the dispositif of metaphysics, revealing the crisis as its criterion. But we can still attempt to escape metaphysics by thinking beyond the crisis and the split between the living and language on which it is based. Infancy is the 'dwelling' of a living being no longer divided as it was in the previous book between the language in which it is immersed and a more authentic destination to which it is called by the voice, a destination in which language is a constraint. For Agamben, the 'habitual experience' of human beings is *ethos*, which does not contain that negative that 'defers' (*differisce*) their most authentic location. In *ethos*, the difference between the living and language is not a split, but is immanent to life; it is life:[3]

> To exist in language without being called there by any Voice, simply to die without being called by death, is perhaps the most abysmal experience; but this is precisely, for man, also his most *habitual* experience, his *ethos*, his dwelling, always already presented in the history of metaphysics as demonically divided into the living and language, nature and culture, ethics and logic, and therefore only attainable in the negative articulation of a Voice. And perhaps only beginning with the eclipse of the Voice, with the no longer taking place of language and with the death of the Voice, does it become possible for man to experience an *ethos* . . . Perhaps man – the animal who seems not to be encumbered by any specific nature of any specific identity – must experience his poverty even more radically. Perhaps humans are even poorer than they supposed in attributing to themselves the experience of negativity and death as their specific anthropogenetic patrimony, and in basing every community and tradition on this experience. (Agamben 2006: 96)

A few years later, in 'Tradition of the Immemorial' published in *il Centauro*, Agamben begins from the questions that *Language and Death* had left open, that is, from the possibility of a community capable of making its *ethos* 'habitual' and thus inhabiting it without its ungroundedness sending it to some ulterior destination:

> Do we experience the principle of all things as anything other than an Unparticipated that destines and historically produces us as *parts*, im-parting us in its incessant participation? Are we truly capable of conceiving the generic and universal essence of human being and its community without presuppositions? Are we capable of thinking of the tradition of truth and language as anything other than an unfounded and yet destining presupposition? (Agamben 1999a: 112)

In order to reflect on community, Agamben had to address the question of the part, which, like Esposito, he links to the French word *partage* (sharing), a term that refers to Blanchot's and above all Nancy's conceptions of the unavowable/inoperative community as an unfounded community.[4] Agamben also poses the question of community in terms of a 'common participation' that is not founded on a specific 'belonging', even that of human nature, but is rather 'participation in an Unparticipated'. What is key here is the part as such, unrepresentable as a part; or, put another way, the part that takes a position without establishing itself as a party:

> We are united only through our common participation in an Unparticipated; we are anticipated by a presupposition, but one without an origin; we are divided, without any inheritance. *This is why everything we can take is always already divided*, and why the community that binds us – or, rather, the community into which we are thrown – cannot be a community of something into which we are appropriated and from which we are subsequently separated. Community is from the beginning a community *of parts and parties*. (The domination and simultaneous devastation of the form of the party, its *destitution of every foundation*, has its root in this epochal situation). (Agamben 1999a: 112–13)

And yet, Agamben holds that Cacciari's mystical as premise and the ungroundedness of Nancy's and Blanchot's community do not entirely escape the dispositif of metaphysics discussed in *Language and Death*. The absence of the presupposition becomes the 'presupposition of nothing' and ungroundedness becomes a negative foundation. In both cases, the community is not a 'habitual dwelling (*ethos*)' but a 'pure destination':

> it is this epochal situation that has been most rigorously considered in France by Jean-Luc Nancy and Maurice Blanchot as 'inoperative community' and 'unavowable community', and it is the constitution of this very figure of presupposition that, in Italy, Massimo Cacciari has sought in the mystical tradition. Our time thus registers the demand for a community without presuppositions; yet without realizing it, it simultaneously maintains the empty form of presupposition beyond all foundations – presupposition of nothing, pure destination. (Agamben 1999a: 113)

This is the result of conceiving community from within negative thought: community as pure destination ends up resembling that community of death with which Esposito concluded the thought of the impolitical.

In order for the community to be unsubjectable to any specific belonging, the focus must shift to the question of subjectivity: belonging to a part is the subjectification of the part. This shift is found in *The Coming Community*: 'What could be the politics of whatever singularity, that is, of a being whose community is mediated not by any condition of belonging (being red, being Italian, being Communist) nor by the simple absence of conditions (a negative community, such as that recently proposed in France by Maurice Blanchot), but by belonging itself?' (Agamben 2007: 84) In line with Esposito, Agamben argues that belonging becomes identity when it is reduced to representation: when it is subjugated. The subject as *sub-jectum* is by definition subservient to a higher power, to a sovereign power. This subjugation is the state's condition of existence. It is therefore in the state that the subjectivity of the identitarian part is represented: the state is the organization of subjects and parties. However, the embodiment of the 'non-State' is not society – on the contrary, society needs a state or a party that recognizes and represents the claims of the new subjectivities that emerge within it – but the community. The coming community is irreducible to subjectification. Belonging to it means belonging to the part as such, and not to its representation. For example, being a communist is belonging to a part that, to be such, does not need to make a party. The coming community is a shared community of 'whatever singularities':

> *The novelty of the coming politics is that it will no longer be a struggle for the conquest or control of the State, but a struggle between the State and the non-State (humanity), an insurmountable disjunction between whatever singularity and the State organization.* This has nothing to do with the simple affirmation of the social in opposition to the State that has often found expression in the protest movements of recent years. Whatever singularities cannot form a *societas* because they do not possess any identity to vindicate nor any bond of belonging for which to seek recognition . . . What the State cannot tolerate in any way, however, is that the singularities form a community without affirming an identity, that humans co-belong without any representable condition of belonging (even in the form of a simple presupposition). (Agamben 2007: 84–5)

Since it is unrepresentable by and in the state and does not have a pre-assumed identity and belonging, the 'whatever singularity' cannot be recognized by power and so cannot be subjugated by it. Like the split between language and the living, the critical and metaphysical split between the subject – the form of life presupposed by state sovereign power – and the living, and the resulting 'indifference',[5] is simply life. The life of the 'whatever singularity' thus has no destination – neither in being-towards-death nor in the state – but is 'at ease' in its *ethos*,[6] here it is in fact 'being *such as it is*': 'The Whatever in question here relates to singularity not in its indifference with respect to a common property (to a concept, for example: being red, being French, being Muslim), but only in its being *such as it is*' (Agamben 2007: 1).

The continuing influence of Agamben's work on an international level – and not only in philosophy – began with the publication of *Homo Sacer* in 1995,[7] which ultimately became the first of a nine-volume project, whose final volume, *The Use of Bodies*, was published in 2014. And yet, the *Homo Sacer* project does not begin *ex novo*, but represents a deviation or line of flight within an idea he had previously proposed.[8] Indeed, the figure of *homo sacer* and the notion of bare life already appear in the final pages of *Language and Death*:

> *At the center of the sacrifice is simply a determinate* action *that, as such, is separated and marked by exclusion; in this way it becomes* sacer *and is invested with a series of prohibitions and ritual prescriptives. Forbidden action, marked by sacredness, is not, however, simply excluded; rather it is now only accessible for certain people and according to determinate rules. In this way, it furnishes society and its ungrounded legislation with the fiction of a beginning: that which is excluded from the community is, in reality, that on which the entire life of the community is founded, and it is assumed by the society as an immemorial, and yet memorable, past.* (Agamben 2006: 105)

The *sacrum facere* (the process of making sacred) reiterates the metaphysical dispositif of ungroundedness: it is the exclusion of *homo sacer* that founds the community.[9] Just as language takes place with the removal of the voice, which remains within language as the destination of the speaker, so too, the banishment of *homo sacer*, which founds the community, is not simply an exclusion, but is also the way this exclusion is assumed within the community, determining its ungroundedness. Thus, *ethos* is the 'dwelling' of the living, because to understand it '*such as it is*' does not presuppose separation (from the community, from language), but is indifferent to separation:

> *In fact, even the sacralization of life derives from sacrifice: from this point of view it simply abandons the naked natural life to its own violence and its own unspeakableness, in order to ground in them every cultural rule and all language. The* ethos, *humanity's own, is not something unspeakable or* sacer *that must remain unsaid in all praxis*

> *and human speech. Neither is it nothingness, whose nullity serves as the basis for the arbitrariness and violence of social action. Rather, it is social praxis itself, human speech itself, which have become transparent to themselves.* (Agamben 2006: 106)

The *Homo Sacer* project then elaborates on these ideas, and it is here that the concept of *homo sacer* most fully expresses its heuristic potential as a deviation within the biopolitical paradigm.

Agamben's biopolitics in *Homo Sacer* is built upon the work of three authors, Arendt, Benjamin and, of course, Foucault, to whom we should add – in keeping with much Italian philosophical-political thought – Schmitt and his theory of sovereignty.[10] Although Arendt's and Benjamin's reflections are not directly biopolitical, Agamben uses Arendt's distinction between *bios* and *zoe* and her analysis of totalitarian power and Benjamin's conception of bare life to elaborate on and correct Foucault's definition of the biopolitical paradigm. Whereas for the Foucault of *The History of Sexuality*, the stress is on 'modern man' as the 'animal whose politics places his existence as a living being in question', through *Homo Sacer* Agamben establishes a connection between biopolitics and sovereignty that returns to the origins of politics, arguing that the peculiarity of the dispositif of sovereignty has always been its production of a biopolitical body. He understands Nazism as an exemplary expression of the biopolitics of the modern state, but also points out that it is only one of its many expressions:

> What this work has had to record among its likely conclusions is precisely that the two analyses [the juridico-institutional and the biopolitical models of power] cannot be separated, and that the inclusion of bare life in the political realm constitutes the original – if concealed – nucleus of sovereign power. *It can even be said that the production of a biopolitical body is the original activity of sovereign power.* In this sense, biopolitics is at least as old as the sovereign exception. Placing biological life at the center of its calculations, the modern State therefore does nothing other than bring to light the secret tie uniting power and bare life. (Agamben 1998: 6)

As Arendt taught us, the classical world had excluded biological and natural life (the *zoe*) from the form of life of humanity (the *bios*) belonging to the political sphere, relegating the former to the *oikos*, the home. Agamben argues that the achievement of modern biopolitics was not so much that it welcomed biological and natural life (the *zoe*) into the *polis*, but that it made the bare life of the *zoe* into *the* form of life of politics.[11] In short, modernity makes *bios* and *zoe* indistinct:

> The Foucauldian thesis will then have to be corrected or, at least, completed, in the sense that what characterizes modern politics is not so much the inclusion of *zoē* in the *polis* – which is, in itself, absolutely ancient – nor simply the fact that life as such becomes a principal object of the projections and calculations of State power. Instead the decisive fact is that, together with the process by which the exception everywhere becomes the rule, the realm of bare life – which is originally situated at the margins of the political order – gradually begins to coincide with the political realm, and exclusion and inclusion, outside and inside, *bios* and *zoē*, right and fact, enter into a zone of irreducible indistinction. (Agamben 1998: 9)

Agamben uses the figure of *homo sacer* to correct Foucault,[12] arguing that the exclusion of *zoe* from the political sphere was not the separation of an autonomous space – the *oikonomia* – but the creation of an *exception* (which derives from *ex-capere*, 'take out of').[13] Thus, the exception excludes bare life from the political order by capturing it within it. The space of the political *bios* is based on its removal; sovereign power is founded on its absence. This is in keeping with Schmitt, who understands sovereignty and the legal order to be based on the exception. Modern biopolitics therefore does not arise with the inclusion of bare life into the political sphere – for it has always been there as *ex-capere* – but begins when the exception becomes the rule:

> At once excluding bare life from and capturing it within the political order, the state of exception actually constituted, in its very separateness, the hidden foundation on which the entire political system rested. When its borders begin to be blurred, the bare life that dwelt there frees itself in the city and becomes both subject and object of the conflicts of the political order, the one place for both the organization of State power and emancipation from it. (Agamben 1998: 9)

The reason the living remains captured by subjectivity, and so the community of the whatever singularity is still subject to the sovereign power of the state, is because its power is primarily biopower – power over bare life, the subjectification of *zoe*. Bare life performs the same function in the dispositif of sovereign power as the voice does in the dispositif of metaphysics. We could argue that biopolitics is the metaphysical dispositif of politics, which, through the exception that has become the rule, makes the ungroundedness of power – bare life – its sole source of legitimation:

> In carrying out the metaphysical task that has led it more and more to assume the form of a biopolitics, Western politics has not succeeded in constructing the link between *zoē* and *bios*, between voice and language, that would have healed the fracture. Bare life remains included in politics in the form of the exception, that is, as something that is included solely through an exclusion. (Agamben 1998: 11)

It is worth noting not only that Agamben first introduced the figure of *homo sacer* in his analysis of the dispositif of metaphysics, but also that it is only in the *Homo Sacer* project that the *sacratio* is clearly distinguished from its meaning in criminal law (which misinterprets the use of *homo sacer* in archaic Roman law) and from religion (which placed it in the order of 'sacrifice'), being understood instead as the original act of sovereign power. *Sacratio* is the sovereign ban, the dispositif that, in making bare life sacred – 'life that may be killed but not sacrificed' – produces that bare life that, as exception, gives rise to the political sphere:

> once brought back to his proper place beyond both penal law and sacrifice, *homo sacer* presents the originary figure of life taken into the sovereign ban and preserves the memory of the originary exclusion through which the political dimension was first constituted . . . *The sovereign sphere is the sphere in which it is permitted to kill without committing homicide and without celebrating a sacrifice, and sacred life – that is, life that may be killed but not sacrificed – is the life that has been captured in this sphere* . . . The sacredness of life, which is invoked today as an absolutely fundamental right in opposition to sovereign power, in fact originally expresses precisely both life's subjection to a power over death and life's irreparable exposure in the relation of abandonment. (Agamben 1998: 83)

What Benjamin had called the 'dogma of the sacredness of life' in 'Critique of Violence',[14] for Agamben does not correspond to mere natural life, which precedes or is outside politics, but to that *zoe* 'taken out' in the exception: it corresponds to bare life. Bare life is thus neither animal life (*zoe*) nor properly human life (*bios*), but the life of *homo sacer*, the 'sacred life': '*Not simple natural life, but life exposed to death (bare life or sacred life) is the originary political element*' (Agamben 1998: 88). Agamben's *Homo Sacer* neither identifies the 'foundation' of politics in the social contract nor in the friend-enemy criterion, but in sovereignty, which begins long before modernity, and which has been continuously reproduced throughout history. We could even argue that Agamben's archaeological method does not simply fail to contemplate a postmodern but dismisses the periodization of history altogether.

The dispositif holding sovereignty and bare life together, making it the '*originary political element*', is the 'ban'. Included in the sovereign ban, thus banned from the community, bare life is a-ban-doned to death, to an indiscriminate capacity to be killed, but at the same time it cannot be sacrificed, because it exceeds the properly human sphere; like the sovereign, it is placed in a zone of indistinction, in which humanity, animal and god are indistinguishable:

> The ban is the force of simultaneous attraction and repulsion that ties together the two poles of the sovereign exception: bare life and power, *homo sacer* and the sovereign . . . And if in modernity life is more and more clearly placed at the center of State politics (which now becomes, in Foucault's terms, biopolitics), if in our age all citizens can be said, in a specific but extremely real sense, to appear virtually as *homines sacri*, this is possible only because the relation of ban has constituted the essential structure of sovereign power from the beginning. (Agamben 1998: 110–11)

After establishing the banishment of bare life as the foundation of politics and the original dispositif of sovereignty, Agamben attempts to identify the fundamental forms of sovereign power throughout history, up to the present, when all citizens are potentially *homines sacri*. The modern state is nothing more than a certain configuration of sovereign power, and yet this configuration is crucial for bringing the biopolitical nature of politics to the fore in the form of the nation state. The reference to birth (*nativitas*) in the term 'nation' represents the inscription of bare life into the state organization. In the subjectivity subjected to the sovereign power of the state, the bare life of the citizen is also included, although only as a part. Indeed, as we have seen, the state always recognizes and represents subjectivity as a part – being a citizen by birth is belonging to state subjectification. The 'people', rather than being a dialectical synthesis that removes partisan differences –

which first the working class and then the multitude opposed – is a sharing of these differences (*con-divisione*):

> It is as if what we call 'people' were in reality not a unitary subject but a dialectical oscillation between two opposite poles: on the one hand, the set of the People as a whole political body, and on the other, the subset of the people as a fragmentary multiplicity of needy and excluded bodies; or again, on the one hand, an inclusion that claims to be total, and on the other, an exclusion that is clearly hopeless; at one extreme, the total state of integrated and sovereign citizens, and at the other, the preserve – court of miracles or camp – of the wretched, the oppressed, and the defeated . . . But this also means that the constitution of the human species in a political body passes through a fundamental division and that in the concept 'people' we can easily recognize the categorial pairs that we have seen to define the original political structure: bare life (people) and political existence (People), exclusion and inclusion, *zoē* and *bios*. The 'people' thus always already carries the fundamental biopolitical fracture within itself. It is what cannot be included in the whole of which it is a part and what cannot belong to the set in which it is always already included. (Agamben 1998: 177–8)

In short, returning to the terms used in this book, the sharing of differences (*con-divisione*) of the 'people' is a sharing of the part as such and the 'Part' in relation to the whole of the state, represented in the party. As Foucault pointed out,[15] this sharing, which was fundamental to class struggle, falls apart when bare life as population is separated from the people. And it is on this point that Agamben confronts Foucauldian analysis with the turning point represented by the biopolitics of the Nazi state. The 'camp', whose prototype is the Nazi *Lager*, is the localization and confinement of the exception in a space where bare life '*such as it is*' is located. *Bios* and *zoe*, human and non-human, citizen and people, are for the first time separated and divided, becoming autonomous from each other:

> the birth of the camp in our time appears as an event that decisively signals the political space of modernity itself. It is produced at the point at which the political system of the modern nation-state, which was founded on the functional nexus between a determinate localization (land) and a determinate order (the State) and mediated by automatic rules for the inscription of life (birth or the nation),

> enters into a lasting crisis, and the State decides to assume directly the care of the nation's biological life as one of its proper tasks . . . The state of exception, which was essentially a temporary suspension of the juridico-political order, now becomes a new and stable spatial arrangement inhabited by the bare life that more and more can no longer be inscribed in that order. The growing dissociation of birth (bare life) and the nation-state is the new fact of politics in our day, and what we call *camp* is this disjunction. (Agamben 1998: 174–5)

What if the exception of the camp became the rule for the biopolitical regulation of space? What if the exception of the biopolitical regulation of the population became the rule for determining the political body of the people? Totalitarian states represent the moment in which biopolitics becomes politically dominant. Agamben argues in *Remnants of Auschwitz* that Nazi biopolitics ends up revealing itself as a thanatopolitics, casting a disturbing light on current democratic regimes as the most advanced stage of biopolitics:

> In Hitler's Germany, an unprecedented absolutization of the biopower to *make live* intersects with an equally absolute generalization of the sovereign power to *make die*, such that biopolitics coincides immediately with thanatopolitics . . . The fundamental caesura that divides the biopolitical domain is that between *people* and *population*, which consists in bringing to light a population in the very bosom of a people, that is, in transforming an essentially political body into an essentially biological body, whose birth and death, health and illness, must then be regulated. With the emergence of biopower, every people is doubled by a population; every *democratic* people is at the same time, a *demographic* people. (Agamben 1999b: 83–4)

If biopolitics is – first covertly and now manifestly – the original paradigm of politics as Agamben claims, then is thanatopolitics its inevitable outcome, as some of his critics held? If Agamben's premise is correct, it is impossible to re-establish the classical distinction between *bios* and *zoe*, between public and private space. Post-democratic spectacular society is not one political regime among others, but the final realization of Western politics. And by destroying the classical distinctions it has revealed their ungroundedness. But it was precisely the emergence of this ungroundedness – in metaphysics, in community, in politics – that made *zoe* politically available in a different way, that same *zoe* whose removal – whose exception – had founded politics. And yet, the fact that politics is at stake in the *zoe* does not lead only to a bio-thanatopolitics but also opens up the possibility of a new politics:

> It is on the basis of these uncertain and nameless terrains, these difficult zones of indistinction, that the ways and the forms of a new politics must be thought. . . . Every attempt to rethink the political space of the West must begin with the clear awareness that we no longer know anything of the classical distinction between *zoē* and *bios*, between private life and political existence, between man as a simple living being at home in the house and man's political existence in the city . . . This biopolitical body that is bare life must itself instead be transformed into the site for the constitution and installation of a form of life that is wholly exhausted in bare life and a *bios* that is only its own *zoē*. (Agamben 1998: 187–8)

Finding a 'new politics' – which anyway has to be a biopolitics[16] – is about maintaining the separation between *bios* and *zoe*, between human and animal, without choosing or electing one of the two terms to the detriment of the other: in fact, in the classical dispositif, it is the 'election' that establishes the primacy of *bios* in the definition of what is authentically human, and thus also the curse of *zoe*. And in the thanatopolitical dispositif, it is still the 'election' of *zoe* to non-human life that abandons it to death. The new politics must instead suspend the decision, the division that implies choice, deactivating the dispositif of the crisis that is still the 'criterion' of the political. It should come as no surprise that the dispositif of crisis is equally influential in biopolitics. As early as Hippocrates, the term *krisis* is not only used in the politico-legal sphere, but also in medicine. According to its Greek etymology, *crisis* means the separation and division into parts and, at the same time, the election and choice of one of the parts. And so, without an elective decision being made between *bios* and *zoe*, the dispositif of crisis is deactivated and their separation remains pending in in-difference and so life is '*such as it is*'. Agamben's discussion of a new politics in *The Open* makes no direct reference to the dispositif of crisis and its deactivation, but does explore the separation of humans and animals, which must be left suspended in in-difference, without any decision being made:

> in our culture man has always been the result of a simultaneous division and articulation of the animal and the human, in which one

> of the two terms of the operation was also what was at stake in it. To render inoperative the machine that governs our conception of man will therefore mean no longer to seek new – more effective or more authentic – articulations, but rather to show the central emptiness, the hiatus that – within man – separates man and animal, and to risk ourselves in this emptiness: the suspension of the suspension . . . Once again, the solution of the *mysterium coniunctionis* by which the human has been produced passes through an unprecedented inquiry into the practico-political mystery of separation. (Agamben 2004: 92)

Thinking a new politics thus consists in deactivating the dispositif of crisis that remains active in the ungroundedness of the metaphysics on which bio-thanatopolitics is 'founded'. Thus, politics is new if, instead of deciding on life, as sovereign power has demanded from the beginning, it frees itself from this decision and thus renders 'inoperative' the separation between *bios* and *zoe* and the election of one part over the other.[17] As we have seen, this election is the presupposition of the curse: it establishes the difference between what is blessed by the language of power and what is cursed by it, between the word that tells the truth and the word that, betraying the oath, does not tell the truth, thus, between the life corresponding to the human (*bios*) and that corresponding to the non-human (*zoe*).[18] Rendering inoperative the decision on the separation between the blessed and the cursed means making speaking and living indifferent. What becomes inoperative is thus the curse of the part that does not correspond to the human being's authentic destination. And so the praxis of the new politics does not consist in electing the part and the party, whether blessed or cursed, but, on the contrary, in making inoperative the decision of belonging. What remains in this suspension is the coming community or the *ethos* as the dwelling of the human:[19] 'a *bios* that is only its own *zoē*' (Agamben 1998: 188).

In *The Use of Bodies*, Agamben returns to this idea, although now characterizing it as 'form-of-life'. But he takes it even further: the form-of-life is not only the deactivation of the form of bare life through which the ontological-biopolitical machine acts on the *zoe*, but reveals inoperativity itself to be the form of the *zoe*, that is, inoperativity as the *bios* of the *zoe*. The 'destituent power' – which he explores in the epilogue of *The Use of Bodies* and throughout the *Homo Sacer* project – is the political life of a *zoe* that is irreducible to bare life. Thus, what this power 'renders destitute' is not the conjunction of *bios* and *zoe*, but rather their separation,[20] the presupposition of every division into parts and therefore of every political form of belonging. Indeed, Agamben had already set out to destroy this presupposition as early as the 1980s: 'One has a political *bios* who never has his *zoè* as a part, as something separable (that is, as bare life), but is his *zoè*, is completely *form-of-life*' (Agamben 2016: 219).

2. Biopolitics and biopower, multitude and empire

In *Fabbriche del soggetto*, Negri shows particular interest in Agamben's *Language and Death*. He understands its thought of crisis as opening up the possibility of an ontology that no longer rests on the ungrounded foundation of the negative – thus is no longer metaphysical – but is instead able to influence political practice. Negri thus senses an opportunity to liberate the voice from the negative that binds being to the metaphysical *logos*. This is the opportunity for an affirmative voice that suggests a political destination for being. Of course, Agamben instead understands the deactivation of the dispositif of metaphysics as 'the eclipse of the Voice', which absolves the living of any destination beyond its being speaking. But the most striking part of Negri's interpretation is his conclusion:

> Are we able to understand the voice that represents our human essence not as a substitute for being but as constitutive of being? . . . Detached from the political functions that have been wrongly entrusted to it and from the mystification that they ended up expressing, the philosophy of *Krisis* could represent a possible introduction to positive thought, to the philosophy of the future. Without being caught in further moves of resipiscence and attempts at new and surreptitious recoveries of the negative. (Negri 1987: 195)

Negri uses the term 'human operativity' (Negri 1987: 195) to describe that political praxis that converts the negative thought of *Krisis* into a positive. This is thus the exact opposite of the inoperativity that defines political praxis for Agamben. A few years later, it became clear that this was no coincidence when Negri started to explore the concept of 'constituent power', which Agamben then confronted in *Homo Sacer*. But despite their differences, in the same period, both of them brought the ontological dimension to the fore.[21]

In *Insurgencies*, Negri identifies a constituent power irreducible to any constituted power, tracing through it the cursed line of modernity and of that political thought – from Machiavelli through Spinoza to Marx – which opposed the dominant line – from Hobbes via Rousseau to Kant and Hegel.[22] The discontinuous cursed line of constituent power, which assumes political primacy in the interruptions of history by the great modern revolutions, is presented as an alternative to the concept of sovereignty:

> the truth of constituent power is not what can be attributed to it, in any way whatsoever, by the concept of sovereignty. It cannot be so, because constituent power is not only, obviously, an emanation of constituted power, but it is not even the institution of constituted power. It is, rather, an act of choice, the precise determination that opens a horizon, the radical apparatus of something that does not yet exist, and whose conditions of existence imply that the creative act does not lose its characteristics in the act of creating. When constituent power sets in motion the constituent process, every determination is free and remains free. On the contrary, sovereignty presents itself as a fixing of constituent power, and therefore as its termination, as the exhaustion of the freedom that constituent power carries. (Negri 1999: 21–2)

Like Agamben, Negri also seems to consider constituent power in its irreducibility to constituted power, thus as *potenza* (power/potential) as such: 'But at the very moment when strength [*potenza*] gets instituted it ceases being strength [*potenza*] and thus declares itself as never having been such' (Negri 1999: 22). And yet, the 'act of choice', which for Negri affirms the autonomy and discontinuity of constituent power from all constituted power, seems to coincide with that decision which for Agamben binds constituent power to constituted power through the dispositif of the sovereign ban. Every decision is included within an ontology that thinks *potenza* in relation to the act: its destination is to pass into the act, thus to become *potere*. In such a dispositif, *potenza* as such is defined as having the possibility of not passing over into actuality, thus as impotence. In *Homo Sacer*, constituent power's being 'taken out' by constituted power, the exception of *potenza*, corresponds to the dispositif of the sovereign ban:

> This is why it is so hard to think both a 'constitution of potentiality' entirely freed from the principle of sovereignty and a constituting

> power that has definitively broken the ban binding it to constituted power. That constituting power never exhausts itself in constituted power is not enough: sovereign power can also, as such, maintain itself indefinitely, without ever passing over into actuality . . . Instead one must think the existence of potentiality without any relation to Being in the form of actuality . . . This, however, implies nothing less than thinking ontology and politics beyond every figure of relation, beyond even the limit relation that is the sovereign ban. (Agamben 1998: 47)

As we have seen, this is about thinking political praxis as inoperativity, whereas Negri explicitly includes constituent power within the thought of crisis:

> Our aim then will be to find a definition of constituent power within the boundaries of this crisis that characterizes it. We will try to understand the radical character of the foundations of the concept of constituent power, and the extent of its effects, from democracy to sovereignty, from politics to the State, from power [*potere*] to strength [*potenza*]. In short, we will try to understand the concept of constituent power exactly insofar as it is the concept of a crisis. (Negri 1999: 2)

The dispositif of crisis becomes fundamental for ensuring constituent power is not reduced to constituted power and sovereignty, for its *potenza* not to be exhausted in *potere*. In fact, it is not enough to affirm the temporal and ontological primacy of struggles – and therefore of constituent power and *potenza* – with respect to constituted power. When the constituent power of revolutions is transformed into constituted power, the separation and difference between the two must be maintained. This is the force of the dispositif of crisis. The crisis is the necessary premise for the affirmation of the autonomy of constituent power, and thus for the possibility of the latter's historical re-proposition and re-emergence; that is, for the possibility of revolution. And yet, Negri seems aware that the crisis can only be a premise, that its dispositif can only keep antagonism within constituted power, which means that a way out must be found from within constituted power by emphasizing the difference between constituent power and constituted power. But by using the crisis in this manner, the *potenza* of constituent power ends up at most being the ungroundedness of constituted power, and thus always remains the expression of a 'negative ontology':

> The crisis is a limit but it is also and, more important, an obstacle. The limit is posed against a will of strength of the multitude that is impossible to limit, and thus it becomes an obstacle. And it is by becoming deeper on this terrain of the negative that the clash and the contradictions become active: the limit does not close but liberates praxis . . . It is the revelation of an 'outside' that has become an 'inside' and the folding in of historical development on this omnipotence that is never actualized but always reproposed. And since this strength [*potenza*] is the strength [*potenza*] of the multitude, here the multitude reveals itself as subject . . . All this in the scenario of a negative ontology. (Negri 1999: 318)

Insurgencies identified the subject of constituent power in the concept of the multitude deriving from Spinoza – a legacy of the cursed line of modernity. Although this offered an alternative to the people as the subject of constituted power, the question of the way out of the crisis, which required the subject of constituent power to be within constituted power, was nevertheless left open. The limit posed by the crisis, while giving the multitude the power to go beyond it, at the very least calls into question the multitude's capacity to make decisions and, therefore, its autonomy and self-valorization.

In his famous tetralogy written with Michael Hardt, made up of *Empire*, *Multitude*, *Commonwealth*, and *Assembly*, Negri explicitly places his philosophical and political proposal beyond the thought of crisis, thus suggesting a positive ontology:

> The means to get beyond the crisis is the ontological displacement of the subject. The most important change therefore takes place inside humanity, since with the end of modernity also ends the hope of finding something that can identify the self outside the community, outside cooperation, and outside the critical and contradictory relationships that each person finds in a non-place, that is, in the world and the multitude. This is where the idea of Empire reappears, not as a territory, not in the determinate dimensions of its time and space, and not from the standpoint of a people and its history, but rather simply as the fabric of an ontological human dimension that tends to become universal. (Hardt and Negri 2000: 384–5)

Negri and Hardt's tetralogy makes numerous philosophical (and other) references and raises many questions that were taken up in the wide and varied debate following its international success.[23] We are most interested here in those passages that address the contribution that the biopolitical paradigm made to the deactivation of the dispositif of crisis. The condition for going beyond the crisis is 'the ontological displacement of the subject': the most authentic destination of human beings is not outside of themselves and the world with its various working and affective relationships established as 'common' institutions; it does not transcend the plane of immanence in which these relationships happen. As Agamben says, the voice that calls humanity to a destination beyond its condition as a living being has finally been eclipsed. And modernity's form of constituted power, the territorial state, is now incapable of reducing the multiple and plural production of subjectivity – the multitude – to the unity of the people, and its life to the unity of the nation. In globalization, the Empire is both the space of the multitude and the form of sovereignty exercised over it. And in the post-Fordist productive regime, capital extracts surplus value from the production of the multitude. The place of production is no longer the factory but the life in common of the multitude, and the immaterial labour of the 'general intellect' becomes productive labour par excellence:

> Empire takes form when language and communication, or really when immaterial labor and cooperation, become the dominant productive force. The superstructure is put to work, and the universe we live in is a universe of productive linguistic networks . . . Production becomes indistinguishable from reproduction; productive forces merge with relations of production; constant capital tends to be constituted and represented within variable capital, in the brains, bodies, and cooperation of productive subjects. Social subjects are at the same time producers and products of this unitary machine. In this new historical formation it is thus no longer possible to identify a sign, a subject, a value, or a practice that is 'outside'. (Hardt and Negri 2000: 385)

When capital is valorized through the collective capacities of the general intellect, the possibility arises for the self-valorization of the multitude. Empire and multitude are expressions of the postmodern, of a discontinuity with the modern that has only now been definitively realized.[24] Thus, the life of the multitude does not correspond to the negative on which modern (metaphysical) politics and capital founded power and profit, but emerges, through its own self-reproduction, as the positive and immediate production of society and wealth. And so biopolitics is a principal characteristic of Empire:

> We can answer the question of how to get out of the crisis only by lowering ourselves down into biopolitical virtuality, enriched by the singular and creative processes of the production of subjectivity . . . The biopolitical, seen from the standpoint of desire, is nothing other than concrete production, human collectivity in action. Desire appears here as productive space, as the actuality of human cooperation in the construction of history. This production is purely and simply human reproduction, the power of generation. Desiring production is generation, or rather the excess of labor and the accumulation of a power incorporated into the collective movement of singular essences, both its cause and its completion. When our analysis is firmly situated in the biopolitical world where social, economic, and political production and reproduction coincide, the ontological perspective and the anthropological perspective tend to overlap. (Hardt and Negri 2000: 387–8)

This is one of a number of passages that demonstrate Negri's grafting of French poststructuralist philosophy (including Foucault, but also and above all Deleuze and Guattari) onto the Marxian and operaist framework, an operation that can also be seen in Negri's earlier work, but which only became fully visible in the tetralogy. He also took inspiration from postcolonial studies, gender studies and cultural studies, all of which had become increasingly influential in the international debate. The influence of Deleuze, for example, is evident in Negri's argument that the ontological excess of desire, which cannot be captured within the post-Fordist mode of production, makes the neutralization and disciplining of the productive force of life impossible. However, what really interests us here is the peculiar turn that the biopolitical paradigm takes when it comes into contact with Negri's operaist premises. At several points, Negri specifies that it is not simply biological life, the bare life of the *zoe*, that is captured by the new imperial sovereignty, but also social life, as the new productive force exploited by capital in the era of post-Fordist globalization. The generic capacities of the human animal, whose collectivity constitutes society, and its activity of immaterial production are both put to work by capital. Social life is thus the sphere of capitalist exploitation and of the sovereign command of the production of subjectivity and sociality. Biopolitics is the maximum intensification and extension of the 'social factory', the full realization of that tendency which Negri had already identified in the 1970s.

When life is the generative *potenza* (power/potential) of all politics, economics and society, what is the difference between constituted power and constituent power, and where is the crisis that in modernity determined subjugation and subjectification, discipline and liberation? If constituted power can no longer be defined as the neutralization of constituent power, if every limit it sets to the latter's *potenza* becomes a limit to the very production from which it draws its power and profit, if, therefore, the immaterial production of subjectivity and sociality can no longer be obstructed but must be encouraged, then biopolitics becomes the sphere in which the distinction between constituted power and constituent power, between inside and outside, between immanence and transcendence disappears: 'The political, the social, the economic, and the vital here all dwell together . . . The practices of the multitude invest this complex and unitary horizon – a horizon that is at once ontological and historical. Here is where the biopolitical fabric opens to the constitutive, constituent power' (Hardt and Negri 2000: 406). Yet for the politics of the multitude to become a politics of liberation from subjugation, the multitude, which is within the Empire, must stand against it. This requires a liberation that does not arise from the modern dispositif of crisis. In order for conflict to be conceived of and emerge on the plane of immanence, Negri and Hardt make recourse to a new dichotomy that is found in the biopolitical, and which produces a new antagonism. While still referring to the crisis when describing the geopolitics of Empire, *Multitude* translates it in biopolitical terms, and, unlike in Foucault, understands the distinction between biopolitics and biopower in a dichotomous and conflictual sense:

> When we say crisis we do not mean that geopolitics is on the verge of collapse, but rather that it functions on the basis of borders, identities, and limits that are unstable and constantly undermined . . . This is a *geopolitics of crisis* . . . [T]hese internal conflicts or contradictions within the concept of geopolitics should be recognized as the conflict between the multitude (that is, the forces of social production) and imperial sovereignty (that is, the global order of power and exploitation), between biopolitics and biopower. (Hardt and Negri 2004: 314–15)

Although the antagonism is no longer between workers and capital or between constituent power and constituted power, the dispositif of crisis entails a conflict and separation within social life: between biopolitics and biopower, between the production of subjectivity and subjugation by the sovereignty of Empire. Again the multitude is called to make a decision to assert its biopolitics against sovereign biopower.

This decision, however, is no longer destined towards a way out, but can only fall within life itself: 'The primary decision made by the multitude is really the decision to create a new race or, rather, a new humanity' (Hardt and Negri 2004: 356). But how is it possible to make a decision within the plane of immanence of life, and so without an 'outside'? Negri and Hardt's answer is that the separation between biopolitics and biopower is due to sovereign command and capital, which poisons the life of the multitude. The biopolitical decision, therefore, does not consist in 'choosing' one side over the other, but is instead an exodus within: 'the exodus of the multitude from the republic of property, from the hierarchies of command over production, and from all other social hierarchies is perhaps the most significant example of a common decision' (Hardt and Negri 2009: 306). Thus exodus is not the choice or election of the part, but rather a 'subtraction' from the command of the sovereign and capital. In exodus, the *potenza* (power/potential) of the multitude – subtracting itself from the biopower that destines it to be 'actualized' in capitalist appropriation – immediately becomes action. As it discovers that it relates exclusively to the production-reproduction of its own life, it discovers itself to be autonomous:

> class struggle in the biopolitical context takes the form of exodus. By exodus here we mean, at least initially, a process of subtraction from the relationship with capital by means of actualizing the potential autonomy of labor-power. Exodus is thus not a refusal of the productivity of biopolitical labor-power but rather a refusal of the increasingly restrictive fetters placed on its productive capacities by capital. (Hardt and Negri 2009: 152)

The crisis is nothing more than a dispositif for governing social life and expropriating – from the outside – the common wealth of biopolitical production. Exodus instead shows that biopower no longer has any hold on life, which can now govern itself and produce autonomously: 'economists are recognizing the increasing importance of factors external to capital because in fact, to reverse the conventional economic formulation, capital is increasingly external to the productive process and the generation of wealth. In other words, biopolitical labor is increasingly autonomous' (Hardt and Negri 2009: 141). Unlike the separation between constituent power and constituted power, the separation between biopolitics and biopower only benefits sovereign power: the liberation of the multitude is no longer *in* the crisis but *from* the crisis. And yet, the crisis still remains necessary, because it gives the multitude the opportunity to decide on exodus and thus practise its autonomy. But if, as Negri and Hardt maintain, the productive autonomy of the multitude does not entail political autonomy – which is still to be organized even if no longer in the form of the party[25] – if, therefore, the decision for exodus is not a political constituent, the question remains as to whether there is indeed the symbiosis between the political, economic and social that they claim. In other words, biopolitics could only correspond to the productive life of the multitude on condition of a further decision by the multitude. That is, politics is not immanent to the working and social life of the multitude and so is not immediately implicated in it. Thus, the question of the division of life returns, with the risk of falling back into something like the much-criticized Arendtian distinction between a working or social life and a political life. At this point, Paolo Virno's argument in *A Grammar of the Multitude* turns out to be much more than a clarification of the relationship between biopolitics and immaterial or cognitive labour. For Virno, biopolitics is only a further form of that 'primary fact' of the general intellect and the productive *potenza* of the multitude being put to work:[26]

> One should not believe, then, that bio-politics includes within itself, as its own distinct articulation, the management of labor-power. On the contrary: bio-politics is merely an effect, a reverberation, or, in fact, one articulation of that primary fact – both historical and philosophical – which consists of the commerce of potential as potential. Bio-politics exists wherever that which pertains to the potential dimension of human existence comes into the forefront, into immediate experience: not the spoken word, but the capacity for speaking as such; not the labor which has actually been completed, but the generic capability of producing. The potential dimension of existence becomes conspicuous only, and exclusively, under the guise of labor-power. (Virno 2004: 83–4)

It is not that Virno believes that the life of the multitude has no political potential. On the contrary, today, when the general capacities of the human animal are at stake in politics, it embodies 'the fundamental form of political existence'. But it is not primarily sovereign biopower that subjugates the life of the multitude and limits and channels its innovative power in a conservative direction. It is rather in the very nature of the multitude – and of the general intellect – to be ambivalent and to oscillate between conservation and innovation, between competition and cooperation. A politics of the multitude must therefore not decide on an exodus as a way out from the crisis but use exodus to produce new political institutions – alternatives to the state, which functioned as long as the multitude was reducible to the unity of the people – to channel the conflictuality of the crisis in a different direction, taking the government of the crisis from sovereignty.[27] Like other thinkers we have already discussed, for Virno, the fundamental question is the location of political conflict: biopolitics is not the 'primary fact', because the multitude is formed historically in the technical-productive capacities of the general intellect, and it is here that crisis and conflict take place. The original location of conflict is not so much between powers or between biopower and biopolitics, but within the life of the multitude, whose 'transindividual reality that Marx called general intellect or "social brain"' is converted in post-Fordism into 'real and true technicoproductive resources' (Virno 2007: 41). As Virno points out in 'So-Called "Evil" and Criticism of the State':[28]

> *multitude* constitutes, today, the fundamental form of political existence. It is no longer an incidental parenthesis, but a stable way of being. In an era when the modern State is waning, and the 'monopoly of political decision making' is falling to pieces, it happens that in every aspect of social organization a plurality of individuals prone to avoid (and even, at times, to obstruct) the circuits of representative democracy becomes ever more valid. . . . Sometimes aggressive, sometimes united, prone to intelligent cooperation, but also to the war between factions, being both the poison and the antidote: such is the multitude. It adequately embodies the three key-words with which . . . we tried to clarify what might be a nondialectic understanding of the negative: ambivalence, oscillation, that which is perturbing. (Virno 2007: 40)

3. *The origin of conflict: An affirmative biopolitics*

From the 1980s onwards, the thought of sexual difference, late operaismo, Marramao's thought, and Agamben's and Negri's conceptions of biopolitics – each in their own way and sometimes in direct conflict with each other – have seen political potential in those deviations from the straight line of power whose corresponding subjectivities were destined to be cursed. However, it is only with the biopolitical paradigm proposed by Esposito that the dispositif of the crisis is radically called into question.

We have seen that Esposito's theory of the impolitical intended to maintain the difference of politics as conflict within the order of the modern political, whose function was to neutralize it through reducing it to representation. And we have seen how a conception of community like that of Bataille, whose commonality is constituted by death, escapes the representation of the political as unrepresentable yet affirmative. And so, a community that is irreducible to and alternative to the political is only positively manifested at the moment of its extinction. *Communitas*, the first volume of a trilogy also composed of *Immunitas* and *Bíos*, while continuing the reflection on community in *Categories of the Impolitical* – which concludes with Bataille – nevertheless radically reverses its perspective. It is to the origin of the community, and not to its final and extreme outcome, that Esposito now looks in order to positively identify its difference from the modern political, concentrating on the *munus* of *communitas*, the common of the community:

> the *munus* that the *communitas* shares isn't a property or a possession [*appartenenza*]. It isn't having, but on the contrary, is a debt, a pledge, a gift that is to be given, and that therefore will establish a lack. The subjects of community are united by an 'obligation' . . . that more precisely expropriates them of their initial property (in part or completely), of the most proper property, namely, their very subjectivity . . . [T]he common is not characterized by what is proper but by what is improper, or even more drastically, by the other; by avoiding [*svuotamento*], be it partial or whole, of property into its negative; by removing what is properly one's own [*depropriazione*] that invests and decenters the proprietary subject, forcing him to take leave [*uscire*] of himself, to alter himself. (Esposito 2010: 6–7)

Although in *Communitas* the influence of deconstruction is still at times detectable,[29] its change of direction is clear: not only – going back to the etymological root of *munus as* a 'gift' that is 'distinguished by its obligatory character' (Esposito 2010: 4) – is there an inversion of the point of view from which the reflection on community begins, starting from its origins instead of its destination – unlike Agamben's 'coming community' and Negri and Hardt's production of the commons; not only is the commons freed from the meaning of shared property and, therefore, from the reference to property that characterizes the public/private dichotomy; and not only, once separated from the idea of property, is community no longer reducible to subjectivity, whether of the individual or of the collective, whether personal or of the state, or to any identitarian concept, such as the 'belonging' of communitarianism; but, and this is the main point, the *communitas*, rather than starting from *cum*, from the relation (a la Nancy), is thought by starting from *munus*. In this way, at its origin, it is the *communitas* itself that activates the neutralizing dispositifs of modern politics, because they are essentially dispositifs of immunization. Modern politics is the immunization of the *communitas*, and *immunitas* also derives from *munus*, from that infinite duty of compensation that the gift of the other necessitates, which constitutes the original community. It is this *munus* that the modern political intends to immunize. In short, *communitas* is not simply the negative that makes modern politics and its order of representation ungrounded, nor simply the 'coming' of a never definitively accomplished deconstruction of the political, but is the raison d'être of modern politics and its dispositifs, not least that of subjectivity:

> Modern political philosophy attempts to respond to this unacceptable *munus*. How? Here reappears that category of 'immunization' that we saw as constituting the most incisive semantic counterpoint of *communitas*. The thesis I would like to advance in this regard is that the category of immunization is so important that it can be taken as the explicative key of the entire modern paradigm, not only in conjunction with but even more than other hermeneutic models, such as those we find in 'secularization', 'legitimation', and 'rationalization', terms that hide or diminish the lexical significance of modernity. The reason is that, yes, there are echoes in these models, distant with respect to the premodern past, but not of the prospective inversion and the negative power [*potenza*] of the negative that juxtaposes directly *immunitas* and *communitas*. The 'immune' is not simply different from the 'common' but is its opposite, what empties it out until it has been completely left bare, not only of its effects but also of its own presupposition'. (Esposito 2010: 12[30])

Unlike the deconstructive approach, Esposito holds that the community is not the negative of the dispositif of *immunitas* of modern political philosophy, but the opposite: *immunitas* is the negation of *communitas*. And yet, the dispositifs put in place by modern philosophy to immunize the *munus* of *communitas* became necessary. In fact, in the original community, the unconditional openness which the common *munus* obliges made everyone vulnerable and exposed to death. At the dawn of modernity, it was in these terms that Hobbes described the 'state of nature' to justify the pact which, in exchange for protection and security, binds people to obedience and subjects them to the sovereign:

> What men have in common, what makes them more like each other than anything else, is their generalized capacity to be killed: the fact that anyone can be killed by anyone else. This is what Hobbes sees in the dark depths of the community; this is how he interprets community's indecipherable law: the *communitas* carries within it a gift of death. From it inevitably arises the following: if community is so threatening to the individual integrity of the subjects that it puts into relation, nothing else remains for us except to 'immunize us' beforehand and, in so doing, to negate the very same foundations of community. (Esposito 2010: 13)

The immunitary dispositif, activated by sovereignty as a response to the fear of death generated by the original community, compensates for the suppression of the *cum* of *communitas* with the constitution of subjectivity, which at the very beginning of modernity fully reveals the original meaning of 'subjection' and 'subjugation' that would then end up being implicit in every process of subjectification. In Hobbes, the two aspects of subjectivity are still sharply divided: the subjection of the subject corresponds to the subjectification of the sovereign. As Foucault teaches, this division disappeared with the evolution of modern politics: the subjugation of a part is the condition for its subjectification. However, unlike in Foucault, in Esposito the separation – arising from the suppression of the *cum* and so the sharing of the *munus* – does not originate in the community, as the dispositif of crisis presupposes, but is instead produced by that immunization of the community that defines the modern political: 'Subjects of such a sovereign are those that have nothing in common since everything is divided between 'mine' and 'yours': division without sharing [*condivisione*] . . . It is this irremediable separation that puts an end to that form of originary *munus* that had still characterized the precontractual social relation' (Esposito 2010: 28–9).

The final deviation from a deconstructionist perspective is completed in the second book of the trilogy, *Immunitas*. Here we see the full development of the specific characteristics of the immunitary dispositif as the paradigm of modern political philosophy. As already partly anticipated in *Communitas*, at an etymological level *immunitas* means that which is lacking the *munus* or negates the obligation derived from the gift that the *communitas* shares [*con-divide*]: it exempts some privileged people from the compensation of the *munus* to which originally everyone, with no exceptions, was equally obliged. The dispositifs of modern politics, starting with Hobbes's conception of the social contract and sovereignty, thus spring from an inappropriable origin, which they however have to presuppose, depending on it in order to become operative. Thus, what is radically called into question by Esposito's idea of *immunitas* is the very possibility of its autonomy, that is, an autonomy of the political, whether this is configured in the state or in the party: 'Latin dictionaries tell us that the noun *immunitas*, with its corresponding adjective *immunis*, is a negative or privative term whose meaning derives from what it negates or lacks, namely, the *munus*' (Esposito 2011: 5). *Immunitas* is thus marked by a 'privation' of the *munus*, and is activated exclusively via the *negation* of that *communitas* which instead becomes the bearer of the common *munus*:

> 'the true antonym of *immunitas* may not be the absent *munus*, but rather the *communitas* of those who support it by being its bearers. In other words, if the privation – that which lacks – is the *munus*, the point of contrast against which immunity takes on meaning is the com through which the *munus* becomes generalized in the form of the *communitas*'. (Esposito 2011: 6)

The difference from other conceptions of community should now be clear, including from those most akin to Esposito's: it is the *munus* that originally determines the relationship between *communitas* and *immunitas*, and that binds them together in a 'single dispositif'. In response to the exposure which the common *munus* obliges, which puts at risk not only the life of the individual but also the possibility of recognizing oneself as such, that is, as distinct and divided from the community, the immune defences react in a way that is proportionate to the danger: 'The more life is hounded by a danger that circulates without distinction throughout all its practices, the more its response is concentrated into the mechanisms of a single device [*dispositivo*]: as risk of the common becomes increasingly extensive, the response of the immune defense becomes increasingly intensive' (Esposito 2011: 5). In order for the relationship between *communitas* and *immunitas* to constitute a 'single dispositif' and to become 'instituting', immunity cannot assert its autonomy from community, it cannot suppress that relationship; instead its representation as the negative of community must be affirmed, as Esposito clarified some years later, in relation to his conception of negation: 'To argue that immunity – or immunization

– is the negative of community means that community must never be folded back on itself and blocked in a self-identity that prevents it from changing' (Esposito 2019: 198).

The fact that *communitas* and *immunitas* converge in a single disposit if has another consequence for those who, despite also interpreting the theme of community ontologically, do not take it back to the original and constitutive link with the immunitary paradigm on which modern politics is based, thus making it untranslatable in political terms, at most remaining confined to the level of ethics, if not metaphysics. But what kind of politics are we referring to, what conception of politics can encompass both *communitas* and *immunitas*, the surplus of life in common and the immunitary protection of the individual body and the political body? The lexicon of *Immunitas* suggests the answer: biopolitics. Unlike other conceptions of biopolitics, the function of immunization, to which the dispositifs of modern politics can be traced, comes from within life itself, whether individual or collective:

> what does it mean to say that politics is enclosed within the boundaries of life? That life is the primary object – and purpose – of politics? What is the horizon of meaning that is given to biopolitics as a result of this co-belonging? In my view, the answer to this question should not be sought in the folds of a sovereign power that includes life by excluding it. Rather, what I believe it should point to is an epochal conjuncture out of which the category of sovereignty makes room for, or at least intersects with, that of immunization. (Esposito 2011: 138–9)

This passage contains a clear reference to and rejection of Agamben's concept of biopolitics, and indeed Esposito distances himself from this conception even more sharply than is implied here. While the dispositif of the sovereign ban, by capturing life within the political, makes it bare and indiscriminately killable, in Esposito, the immunization of the political springs from life itself, in order to protect it. It is politics that is 'enclosed within the boundaries of life' – or, in other words, it is not sovereignty that encloses bare life in the camp but the original limitlessness of life that produces its immune confinement by the political. In short, while in Agamben it is the dispositif of sovereignty that produces bare life – thus making biopolitics the most recent expression of sovereignty as the paradigm par excellence of Western politics – in Esposito it is life that historically determines sovereignty, among other immunitary dispositifs. Esposito therefore follows Foucault in tracing the 'birth of biopolitics'[31] to the modern era, in the sense that, although the ontological nexus of *communitas-immunitas* is at the origin of the political *tout court*, it is in late modernity that it directly and immediately involves life, making it the object of immunization in an increasingly intensive way, ending up in the thanatopolitical outcome of Nazi biopolitics. Thus, biopolitics appears in history with an undoubtedly negative connotation:

> The purpose of biopolitics is not to distinguish life along a line that sacrifices one part of it to the violent domination of the other – although that possibility can never be completely ruled out – but on the contrary, to save it, protect it, develop it as a whole. But the point we have focused on from the outset is that this objective involves the use of an instrument that is bound to it through the negative, as if the very doubling that life experiences of itself through the political imperative that 'makes it live' contained something that internally contradicted it. (Esposito 2011: 139)

Just as the *immunitas* of politics intervenes to safeguard people from the danger of death that pervades the original *communitas*, but can end up rendering them nothing more than individuals subject to the sovereign's power to 'take life or let live' (Foucault 1978: 281), biopolitical immunization is the defence of life itself, which is activated to react to the 'contagion' of disease, but can end up turning against the life it is supposed to protect, denying it and suppressing it. This is what happens in autoimmune diseases, when the immune system attacks the body instead of defending it. And this is what happened in the body politic when Nazi autoimmune politics had broadened the range of contagious human types to such an extent that it ended up turning against the German population itself. This could also happen with today's securitarian policies, created as a response to various threatened contagions, such as immigration. And perhaps this is what we saw in the economic policies of austerity implemented in Europe after 2010 to contain the contagion of the sovereign debt crisis.

The immune system is a necessary filter to protect the life of the individual and the community from the risk of death that would result from indiscriminate exposure to *communitas*. But loosening the ties of security, by rendering borders more porous, further opening up the immune system's filter, would not expose society to the contagion of nothingness or the absence of values, as nihilism and its adversaries would have it, and neither would it abandon it to the civil war of all against all, as political realism holds. Immunization does not have nothingness or war as its premise: its premise is the community. This is what differentiates Esposito's position from much of the philosophical-political tradition. Community and immunity constitute a single dispositif: less immunity entails more community. But, Esposito asks, how can the relationship between *communitas* and *immunitas* find an equilibrium, so that the protection of life is not converted into its suppression, if – this time in agreement with Agamben – the traditional dispositifs of modern politics have today been interpreted within a negative biopolitics? How can the protection of life be converted into the strengthening [*potenziamento*] of life rather than its negation? In short, is an affirmative biopolitics possible, thus one which is not conceivable exclusively in terms of a praxis of inoperativity? The conclusion offered in *Immunitas* once again refers to the human body: the relationship between mother and child during pregnancy. Translated into political terms, this answer may seem surprising, if not paradoxical. That which can enhance and regenerate political life, if regulated by the filter of immunity, is in fact conflict – the same conflict that the modern paradigm of immunization introduced by Hobbes intended to neutralize:

> This is the ultimate – and prime – issue around which the entire immune paradigm wraps itself until reaching the point where it becomes indistinguishable from its opposite, 'community': the force of the immune attack is precisely what keeps alive that which it should normally destroy. The mother is pitted against the child and the child against the mother, and yet what results from this conflict is the spark of life. Contrary to the metaphor of fight to the death, what takes place in the mother's womb is a fight 'to life', proving that difference and conflict are not necessarily destructive. (Esposito 2011: 171)

If we remember how Esposito had previously elaborated the question of the impolitical, his solution is unsurprising: the thought of the impolitical was precisely intended to safeguard the difference between politics as conflict and the modern political, whose order of representation – or of immunization, as we could now call it – functions to neutralize conflict and, with it, politics itself. Reacting to the deadly imbalance between *communitas* and *immunitas* produced in late modernity, the search for an equilibrium – however precarious and contingent – capable of strengthening (*potenziare*) life takes place through the strengthening (*potenziare*) of the conflict between the common and the immune, and therefore through strengthening (*potenziare*) politics at the expense of the modern political: less immunity and more community.

The questions which *Immunitas* poses are taken up and more explicitly articulated in biopolitical terms in *Bíos*, which also begins from the questions left open by Foucault himself. *Bíos* considers the possibility of an affirmative biopolitics, which from this point onward defines Esposito's specific position in the international debate:[32]

> if life is stronger than the power that besieges it, if its resistance doesn't allow it to bow to the pressure of power, then how do we account for the outcome obtained in modernity of the mass production of death? . . . This is the paradox, the impassable stumbling block that not only twentieth-century totalitarianism, but also nuclear power asks philosophy with regard to a resolutely affirmative declension of biopolitics. How is it possible that a power of life is exercised against life itself? (Esposito 2008: 39)

How is it possible that biopolitics, instead of describing a 'power of life', has ended up being associated with historical events that have exercised 'power over life'? Why has it been historically experienced exclusively in terms of the denial of life? Does biopolitics necessarily mean that the relationship between politics and life is configured in the government of the former over the latter, that is, in the reduction to bare life brought about by the different historical forms of the sovereign dispositif?

> Does [a political government of life] concern a governing of or over life? It is the same conceptual alternative that one can express through the lexical bifurcation between the terms, used indifferently sometimes, of 'biopolitics' and 'biopower'. By the first is meant a politics in the name of life and by the second a life subjected to the command of politics. But here too in this mode the paradigm that seeks a conceptual linking between the terms emerges as split, as if it had been cut in two by the very same movement. (Esposito 2008: 15)

As we have already seen, Negri and Hardt take the distinction between 'biopower' and 'biopolitics' present in Foucault, although never explicitly elaborated by him, and make it antagonistic. If biopower means the sovereign power exercised over life, biopolitics should instead mean a politics of life: in the first case, power influences life from outside in order to deny it or, in Negri's terms, to exploit it, and in the second, politics is produced within life itself in order to affirm its *potenza* (power/potential). For Esposito, however, this does not solve the problem, as it is not a question of 'choosing' biopolitics *against* biopower: indeed, how can we conceive of an affirmative biopolitics if the very life that is supposed to produce it is subjugated to biopower? We know Negri and Hardt's answer: it is the decision of exodus that liberates life from the exploitation of biopower, although liberation from power over life is not immediately convertible into a 'politics' of life. And we also already know Esposito's answer: the distinction between biopower and biopolitics is fictitious, because also so-called biopower is produced by life. Biopower, in fact, corresponds to the degeneration of that immune paradigm that arises from life itself in order to protect it:

> Yet the category of immunization enables us to take another step forward (or, perhaps better, laterally) to the bifurcation that runs between the two principal declinations of the biopolitical paradigm: one affirmative and productive and the other negative and lethal. We have seen how the two terms tend to be constituted in an alternating and reciprocal form that doesn't take into account points of contact . . . Now the hermeneutic advantage of the immunitary model lies precisely in the circumstance that these two modalities, these two effects of sense – positive and negative, preservative and destructive – finally find an internal articulation, a semantic juncture that organizes them into a causal relation (albeit of a negative kind). This means that the negation doesn't take the form of the violent subordination that power imposes on life from the outside, but rather is the intrinsically antinomic mode by which life preserves itself through power. (Esposito 2008: 46)

In origin, then, there are not two lives – *bios* and *zoe*, one capable of subjectification and the other subjugated, one blessed and the other cursed – and therefore neither are there two forms of biopolitics. Instead, they constitute, like *communitas* and *immunitas*, a single dispositif – they are two sides of the same coin. Considered in its biological materiality, life is not the new object on which politics is exercised, but, as it has always been, the origin of every form of politics. The deviation that has taken place in late modernity has not so much been a paradigm shift – *immunitas* is still the paradigm through which life preserves itself – as the degeneration of the immunitary dispositifs of modern politics from protecting to denying life:

> what has a clear ontological relevance is always interpreted politically; not in the sense of any form that is superimposed from the outside onto the material of life . . . But, as the constitutive character of life itself, life is always already political, if by 'political' one intends not what modernity wants – which is to say a neutralizing mediation of immunitary nature – but rather an originary modality in which the living is or in which being *lives*. (Esposito 2008: 81)

In order for an affirmative biopolitics to be possible and conceivable, our aim cannot be a sort of adequation of politics and life. It is not through conceiving new political categories that are closer to life that biopolitics frees itself from its negative meaning. Life must be protected, but its immune defence will again turn into the negation of life if politics is not simultaneously also the reproduction and strengthening (*potenziamento*) of life. The categories of an affirmative biopolitics must therefore come from life itself. And Esposito argues that these are the same categories from which the immune delirium of Nazi thanatopolitics unleashed its power of negation. They are, in addition to the category of life, the categories of body and birth. As we now know, loosening *immunitas*'s hold on them means returning them to the *communitas*, from which they derive their original vital power:

> The attempt we want to make is that of assuming the same categories of 'life', 'body', and 'birth', and then of converting their immunitary (which is to say their self-negating) declension in a direction that is open to a more originary and intense sense of *communitas*. Only in this way . . . will it be possible to trace the initial features of a biopolitics that is finally affirmative. No longer over life but of life, one that doesn't superimpose already constituted (and by now destitute) categories of modern politics on life, but rather inscribes the innovative power of a life rethought in all its complexity and articulation in the same politics. (Esposito 2008: 157)

However, political praxis consists in deactivating the dispositif of the election of the part with which the modern political has, through the decision, separated the body from the political body of the people, birth (*nascita*) from the nation, and life from the legal person, thus excluding the *zoe* from the dimension of the *bios*. This deactivation does not merely entail the suspension of the decision to choose between the two separated parts – which curses the part that is not chosen – but also returns these political categories of life to their original common dimension, which Esposito identifies in flesh (common to the animal and the human, i.e. the living), in birth (a common origin that crosses and transcends all personal and national distinctions) and in the norm of life (the juridical norm does not rule over the person, but is generated in life in common). At the origin, which for Esposito is not just at the beginning, but repeats itself throughout history,[33] there is not separation and crisis – presupposed by every conception of politics that refers to the decision in order to overcome them – but rather the unity and community of life which is the only presupposition of an affirmative biopolitics. Thus, in order for there to be a politics of life, this affirmative biopolitics does not begin from life's division into parts:

> That such a unique process crosses the entire extension of life without providing a continuous solution – that any thing that lives needs to be thought in the unity of life – means that no part of it can be destroyed in favor of another: every life is a form of life and every form refers to life. This is neither the content nor the final sense of biopolitics, but is a minimum its presupposition. (Esposito 2008: 194)

The deactivation of the dispositif of crisis is directly implicated in the deactivation of the 'dispositif of the person', as addressed by Esposito in *Third Person*. Dating back to Roman law, the person was initially a juridical dispositif, and over time became a keystone of the Western legal system, which separates one part from another. In the Roman world, this dispositif separated and distinguished person and *homo* in a hierarchical sense, such that the status of the latter could border on that of the thing (the slave being the clearest example). In the modern era, the dispositif of the person returns in the Cartesian distinction between mind and body, or in that between the rational and the irrational, which inaugurates the constitution of subjectivity itself. In the biopolitical era, it is directly within the living – the individual and the population – that the distinction between the human and the animal takes shape. The dispositif of the person is ancient and has taken on various different historical forms, including the subjectification-subjugation of subjectivity, which returned with great force in response to the annihilation it suffered under Nazism. In fact, the rights that totalitarianisms denied are attributed to the person. However, Esposito sees the dispositif of the person as resulting in thanatopolitics, for it suggests the separation and discrimination between a human part, 'elected' as the depository of rights, and a cursed part, excluded from humanity and subjected to that human part: '[The dispositif of the person] is based on the assumed, continuously recurring separation between person as an artificial entity and the human as a natural being, whom the status of person may or may not befit' (Esposito 2012b: 9). What the dispositif of the person – like the complementary dispositif of the crisis – does not presuppose, and indeed denies in order to make use of it, is the original unity of life. Deactivating the immunitary dispositif of the person does not mean depriving the living person of their basic rights, abandoning them to blind and indiscriminate violence, but – as Esposito argues in *Bíos* – restoring the origin of the juridical norm to life and the community, thus restoring it to that sphere which, in *Third Person*, Esposito calls the 'impersonal'. Much like the impolitical with respect to the political, the impersonal is not the negation of the rights attributed to the person, but their relocation in a more original domain than that presupposed by the dispositif of the person and by any exclusively immunitary dispositif, which do not allow the vital power of the community to filter through. In the sphere of the impersonal – inscribed on the plane of the immanence of life[34] – the juridical norm neither derives from nor is applied to a transcendental (that of the person), and thus does not choose between two different parts:

> Life is the tangent, the line of force, along which immanence folds back on itself, eliding any form of transcendence or any ulteriority beyond being a living substance as such. It refers neither to a rational subject nor to a bare material substrate. But above all, if understood in its impersonal, singular dimension, life is what does not allow – what contradicts at its roots – the hierarchical division between these two entities within the separating dispositif of the person. (Esposito 2012b: 147)

Here, each of the categories of Esposito's affirmative biopolitics ends up finding its origin in life: community, politics and the impersonal. And they are all located on the same plane of immanence.

Chapter 5

OLD AND NEW PATHS

The dispositif of crisis is fundamental to the production of conflict. The premise of conflict is a division and separation into parts. As both operaismo and feminism have shown, when a part is cursed it allows for subjugation to be converted into subjectification, for it enters the domain of conflict and thus the political sphere. But can there be conflict without a division into parts in which one is elected and the other cursed? Can there be a conflict that does not presuppose crisis, and so would not produce the elective and selective decision? Could a conflict on the level of the immanence of life – an affirmative biopolitics – support separation without decision, a division without a curse? These questions are similar to those posed by Esposito in relation to postwar Italian philosophy, beginning from Tronti's *Workers and Capital*. How can immanence and conflict be thought together, how can we be both within and against? In *Living Thought*, Esposito argues that when Italian political philosophy attempted to ask that question, it ended up deciding on either one or the other: immanence or conflict.[1] I would add that this was because it presupposed crisis. This question in fact stretches back to Machiavelli, who was the first to elaborate a conception of political order that did not exclude conflict, and, following that attempt, was the first to reveal the antinomy of the relationship between immanence and antagonism:

> It is here – in his development of a completely new theory of conflict, now viewed not as a residue or opposite of order, but as a form of order – that Machiavelli opens up a whole new horizon of meaning to political thought . . . I am referring to the problematic, and in some ways even antinomic, relationship between antagonism and immanence that is to be found, in different forms, in other phases of Italian thought. The problem of this relationship lies in the fact that the plane of immanence is at once enabled and undermined by its conflictual makeup. (Esposito 2012a: 53)

Or, following Negri, we could say that the 'cursed line' of Western political thought, beginning with Machiavelli and continuing in Spinoza, poses the dilemma of the relationship between antagonism and immanence without resolving it: 'For both Spinoza and Machiavelli, although the logic of antagonism is inscribed in the plane of immanence, there is always a point beyond which they enter into potential friction' (Esposito 2012a: 54). Esposito's solution to this problem should be clear by now: the only politics able to hold immanence and conflict together is an affirmative biopolitics, that is, a politics that originates in life. And yet Italian thought also provides another solution, that of political theology, which understands the link between antagonism and immanence as one between conflict and order, following Machiavelli's position that conflict and order are not mutually exclusive.

1. Political theology

Political theology, which became central to Italian philosophy in the 1980s, is today seen as a key part of Italian thought, alongside and in tension with biopolitics. Although these two trajectories occasionally overlap in their responses to the dispositif of crisis, they have very different interpretations of it, which have diverged even more radically in response to recent crises and the use neoliberal capitalism has made of them.

Political theology has returned to the international debate, particularly in so-called 'critical thinking', including in some cultural and political contexts in which it was previously absent. This can be seen in the work of thinkers such as Alain Badiou, Slavoj Žižek, Peter Sloterdijk, Terry Eagleton and Simon Critchley.[2] At times, political theology has also been reformulated as economic theology. Indeed, the debate on political theology significantly intensified around the time of the 2007–10 crisis, when the theological dispositifs permeating the neoliberal economy's art of government were fully revealed (above all, the issue of private and public debt, but also the politics of 'austerity' in Europe following the debt crisis).[3] Economic theology then became a possible lens through which to read conflict.

However, the adoption of political theology by the Italian left goes back much further, at least to the 1980s. In fact, Cacciari argues that the '80s was the true decade of political theology, which came to an end with the onset of neoliberal globalization. Carl Schmitt was one of the biggest influences on Italian thinkers at the time, with his thought being subject to much broader and deeper analysis in Italy than elsewhere. The early adoption of political theology in Italy also seems to be rooted in a certain interpretation of the crisis at the beginning of the 1980s.

In the 1970s, in line with Marx's interpretation of crisis in the *Grundrisse*, the thinkers of late operaismo proposed a political and antagonistic use of capitalist crisis. But by the 1980s, crisis had started to become a dispositif of restoration, which, little by little, took on the governmental character it has in neoliberalism today. It was in this passage from the antagonistic to the governmental use of crisis – when the left was increasingly on the defensive – that the first experiments in political theology began. Cacciari's argument that political theology then exhausted its usefulness by the end of the 1980s could help us to cast a critical eye on the return to political theology during and after the 2007–10 crisis. For perhaps that crisis demanded not a revival of political theology, but a new economic theology.

Mario Tronti had fully embraced political theology by the 1980s, even applying it to operaismo. In *Noi operaisti*, a text written forty years after the end of operaismo's first phase, Tronti suggests that political theology could be used as a key for interpreting operaismo:

> Using the language of political theology – which, whatever people say, is the most fruitful for telling the truth about the last century – we can say that while operaismo was being expressed in the early 1960s it had an eschatological aspect: of course its aim was not to bring the history of salvation to a close in the best possible way, but, more modestly, to give a political outcome to workers' struggles. Rereading operaismo today, its active oppositional function comes to the fore, which consisted in withholding and delaying the philanthropic-humanitarian drift of the figure of the factory worker, the last stronghold to be conquered by bourgeois universalism. (Tronti 2009: 63–4)

Whereas in the 1960s operaismo seemed to advocate for an eschatological political force (breaking the yoke of the Fordist factory to escape from capital's economic domination), Tronti argued that in retrospect working-class politics had only slowed down the subsequent globalization of post-Fordist capitalism.[4] What particularly interests me in Tronti's *a posteriori* interpretation of operaismo is his treatment of the separation between the economic and the political, and the relationship that the use of a political-theological dispositif creates between them. Both politics as *éschaton* (the *potenza* – power/potential – that breaks capitalist economic power) and politics as *katéchon* (the *potere* – power – that 'withholds' the expansion of economic *potenza*) are rooted in a conflict that presupposes a radical distinction between economics and politics. In his text *Politica e Destino* (Politics and destiny), Tronti elaborates on and develops the concept of the katechontic function through his discussion of 'the autonomy of the political'.[5] Looking back to the crisis of the 1970s, Tronti argued that the *katéchon*'s functions would have had to have been assumed by the state when it was conquered by the working class: 'When I look back I see a surplus of "*éschaton*" in the operaist phase, corrected in the phase of the autonomy of the political with a surplus of "*katéchon*"' (Tronti 2006: 27). Although Tronti later considered the autonomy of the political represented by the state to be increasingly compromised, he nevertheless continued to argue that it was essential to preserve a certain place for the autonomy of the political – by which he meant 'modern' politics, since for Tronti that was the only politics – to protect it against the encroachment of democratic society and the economy. And he argued that only political theology could grant this margin of autonomy. Conflict, which is anchored in Schmitt's friend-enemy criterion, is hence played out between the level of immanence – in which we find the social and the economic – and the level of transcendence – in which we find the political and the theological. And so, in this conflict, politics and theology end up finding themselves on the same side, belonging to the same 'part'.

Political theology is called upon to preserve the dichotomy between politics and economy. Yet, in times of crisis, politics can take on the function of the *katéchon* – a force withholding the dominant power of the economy that subjugates politics. As Tronti writes: '[neoliberal fundamentalism] did not abolish politics, it subjugated it, overturning its primacy and suppressing its autonomy. This is one of the reasons for its crisis in recent years' (Tronti 2013: 82). The need for political-theological thought becomes even stronger when the ruptures of crisis do not offer any revolutionary possibility. The task of politics then becomes that of containing and stemming crisis; it becomes katechontic. And so politics becomes exclusively an art of government. As Tronti writes: 'Political theology is not liberation theology. It does not assault power from outside or from below. It aims to manage power through the exercise of authority' (Tronti 2011: 86).

Massimo Cacciari holds an opposite but complementary position to Tronti on this issue.[6] For Tronti, political-theological thought recognizes the power to govern the crisis, which gives politics authority to rule over the domination of the economy. While Cacciari also believes that political theology is fundamental for understanding and governing certain crises, he argues that this only applies to the crises of the twentieth century. The 2007–10 crisis and those that followed (what we might call 'neoliberal crises') are of a different nature. Since they have a governmental function, no *katéchon* can contain or govern them. Unlike in the 1970s and 1980s, Cacciari holds that today the crisis is no longer the prerogative of political organization, whether in the form of nation states or of political institutions, but is instead the prerogative of the economy, understood as 'administration'.

Like for Tronti, Cacciari's reference in *The Withholding Power* was *The Second Epistle to the Thessalonians* by Paul the Apostle. The enemy, the Antichrist that the power of the *katéchon* must withhold, is an 'anomie' that deviates and is 'de-lirious' (literally, is out of the furrow/limit), for which the *katéchon* has to provide a political *nomos*: boundaries, form, order, in short, government. Thus, the *katéchon* returns order, bringing back into line that which deviates through governing the crisis. But this *katechontic* function works only if we understand crisis according to the modern paradigm of the political. The premise of the *katéchon* in political theology is that the 'anomie' can't self-govern. And yet the neoliberal crisis does govern itself:

> From this crisis there emerges neither the absolute and simple absence of law and command, nor anarchy . . . Anomie is a new order; it is a new *nomos* . . . [The Antichrist] works to 'de-substantialize' all political power. But such work remains political praxis! The energy that moves it is spurred by intolerance of any *auctoritas* deriving 'from above', of any super-ordained command, and the law which propels his activity ever further springs from his own nature. It does obey but always obeys itself. (Cacciari 2018: 69–71)

Cacciari calls this self-governing anomie, that is indifferent to any katechontic demand by the modern political, the 'technico-administrative apparatus' (Cacciari 2018: 115). The neoliberal crisis is ungovernable by the modern political because it has its own politics of government. The politics of neoliberalism does not even contemplate the level of the political. This is what one of the most influential neoliberal thinkers, Friedrich von Hayek, claimed almost fifty years ago, when he chose not to refer to the spontaneous order of the market simply as 'economics', instead defining it as 'catallaxy', which means exchange but also has a political meaning of 'to admit into the community' and 'to turn from enemy into friend' (Hayek 1967: 164).

As the dualism between economics and politics disappears, the *katéchon* loses its raison d'etre. And perhaps this was why the debate on political theology's capacity to govern the crisis also began to wind down. Indeed, for Cacciari, the conservative function of the crisis was no longer performed by the *katéchon* and thus by political theology: 'The *katéchon* is as strong in containing as it is impotent in foreseeing . . . He fears the threat of the *exception* rather than the reproduction of the ever-same, of which this very moment of crisis is an essential element. What he cannot realize is that it is precisely the energy [the crisis] that conserves' (Cacciari 2018: 76–7).

2. Economic theology

In *The Mystery of Evil*, Agamben, like Cacciari and Tronti, offers a reading of Paul the Apostle's interpretation of political theology, although his reading in some ways differs from theirs and leads to very different conclusions. Although I do not want to reduce Agamben's reflections on political theology – which are wide-ranging and various – to this brief text, it is significant in offering a possible take on the political theology within his economic theology. Moreover, it shows that also Agamben, through the figures of the *éschaton* and the *katéchon*, interrogates the current relationship between economics and politics. However, he shifts the focus from the *potere* (power) of the *katéchon* to the *potenza* (power/potential) of the *éschaton*. Just as Tronti recognized in the *eschaton* the political dimension of 1960s' operaismo, so for Agamben the *éschaton* has to find a political expression today:

> From the perspective of the laissez-faire ideology that is dominant today, the paradigm of the self regulating market has taken the place of that of justice and pretends to be able to govern an ever more ungovernable society according to exclusively technical criteria. Once again, a society can function only if justice (which corresponds to eschatology in the Church) does not remain a mere idea, entirely inert and impotent in the face of law and economy, but succeeds in finding political expression in a force capable of counterbalancing the progressive leveling out onto a single technico-economic plane. (Agamben 2017: 17–8)

Agamben argues that the eclipsing of the eschatological dimension allows for today's uncontested domination by the worldly economy. The worldly economy – what Agamben calls the 'technico-economic plane' – has indeed become infinite and aimless. Cacciari associates these same qualities with what he calls the 'technico-administrative apparatus', but for him these qualities derive not from the eclipsing of eschatological power but, on the contrary, from the fact that this apparatus has an eschatological power, which is 'delirious' because it is no longer oriented towards an end.

While these two interpretations seem to be in agreement in their analysis of economics under neoliberalism, they have opposing political theologies. For Agamben, the real eschatological power is that of political action, which the technico-economic plane withholds. And it is only political action that can reveal this withholding. For him, the technico-economic plane consists in moving from one crisis to the other with the sole aim of deferring the final crisis, which is the eschatological crisis.[7] Agamben therefore contemplates a political alternative that is able to contend with the supremacy of neoliberal economics. This cannot be manifested at the katechontic level of the modern political but only on the eschatological level of an alternative politics. The aim is to reactivate the dualism and conflict between economics and politics by removing political initiative from the economy. While Agamben agrees with Tronti and Cacciari that the contemporary crisis has a governmental function that can be explained through economic theology, for him it is nevertheless *political* theology – understood as an eschatological politics – that can provoke the 'final, decisive crisis'. This final crisis is deferred by the contemporary crisis (understood as an art of government), which has an eminently katechontic function:

> 'Crisis' in ancient medicine meant a judgement, when the doctor noted at the decisive moment whether the sick person would survive or die. The present understanding of crisis, on the other hand, refers to an enduring state. So this uncertainty is extended into the future, indefinitely. It is exactly the same with the theological sense; the Last Judgement was inseparable from the end of time. Today, however, judgement is divorced from the idea of resolution and repeatedly postponed. So the prospect of a decision is ever less, and an endless process of decision never concludes. (Agamben 2013)

Whether the *katéchon* has a political or an economic connotation (and, consequently, whether the *éschaton* takes on the opposite connotation in each case, i.e., an economic or political one respectively), the problem remains as to the separability of these two moments within the political-theological dimension. This is the issue that Roberto Esposito addresses in his book *Two*:

> one can well say that the both the *ius publicum europaeum* and the bipolar world of the postwar period as well as the globalized world (also structured along exclusionary division lines) all lie within the political-theological horizon, still subject to the restraining force of the *katechon*. If this is the case, a fundamental question still remains to be answered concerning the possibility – but also the absolute difficulty – of exiting that horizon . . . This question, which has been asked and answered in the negative every time the threat of revolution looms up in the West, resounds once again when the crisis takes on a global aspect, that is apparently unresolvable using mechanisms of a technical nature. (Esposito 2015b: 81)

For Esposito, every dichotomy and opposition that we have mentioned so far is part of the politico-theological dispositif. Within this dispositif, all distinctions between politics and economics now fall within political theology as economic theology. Economic theology is thus the form taken by political theology in neoliberalism.

> instead of talking about the end of political theology, we should be talking about its transformation into an economic theology, one that is itself endowed with political attributes, including the supreme one of deciding on the possible survival of subjects. The . . . two paradigms of political theology and economic theology are not opposites, and they should not be ordered in a chronological sequence but integrated into a single meaningful block. (Esposito 2015b: 204)

If it is true that economic theology is the current configuration of political theology, then its political-economic dispositif does not simply maintain the distinction between economics and politics, but also and at the same time creates a relationship between them in which one subjugates and manages the other. The result is a politics of neoliberal economy that gives the crisis a conservative and governmental function. Thus, according to Esposito, the affirmation of the 'anomie' of the 'technico-economic apparatus' does not lead to the end of political theology as Cacciari claims, for this apparatus in all respects remains a political theology, sharing its dispositif. In an exchange with Cacciari, Esposito makes their different positions clear:

> Probably the difference between Massimo Cacciari and me is the following: I believe that also the last phase – which for him is the crisis or the end of political theology – can, despite everything, still be interpreted in the terms of [political theology's] dispositif. By which I mean that the domination of technique or of economics is itself susceptible to being interpreted as a theological-political 'figure'. (Cacciari and Esposito 2014: 7–8)

3. *Within and against biopolitics*

What if no alternative to this crisis presented itself at the political-theological level? The debate on political theology in Italy concluded that political theology offered no new alternatives but instead governed alternatives as economic theology. Then, in the 1990s, the debate on biopolitics started to emerge in Italy, joining political theology in shaping contemporary Italian thought. This raised the question as to whether the neoliberal crisis was better understood as a crisis of biocapitalism, and whether it was thus on the biopolitical level that possible alternatives might be found.[8] For, as Negri argued in 'From the end of national Lefts to subversive movements for Europe', the technico-administrative government of the crisis does not allow any alternative (Negri 2013).[9] So what does the crisis of biocapitalism produce and what does it affect? Forms of the modern political or forms of life?

While political theology aspires towards a government of the crisis, biopolitics configures the crisis as the government of life. Political theology and biopolitics also refer to different modes of judgement and, as Agamben reminds us, crisis is a form of judgement. While political theology understands judgement through the model of the final judgement (that properly 'eschatological' judgement whose deferral is governed by katechontic power), biopolitics takes its mode of judgement from medicine (a judgement aimed at keeping the ill patient alive through re-establishing the health conditions that preceded the organic conflict between life and death). The distinction between the mode of judgement of the theologico-political crisis and the mode of judgement of the biopolitical crisis is that the art of biopolitical government does not have the character of a state of exception (in the Schmittian sense), since what determines the latter is the judgement of political theology.

The overlapping of these two distinct models of crisis was characteristic of the debate in Italy during the Covid-19 pandemic. Indeed, in 2021, despite their different starting points, Agamben and Cacciari both took part in the Commissione dubbio e precauzione (Doubt and Precaution Commission; abbr. DuPre), which opposed the government's decision to limit the freedom of movement of the unvaccinated, arguing that this extension of the state of emergency threatened to become permanent. Thus, Agamben and Cacciari both criticised the state's legal – or, more precisely, theological-political – government of the crisis as a state of exception, but neither of them seemed to fully consider the biopolitical nature of the crisis, which lies beyond the sphere of the state and its laws.

The Covid-19 pandemic seemed to provide further proof that the neoliberal government of the biopolitical crisis consists in leaving no room for alternatives – not only in relation to the health crisis, but also to other crises regarding ecology, migration, society, and so on. It made it even more clear that the only alternative to preserving the existing order is death, meaning that the biopolitical paradigm does not allow for a real and final decision: the apparent choices within this biopolitical dispositif are in fact always forced. As the only alternative is death, we accept technical governments, austerity, indebtedness and precarious work. Thus, the unsustainable nature of neoliberal hegemony begins to become clear, as well as its failure in the face of the biopolitical nature of the crisis of the pandemic, all of which points to the need for another type of governmentality. We could find the starting point for this alternative governmentality in Michel Foucault's search for a political space within this intertwining of governmentality and biopolitics.

In a lecture in his course *The Birth of Biopolitics*, Foucault considers the possibility of a 'socialist governmentality' as an alternative to neoliberal governmentality.[10] He saw the limitations of the socialism of his time lying in its restriction to the 'reason of state', without having produced a governmental reason that could contemplate other forms of governmentality and institutions. Although Esposito critiques Foucault's understanding of the institution as tending to have a repressive function, it seems to me that he poses the same problem as Foucault:[11] that of the relationship between critique and government, between social counter-conduct and governmentality, and between social movements and institutions. Indeed, in recent years, it has been through his analysis of the concept of the institution that Esposito has elaborated on the relationship between order and conflict in the age of biopolitics: 'The logic of the institution – or rather of what . . . we will call "instituting praxis" – implies a continuous tension between inside and outside. [Protest movements] express an instituent energy that institutions should also keep alive in order to "mobilize" and, in some ways, surpass themselves' (Esposito 2022: 9–10).

Esposito begins his reflections on institutions from a position of defeat, seeing the epochal transition that took place in the 1960s and 1970s as a missed opportunity for links to be made between social movements and institutions, whose negative effects are still being felt today: 'This two-fold need for institutionalization and mobilization was obscured especially between the 1960s and 1970s, with the gradual rise of a rigid opposition between institutions and movements . . . The result of this divide has been an increasingly stark disconnection between politics and society' (Esposito 2022: 10). Although using different terms and vocabulary, Esposito's proposal for an instituting praxis and thought seems in some ways to re-propose the Foucauldian idea of a socialist governmentality or, more generally, an alternative governmentality.

Esposito's interest in an 'instituting praxis' has led him to reconsider or, better, elaborate on his conception of biopolitics. He increasingly analyses the 'politics of life' – an 'affirmative biopolitics' – from the perspective of political-legal instituting forms. Applying the terms of his biopolitics to his more recent work on the concept of the institution, it could be argued that Esposito understands the affirmative force of a politics of life from the perspective of *immunitas*, whose politico-legal dispositifs function to protect the body of the individual from the indiscriminate exposure of life in common. While *immunitas* remains the negative of *communitas* it nevertheless has an affirmative function within an instituting praxis. In *Common Immunity: Biopolitics in the Age of the Pandemics*, Esposito takes up the concept of 'common immunity' introduced at the end of *Immunitas* (Esposito 2011: 165–71) and applies it to the context of the Covid-19 pandemic and the immune dispositifs activated to confront it. He argues that the 'current biopolitical turn' can be understood in terms of an 'immuno-politics' (Esposito 2023: 8). Indeed, it is only politics that is able to 'inoculate' that dose of change and conflict that can produce the antibodies that the political immune system needs. Thus, for Esposito, the conflict introduced by an affirmative biopolitics – as an alternative to neoliberal biopolitics and its governing rationality – emerges on the plane of institutions, that is, at the level of *immunitas*. This means recognizing social movements and the critique they offer as having an institutional capacity, enabling them to renew existing institutions and create new ones where existing institutions have failed.

4. *The return to Gramsci*

Esposito's 'instituting' philosophy proposes a return to the problem that characterized Italian thought from Machiavelli onwards: the relationship between order and conflict. Although from different, if not opposing, positions, both biopolitics and political theology insist on stabilizing the relationship between order and conflict in a non-dialectical way, such that one term is not made superior to or the negation of the other. This goes against the Western tradition of political thought from Hobbes onwards, in which conflict is the 'cursed' term that the sovereign order must overcome and resolve. Whether as a dynamic equilibrium between order and conflict or an order that arises from or is renewed by conflict, neither Italian political theology nor Italian biopolitics curse conflict.

And this is even more relevant today, when various neo-sovereignisms are taking power as the 'party of order', to use Marx's expression in *The Eighteenth Brumaire of Louis Bonaparte* (2010). Today Italian thought is trying to establish a new way of thinking about conflict, a new path that, as the history I have traced in this book shows, also means retreading old paths. We thus conclude this book where we began: with Gramsci.

In the *Prison Notebooks*, Gramsci had already understood that, in a situation of crisis in which the subordinate classes are in disarray and the ruling class has lost its authority, the entire social body gathers 'under the banner of a single party' or under a 'charismatic leader' (Gramsci 1971: 211). Like Foucault and Esposito, Gramsci begins his thinking from a position of defeat: in analysing the reasons for the defeat of the workers' movement at the time and the rise of fascism in Italy, Gramsci suggests that government is not the exclusive and direct emanation of the state – which operates through domination and coercion – but also arises from the people governing its own conduct and giving form to its life. Gramsci elaborates the category of 'hegemony'[12] as the seizure of power by the subordinate classes in the absence of a revolutionary dynamic like that seen in 1789 in France, thus, in the absence of 'the molecular accumulation of elements destined to produce an "explosion"' (Gramsci 1971: 279–80). The conquest of hegemony essentially involves the production of favourable power relations for the subordinate classes. This allows them to direct those relations, moving from subalternity to leadership. Gramsci argues that hegemony is constituted over time – and thus not through an explosive revolution – by first shaping the 'superstructure', that is, the social and cultural institutions, then the political institutions, and only afterwards, the state: 'the philosophy of praxis conceives the reality of human relations of knowledge as an element of political "hegemony"' (Gramsci 1995: 306).

With his conception of hegemony, Gramsci invites us to consider conflict – as indicated by its etymology in *cum-fligo*, 'beat/strike together' – above all in its capacity to generate relationships within a context of the fragmentation of subaltern social groups, thus more in its 'instituting' praxis than in its destruction of relationships. We can find traces of an instituting capacity of conflict in the notes Gramsci dedicates to the 'history of subaltern social groups', a history which is 'necessarily fragmented and episodic'. Conflict becomes the expression of 'a tendency to (at least provisional stages of) unification in the historical activity of these groups', that is, in the absence of an already defined economic and political class, it is first and foremost a tendency towards composition in terms of partisanship, subjectivity and forms of life. But 'this tendency is continually interrupted by the activity of the ruling groups' (Gramsci 1971: 54–5) in their attempt to neutralize conflict. In *Assembly*, Negri and Hardt write that 'Gramsci's concept of hegemony defines something like the path' they take in the book (Hardt and Negri 2016: 279). For this Gramscian notion reflects their aim to bring together fragmented, disorganized and competing subaltern groups, thereby composing a new subjectivity. Negri and Hardt sustain that the struggle for political hegemony must be waged through counterpowers that institute new types of social relations and new forms of common knowledge production:

> Hegemony in Gramsci . . . comprises both the party moment (or, rather, the production of subjectivity and the constituent power that gives it flesh) and the dynamic of class and social struggle that transforms society (including modifications of the legal order through trade union counterpowers, for example, and appropriations of machinic knowledges) – and into all of this are interwoven constituent powers. (Hardt and Negri 2016: 279)

In the individualization and atomization of the present – from which arises that demand for security that neo-sovereignties attempt to answer – conflict must above all create partisan relations. Every alternative to the dominant order arises from being partisan, from taking a side, without that side or part necessarily having to be cursed. And it is from this partisan belonging that the struggle for hegemony begins.

NOTES

Introduction

1 A number of edited collections have introduced Italian thought to English-speaking readers, each focusing on different themes and authors. See, for example, Borradori, G., ed. (1988), *Recodings Metaphysics: The New Italian Philosophy*, Evanston: Northwestern University Press; Benso, S. and B. Schroeder, eds (2007), *Contemporary Italian Philosophy: Crossing the Borders of Ethics, Politics, and Religion*, New York: State University of New York; Chiesa, L. and A. Toscano, eds (2009), *The Italian Difference: Between Nihilism and Biopolitics*, Melbourne: re.press; VV. AA. (2010), 'New Paths in Political Philosophy', *The New Centennial Review*, 10 (2); Serratore, C., ed. (2013), 'La política y la vida: una genealogía del pensamiento político italiano contemporáneo', *Revista Pléyade*, 12; Chiesa, L., ed. (2015), *Italian Thought Today: Bio-economy, Human Nature, Christianity*, London-New York: Routledge.

2 On the international reception of Gramscian thought, see Thomas, P. (2009), *The Gramscian Moment: Philosophy, Hegemony and Marxism*, Leiden-Boston: Brill. See also Filippini, M. (2011), *Using Gramsci: A New Approach*, London: Pluto Press.

3 The most important book to make this claim is Fukuyama, F. (1992), *The End of History and the Last Man*, New York: Free Press.

4 For example, while both Tronti and Negri begin their political genealogies from Machiavelli, Tronti places him at the start of a line of *potere* (power) – passing through Hobbes, Marx, Weber and Schmitt – and Negri at the start of a line of *potenza* (power/potential) – passing through Spinoza and Marx, right up to Foucault and Deleuze.

5 The theme of divisions – also understood in a positive sense – is used by Bodei to analyse the history of ideas in republican Italy. The peculiar nature of the Italian political parties in the postwar period is fundamental here: 'In the immediate postwar period (and at least in the first three decades of republican Italy) the relationships of loyalty and complete dedication to a cause tended to no longer be immediately associated with the ideas of a "nation" or "fatherland" as such. They instead appeared to be linked with a kind of political synecdoche (*pars pro toto*) of just one part, the party as the bearer of global demands . . . A part that in some cases presents itself as a whole, insofar as the main parties, the PCI and the DC, refer to ideal communities with a totalizing scope that encompass and transcend the "homeland"' (Bodei 1998: 20–1).

6 In *Living Thought*, Esposito (2012: 12–21) points out that Italian political thought first emerged before and beyond the state, arguing that this was characteristic of Italian thought from the beginning.
7 Here I refer above all to Jürgen Habermas and John Rawls, both in their conceptions of the ethics of communication and public ethics and, to a certain extent, in their cosmopolitanism. For a discussion of these positions within an interpretation of globalization that privileges conflict, see Marramao (2012).
8 'In fact, *sinistra* presupposes social dualism. The division into classes and the theory of this division establish once and for all the sociological connotations of the concepts "left and right"' (Tronti 1981: 137).
9 Carlo Galli interprets the permanence of the categories of right and left in the political debate as being due to the persistence of the modern conception of politics and its structural dualism (in Italy in particular). See Galli, C. (2010), *Perché ancora destra e sinistra*, Roma-Bari: Laterza.
10 For a genealogy and analysis of the 'dispositif of crisis', see Gentili, D. (2022), *The Age of Precarity: Endless Crisis as an Art of Government*, London-New York: Verso.
11 'We call *sinistra* that part that organizes internally and operates on the basis of the recognition of the catastrophic nature of antagonism. This [definition] lacks a secure *episteme*? It lacks a dictator-principle? It lacks any rooting in the philosophy of history and dualistic sociologies? It lacks the myth (the Class and the promise that it embodies)? *On the contrary*, it would be tempting to say that the sinistra is precisely the acute sense of these losses.' (Cacciari 1982: 19).
12 'It is worth beginning to acknowledge that with the dissolution of its theoretical content, the concept of sinistra *did not* also lose its way. There is something in the conceptual system that characterizes the idea of the left that – at least in my opinion – has escaped this theoretical erosion and even the backlash following the end of the model of real socialism. This is taking the side of (*presa di partito*) the excluded, the "cursed part", the subjugated . . . As it has always been on the left, taking the side of (*presa di partito*) the subjugated is still an original fact, which is not determined by prior rational motives'. (Vattimo 1982: 82–3).
13 It would be interesting to explore whether the 'difference' of Italian biopolitics stems from the peculiarity of the Catholic tradition of the government of bodies with respect to other forms of the government of bodies, for instance, that of the welfare state. The interweaving of biopolitics and political theology seen in authors such as Agamben could be a consequence of this.

Chapter 1

1 For more on the relationship between the liberal Bobbio and Marxism, see Bobbio, N. (1997), *Né con Marx né contro Marx*, ed. C. Violi, Roma: Editori Riuniti.

2 The titles of the various volumes of the Togliatti editions (officially edited by Felice Platone) are, in order of publication: *Gli intellettuali e l'organizzazione della cultura (Intellectuals and the organisation of culture), Il Risorgimento (The Risorgimento), Note sul Machiavelli (Notes on Machiavelli), Sulla politica e sullo Stato moderno (On politics and the modern state), Letteratura e vita nazionale (Literature and national life)*, and *Passato e presente (Past and present)*. Bobbio's commentary on the publication of the critical edition of the *Prison Notebooks* is also interesting: 'Looking back today, we could say that publishing the notes of the *Prison Notebooks* not in chronological order but in order of their themes was perhaps not completely philologically correct but was very wise, because it allowed one to immediately identify and highlight the major themes of Gramscian thought' (Bobbio 1990: 100).

3 The continuity between the idealistic tradition and Marxist thought is a recurrent theme in Gramsci, which first appears in his early works. Exemplary in this sense is 'The Revolution against *Capital*' an article written to celebrate the October Revolution in Russia, in which Gramsci has no qualms in recognizing in Lenin more coherence with the idealistic premises of Marxist thought than with certain 'positivist and naturalistic' repercussions of Marx himself: '[The Bolsheviks] live Marxist thought – that thought which is eternal, which represents the continuation of German and Italian idealism, and which in the case of Marx was contaminated by positivist and naturalist incrustations' (Gramsci 2000: 33).

4 Eugenio Garin, another intellectual who was influential in the cultural politics of the time, expresses a position that is in some ways similar to Colletti, although coming from a different perspective: 'When fascism seemed to be defeated on the cultural level that we are discussing, Italy discovered Antonio Gramsci, who was read together with Marx. With skillful editing and clever strategy, Gramsci's legacy was disseminated, almost taking the place, on the cultural level, of that which for some years had been the magisterium of Croce, obviously with different resonances and insights, but also with some significant convergences at their base' (Garin 1997: 108).

5 For an analysis of Italian philosophical tradition through four of its paradigms (Bertrando Spaventa, Giovanni Gentile, Eugenio Garin and Roberto Esposito), see Claverini, C. (2021), *La tradizione filosofica italiana. Quattro paradigmi interpretativi*, Macerata: Quodlibet.

6 '[Culture] undoubtedly means a coherent, unitary and nationally diffused "conception of life and of man", a "secular religion", a philosophy that has become "culture", that is, has generated an ethics, a way of life, a civil and individual conduct. This demanded above all the unification of the "cultured class" . . . but it particularly demanded a new attitude towards the popular classes, a new concept of what is "national", different to that of the historical right, broader, less exclusive, we might say less "policing" . . . In short, the type of literary criticism suitable for the philosophy of praxis is offered by De Sanctis, not by Croce or by anyone else' (Gramsci 1975: 2185–6, 2188). For a critical analysis of the importance of De Sanctis to Italian Hegelian idealism, see Asor Rosa, A. (1975), 'L'idea e la cosa: De Sanctis e l'hegelismo', in *Storia d'Italia*, vol. IV/2, 850–78. Torino: Einaudi.

7 'The modern prince, the myth-prince, cannot be a real person, a concrete individual. It can only be an organism, a complex element of society in which a collective will, which has already been recognised and has to some extent asserted itself in action, begins to take concrete form. History has already provided this organism, and it is the political party-the first cell in which there come together germs of a collective will tending to become universal and total' (Gramsci 1992: 129).

8 For an analytical reconstruction of the different moments characterizing the reception of Gramscian thought over time, see Liguori, G. (2012), *Gramsci conteso: Interpretazioni, dibattiti e polemiche. 1922–2012*, Roma: Editori Riuniti.

9 For a history and summary of the various twentieth-century Italian Marxisms, see Corradi, C. (2005), *Storia dei marxismi in Italia*, Roma: manifestolibri.

10 'It was in these conditions that Della Volpe became the symbol of a commitment to the rigorous study of Marxism where Marxism is actually to be found, that is, in the writings of Marx himself. For Della Volpe, the *Critique of Hegel's Philosophy of Right*, a text written by the young Marx, was the fundamental starting point. But this was of course just the beginning of his direct knowledge of Marx's work, which necessarily culminated in the intense study and analysis of *Capital* itself' (Colletti 1975: 13).

11 For an analysis of the relationship between Hegel and Marx that discusses Della Volpe's work and the debate it inspired, see Finelli, R. (2016), *A Failed Parricide: Hegel and the Young Marx*, trans. P. Thomas, Leiden: Brill.

12 'This example of labour shows strikingly how even the most abstract categories, despite their validity – precisely because of their abstractness – for all epochs, are nevertheless, in the specific character of this abstraction, themselves likewise a product of historic relations, and possess their full validity only for and within these relations' (Marx 1973: 38).

13 As one of the closest followers of Della Volpe's thought, Colletti proposed a critique of the democratic system as neutralizing more properly socialist

demands. In Della Volpe's later thought, however, he tried to insert Marx into a democratic-egalitarian line going back to Rousseau. The successive editions of *Rousseau e Marx* (from 1957 to 1964) imply an ever-closer relationship between democracy and socialism. See Della Volpe, G. (1997), *Rousseau e Marx e altri saggi di critica materialistica*, Roma: Editori Riuniti.

14 This is the passage – which was actually a critique of Giovanni Gentile – in which Gramsci defines the philosophy of praxis as 'Philosophy of the act (praxis, development), but not of the "pure" act, but rather of the real 'impure' act, in the most profane and worldly sense of the word' (Gramsci 1971: 372).

15 Tronti summarizes what he understands to be Gramsci's position in this way: 'Marxism is the *reform of the Hegelian dialectic*; it is the last, positive conclusion of the various attempts that Italian idealism made to review and update the logical instrument of the Hegelian method. Here then is the flaw of a certain Italian cultural tradition: it is too little Hegelian; it has not been able to draw conclusions from all the work of classical German philosophy, it is not successful at *concluding*, at *completing* Hegel; Marxism has arrived or must arrive at this *conclusion*. I do not believe that I have over-stretched [*forzato*] Gramsci's thought with this point' (Tronti 2016b).

16 Tronti also cites the following lines by Della Volpe: 'Marx (not the academic Marxist!) in his positive, scientific research in fact only "flirted" with the formulas of the "dialectic", using them as innocent *metaphors* to effectively summarize, in the cultured "imaginative" intellectual language of the time, the historical *processes* whose *scientific* laws he had discovered . . . the only dialectic that interests Marx and authentic Marxism is the *determinate dialectic*, which is that coinciding with *scientific law*' (Della Volpe 1949: 12).

17 '[Croce] thinks he is dealing with a philosophy and he is instead dealing with an ideology; he thinks he is dealing with a religion and it is instead a superstition; he thinks he is writing a history from which every element of class has been exorcised and he is, instead, producing a highly accurate and praiseworthy description of the political masterpiece whereby a particular class manages to present and have the conditions for its existence and development as a class accepted as a universal principle, as a world view, as a religion. In other words he is describing in the very act the development of a practical means of government and of domination' (Gramsci 1995: 352–3).

18 These divergences culminate in Colletti's interpretation of Marx as an epigone of Hegel and in denying Marxism a scientific status – or rather in rejecting the bases of Della Volpe's theoretical teaching: 'the paradox reaches its climax when we consider that, unlike Hegel's philosophy, Marxism aspires to be a "scientific" conception of reality. It intends to be a science – science in the full sense of the word. And yet it continually

speaks of "contradictions", contradictions that exist in nature and society. Whereas for science – as is well known – contradictions are only logical, they are always only to be eliminated . . . In strong contrast to our present representation of Marx as an epigone of Hegel, stands the highly positive judgement and appreciation that had been expressed in Italy (particularly in Della Volpe's work) of Marx's youthful critique of Hegel's dialectic' (Colletti 1986: 127–9).

19 See L. Colletti (1975), 'Il marxismo come sociologia', in *Ideologia e società*, 3–59, Roma-Bari: Laterza.

20 For a history of operaismo, see Wright, S. (2017), *Storming Heaven: Class Composition and Struggle in Italian Autonomist Marxism*, London: Pluto Press and Roggero, G. (2023), *Italian Operaismo: Genealogy, History, and Method*, Cambridge, MA: MIT Press.

21 André Tosel and Jean-Pierre Potier also stress the subjectivist approach of the operaisti in their reading of Marx (Tosel 2009: 75; Potier 1986). See also S. Mezzadra (2000), 'Operaismo', in R. Esposito and C. Galli (eds), *Enciclopedia del pensiero politico*, 497–8, Roma-Bari: Laterza.

22 Asor Rosa's most important book during the operaist period is on the question of 'popular culture'. See Asor Rosa, A. (1965), Scrittori e popolo. Il populismo nella letteratura italiana contemporanea, Torino: Einaudi.

23 It is thus no surprise that many years later Negri named Gramsci as one of the three thinkers, along with Luisa Muraro and Tronti, that best expressed the 'Italian difference' and the 'fundamental breaks, not only in the continuity of the history of Italian philosophy between the nineteenth and twentieth century, but, at the same time, in the material texture of the intellectual life of Italian society, in its politico-linguistic structure' (Negri 2009: 16).

24 Sandro Mezzadra explores the relationship between the part and the totality in Mezzadra, S. (2008), 'Senza lacrime per le rose: *Operai e capitale* di Mario Tronti e l'operaismo italiano', in M. Baldassari and D. Melegari (eds), *La Rivoluzione dietro di noi. Filosofia e politica prima e dopo il '68*, 61–77, Roma: manifestolibri.

25 In *Noi operaisti*, which is a sort of personal and theoretical summary of the operaist experience, Tronti returns to many of the main problems in *Workers and Capital* in light of his later reflections and the book's continuing relevance (or not) to the present. When discussing the question of the party he refers to the Gramscian concept of the party-prince: 'And if the form of this realization is presented as the *Prince*, the next step is that of defining its political practice, most importantly its forces, in the sense this time of the means and the procedures capable of achieving success. As Gramsci would then see, here Machiavelli passed [the theory of the prince] to Lenin. But while Gramsci saw the prince in the party, we saw it directly in the class. Not because the class could be successful without the party. But because the class-form was the true

subject and its self-realization in politics could only be given by the party instrument. Although the workers can fight the boss, to fight capital you need a party. But the struggle comes first. In this sense the class comes first'. However, he then adds: 'It is the prince that becomes party, it is the leadership of processes that acts as a collective entity: it does not correspond to the masses, it does not follow them, it does not separate from them, but it guides them, just one step ahead, one eye looking back to see if they are following and one eye looking ahead to work out where to go' (Tronti 2009: 68, 95). Negri and Hardt also use the Gramscian version of the Machiavellian prince in *Commonwealth*, describing 'the "becoming-Prince" of the multitude' (Hardt and Negri 2009: 367).

26 Roberto Esposito raises similar questions in his interpretation of *Workers and Capital*. Posing the working class as at the same time within and against capital – in Esposito's terms, keeping together immanence and conflict – in the passage from the economic to the political level leads to a logical contradiction that calls into question the philosophical-political tenability of the working class as an antagonistic subject (Esposito 2012a: 217–22).

27 One thinker from the bourgeois tradition of political realism who was fundamental to Tronti was Max Weber; see Caygill, H., ed. (2021), *Vocation of the Political: Mario Tronti & Max Weber*, London: CRMEP Books.

28 This is the argument in *Noi operaisti*: '1960s' Italian operaismo began with the birth of *Quaderni rossi* and ends with the death of *classe operaia*. Full stop. This is the thesis'. Tronti, M. (2009), *Noi operaisti*, 7, Roma: DeriveApprodi.

29 Tronti thoroughly engages with this periodization in *Twilight of Politics* (Tronti 2025), in which he locates the struggles of the 1960s in the twilight phase of the workers' movement, which was definitively laid to rest precisely at that moment.

30 In the fourteenth thesis of his *Theses on the Concept of History*, Benjamin writes: 'History is the subject of a construction whose site is not homogeneous, empty time, but time filled full by now-time [*Jetztzeit*]. . . . The same leap in the open air of history is the dialectical leap Marx understood as revolution' (Benjamin 2006: 395). W. Benjamin (2006), '*On the Concept of History*', in H. Eiland and M. W. Jennings (eds), *Selected Writings. Volume 4, 1938–1939*, 395, Cambridge, MA: Harvard University Press. In his 'Theses on Benjamin' in *The Twilight of Politics*, Tronti (2025) no longer sees in the present the conditions of Benjamin's now-time.

31 In fact, more recently Tronti wrote: 'The large factory is the opposite of the non-place, that today creates the consistency, or, rather, the inconsistency, of the postmodern. The large factory is a classic of the modern. The concentration of labourers in the workplace defined the masses, without making them [simply] a mass' (Tronti 2009: 94–5).

32 Again in *Noi operaisti*: 'The worker-capital friend-enemy was not a literary-philosophical invention. It was a socio-economic fact. It was there before everybody's eyes, and nobody saw it. Or rather, it was seen through the glasses of the bosses or the binoculars of the union, but nothing was seen with the eyes of politics, and of political thought, because they were looking elsewhere. So operaismo put an image into focus, turned on a light within the factory, and took a photograph' (Tronti 2009: 39).

Chapter 2

1 As we have seen, the idea of the 'twilight of the working class' was already present in embryonic form in the 'Postscript of Problems', the final chapter of the 1971 edition of *Workers and Capital*. But in his later texts, such as *Con le spalle al futuro* (With our backs to the future), it would be made even more explicit: 'The facts of the epoch, the core of the need for new synthesis, the element linking the events and explaining their outcomes, is "in the last instance" singular: it is the twilight of the working class. The final episode of the twilight of the West, which traversed the whole century and now brings it to a close, hastening it on, not therefore with the upsurge of desired actions but with the decline of inescapable facts' (Tronti 1992: X). Also Franco Berardi Bifo, when looking back from the present, sees in the 1970s the 'last glimmers of the modern' and the twilight of the working class as the subject of universal emancipation; see Berardi Bifo, F. (2023), Ultimi bagliori del Moderno. Lavoro, tecnica e movimento nel laboratorio di Potere operaio, Verona: ombre corte.

2 These are Tronti's words: 'I have this idea of a strongly hegemonic thought that also captures that which does not belong to you [to the traditions of the workers' movement]. This idea was already fully present in *Contropiano*. I was a bit outside in the sense that, I repeat, I watched 1968 from the window, precisely because for those of us who came from the experience of the workers' struggles it frankly seemed to be a minor movement, even if it resonated a lot more' (Borio, Pozzi and Roggero 2005: 302).

3 Negri describes that project in an interview: '*Contropiano* was an attempt to bring together this sort of intellectual discourse, that ultimately had some autonomy, with the university. It was extremely important to keep them together precisely as the production of cultural discourse as such. Asor Rosa tried to do this. Except that then we found ourselves in the midst of 1968. At that point what do you do? You could no longer maintain the relative autonomy of the cultural and university discourse. At that point a completely different story begins, there the paradigm itself changes' (Borio, Pozzi and Roggero 2005: 244).

4 Significantly, the Italian translation of the first volume of *Grundrisse* was published in 1968. For an analysis of its influence on the strand of Marxism that began in the 1960s, see Musto, M., ed. (2008), *Karl Marx's* Grundrisse: *Foundations of the Critique of Political Economy 150 Years Later*, New York-London: Routledge.

5 Negri contests the division of operaismo into two phases, insisting on its coherent internal development. See Negri, A. (2018), 'Post-operaism? No, Operaism', in D. Gentili, E. Stimilli and G. Garelli (eds), *Italian Critical Thought: Genealogies and Categories*, 23–32, Lanham: Roman & Littlefield.

6 The notion of 'non-place' entered the postmodern lexicon with French anthropologist and ethnologist Marc Augé. See Augé, M. (2023), *Non-Places: An Introduction to Supermodernity*, London-New York: Verso.

7 For a comparison between Tronti and Negri, see A. Toscano (2009), 'Chronicles of Insurrection: Tronti, Negri and the Subject of Antagonism', in L. Chiesa and A. Toscano (eds), *The Italian Difference*, 109–28.

8 'The Fragment on Machines' was part of the operaist canon from the start: it was translated by Renato Solmi for the fourth issue of *Quaderni rossi* (1964). In the following decades, in which the general intellect was fully embraced by late operaismo, Paolo Virno, among others, critically engaged with and updated the dominant 1960s' and '70s' interpretations of the 'Fragment'. Here he summarizes those previous interpretations: 'The 1970s' reading of the "Fragment" tried to destroy the claims to neutrality made by science and knowledge in general. Against the immoral fairytales of the progressivists and theorists of "human relations", emerged the indestructible nature of technology and command, of machines and hierarchies. In the 1970s, the "Fragment" was brandished to criticize socialism . . . Furthermore, in those pages a sign of the current relevance of communism can be found: the abolition of the wage demand and the withering away of the State. In the fact that work becomes a *quantité negligeable* in the production of wealth we glimpse the possibility for modern workers to shake off the stigmas of the commodity of labour power. The affirmation of the *general intellect* seems to correspond to the affirmation of a powerful antagonistic subjectivity. Today, between the 1980s and the 1990s, a different interpretation of the "Fragment" has become necessary' (Virno 2002: 161).

9 In the same period, *La teoria politica delle classi nel 'Capitale'* by Biagio de Giovanni followed a similar line, shifting the centrality of class antagonism to the level of the reproduction-circulation of capital, arguing that it did not simply have an economic character, but one that was directly political and thus located at the level of the state: 'Relating circulation to class antagonism leads to an enlargement of the range of action of classes to the entire structure of capitalist social reproduction, and as a result expands the organic link of the workers' movement with

the general form of politics, and, *critically*, with the whole fabric of the State' (de Giovanni 1976: 13).

10 'The accumulation of knowledge and of skill, of the general productive forces of the social brain, is thus absorbed into capital, as opposed to labour, and hence appears as an attribute of capital, and more specifically of fixed capital, in so far as it enters into the production process as a means of production proper' (Marx 2015: 694).

11 Cacciari's target here is Lukács in *The Destruction of Reason* (1954) which, in promoting realism as the canon of Marxist aesthetics, silenced the negative thought of romanticism and irrationalism. It is interesting that, in the 1970s, at the same time as his position on aesthetics was being criticized, his earlier work was being discovered and praised in Italy – for instance, that of *Soul and Form* (1910) and *The Theory of the Novel* (1916 and 1920) – which has a lot in common with negative thought and its thinkers.

12 Later we will look more closely at how Negri, unlike Cacciari, placed Nietzsche on the Spinozian line of *potenza* (power/potential) and constituent power. This divergence is in part justified by the ambivalence and ambiguity of the German word *Macht*, which can be translated into Italian both as '*potere*' and as '*potenza*'.

13 The tragic – a specific form resulting from the crisis of dialectical synthesis – was an important theme in Italian thought. See in particular Givone, S. (1989), *Disincanto del mondo e pensiero tragico*, Milano: il Saggiatore.

14 'To view the world *sub specie aeterni* is to view it as a whole – a limited whole. Feeling the world as a limited whole – it is this that is mystical' (Wittgenstein 2001: 88).

15 'There are, indeed, things that cannot be put into words. They *make themselves manifest*. They are what is mystical' (Wittgenstein 2001: 89).

16 The motive for this 'Can this be all?' can also be found in another conception of the negative found in *Negative Dialectics* by Adorno, although here as a critique of the totality: 'Pure metaphysical experience grows unmistakably paler and more desultory in the course of the secularization process, and that softens the substantiality of the older type. Negatively, that type holds out in the demand "Can this be all?" – a demand most likely to be actualized as waiting in vain' (Adorno 2004: 375).

17 In *Dialettica e critica del Politico*, Cacciari identifies symptoms of the crisis in the Hegelian political, for example in the non-dialecticalizable figure of the plebe. Other thinkers in the same period would also point to the 'complexity' of the Hegelian system, although in different ways: see de Giovanni, B. (1970), *Hegel e il tempo storico della società borghese*, De Donato: Bari; Bodei, R. (1975), *Sistema ed epoca in Hegel*, il Mulino: Bologna; Tronti, M. (1975), *Hegel politico*, Istituto dell'Enciclopedia italiana: Roma.

18 On the function assumed by the crisis-state, which also includes economic class conflicts as part of the political, a convergence begins to emerge between Cacciari and the Gramscianism of de Giovanni, which becomes clearer in the 1980s in their collaboration for the journal *il Centauro*: 'It is the modern capitalist State that poses itself as the terrain of confrontation. It thus does not create *automatic* conditions for the resolution of antagonism into a higher form of social life. However, the very way in which it transforms its own relation with production . . . encourages the *political* generalization of the contradiction and creates possible grounds for unification and alliance between the forces pushing for a *positive* acceleration of the tendency to crisis. The process of hegemony is linked to the crisis and penetrates it internally to alter its movement' (de Giovanni 1976: 311). For an introduction to the neo-Gramscian school, the so-called *Ecole barisienne*, in which de Giovanni was one of the key players, and which also included Giuseppe Vacca and Franco Cassano, see Blasi, F. (2007), *Introduzione alla Ecole barisienne*, Roma-Bari: Laterza.

19 Cacciari was particularly interested in the field of architecture and urban planning, for which one of his key points of reference – in keeping with his philosophical and political position – was Adolf Loos, a destroyer of ornament and theorist of functionality. See in particular Cacciari, M. (2002), *Adolf Loos e il suo angelo: «Das Andere» e altri scritti*, Milano: Electa. For an analysis that explores the parallels between the radical Italian architectural theory of the 1970s and operaismo-inspired political thought see Aureli, P. V. (2008), *The Project of Autonomy: Politics and Architecture within and against Capitalism*, New York: Princeton Architectural Press. The architectural theorist Manfredo Tafuri played a fundamental role in strengthening the relationship between operaismo and architecture. He also collaborated with *Contropiano*; see Assennato, M. (2019), *Progetto e metropoli. Saggio su operaismo e architettura*, Macerata: Quodlibet. On the relationship between operaismo and the arts in general, see Galimberti, J. (2022), *Images of Class: Operaismo, Autonomia and the Visual Arts (1962–1988)*, London-New York: Verso.

20 'The Political prevents an "autonomy", a specific form of production, from setting itself up as Law. Since this would block the process of transformation, it would make the games into paradigms. And so the Political is not neutral, but a specific activity, a specific technique, functional to the continuous mutation of mutual boundaries, in order that this dynamic is not interrupted by the prepotency (*pre-potenza*) of a game' (Cacciari 1978b: 133–4).

21 In the 1970s, in particular in *Il Politico e le trasformazioni*, Marramao's thought moved along similar lines to those of Cacciari in *Krisis* – the critique of the political and the crisis of the planner-state as providing a possibility for transformation within the political system – although in relation to different authors and schools of thought, many of which

would be widely cited in Italian philosophy in the following decades (not only Carl Schmitt but also the Frankfurt School – Habermas in particular – and Luhmann's systems theory): 'To claim that the turn of the 1930s did not suppress but "internalized" the pluralistic-conflictual structure inherited from the mass society produced by the great processes of rationalization-socialization [means] introducing the question of the complex status that "contradiction" assumes in contemporary capitalism and the *specific modalities* in which it is configured *within* the political system, thus basing the discourse about the "practicability" of the institutional terrain on this *analysis*, and not on abstract *petitio principii*' (Marramao 1979: 58).

22 'It is not the relationship with the system that can produce alternatives within it, it is not command that can guarantee them, it is not organization that modifies the capital relation in development: it is only the struggles of worker and proletarian autonomy – those that some go to enormous lengths not to see' (Negri 1976: 194).

23 For a comparison between Cacciari and Negri beginning from *Krisis*, see Mandarini, M. (2009), 'Beyond Nihilism: Notes towards a Critique of Left-heideggerianism in Italian Philosophy of the 1970s', in L. Chiesa and A. Toscano (eds), *The Italian Difference*, 55–79. For an interpretation of the thought of crisis in Cacciari and Negri (in light of the gradual loss of hegemony by the historical parties of the Italian left in favour of the neopopulist right), which explores the similarities in their theoretical approaches more than the differences in their aims, see Serra, P. (2002), *Americanismo senza America. Intellettuali e identità collettive dal 1960 ad oggi*, Bari: Dedalo.

24 'The mission of the democratic idea consists in the perfecting of this decay of the state, of the political as totality, in the concourse of the different subjects that by now autonomously make it up. But this decay is at the same time the greatest extension of the political, the perfection of the *Politisierung*: everybody makes politics and organizes himself politically – but only because the political has lost any aura' (Cacciari 2009a).

25 Heidegger understands Marxism as included within the question of technology as the destiny and fulfilment of metaphysics: 'Homelessness is coming to be the destiny of the world. Hence it is necessary to think that destiny in terms of the history of Being. What Marx recognized in an essential and significant sense, though derived from Hegel, as the estrangement of man has its roots in the homelessness of modern man. This homelessness is specifically evoked from the destiny of Being in the form of metaphysics, and through metaphysics is simultaneously entrenched and covered up as such. . . . The essence of materialism does not consist in the assertion that everything is simply matter but rather in a metaphysical determination according to which every being appears as the material of labor . . . The essence of materialism is concealed in the

essence of technology, about which much has been written but little has been thought' (Heidegger 1993: 243–4).

26 'Marx demands that "man's humanity" be recognized and acknowledged. He finds it in "society". "Social" man is for him "natural" man. In "society" the "nature" of man, that is, the totality of 'natural needs' (food, clothing, reproduction, economic sufficiency) is equably secured . . . Every humanism is either grounded in a metaphysics or is itself made to be the ground of one' (Heidegger 1993: 224–5).

27 Translator's note: In official English translations of both Cacciari and Agamben, this concept is either translated as premise or as presupposition. Both will be used in this text, in keeping with the translation used in the citations being discussed.

28 See Cacciari, M. (1990), *Dell'Inizio*, Milano: Adelphi; Cacciari, M. (2004), *Della cosa ultima*, Milano: Adelphi. Also dedicated to the re-proposition of metaphysics are the more recent Cacciari, M. (2014), *Labirinto filosofico*, Milano: Adelphi and Cacciari, M. (2023), *Metafisica concreta*, Milano: Adelphi.

Chapter 3

1 For Judith Revel, the split within operaismo in 1966 and the entry of a number of operaisti into the PCI was an important turning point and key to reading Italian Theory as such. See Revel, J. (2018), 'Italian Theory and Its Differences: Subjectivation, Historicization, Conflict', in D. Gentili, E. Stimilli and G. Garelli (eds), *Italian Critical Thought*, 47–57.

2 Bodei makes a similar point about the changes in Cacciari's thought from the beginning of the 1980s: 'Through an ever-closer confrontation not only with classical metaphysics but also with theology, Cacciari – who has learnt to clearly distinguish philosophy from politics, thus marking a shift from the Italian tradition – in recent years has deliberately become "untimely"' (Bodei 1998: 120).

3 'The mode of being of the new intellectual can no longer consist in eloquence, which is an exterior and momentary mover of feelings and passions, but in active participation in practical life, as constructor, organiser, "permanent persuader" and not just a simple orator (but superior at the same time to the abstract mathematical spirit); from technique-as-work one proceeds to technique-as-science and to the humanistic conception of history, without which one remains "specialised" and does not become "directive" (specialised and political)' (Gramsci 1971: 10).

4 Bodei summarizes the epochal shift in the history of the Italian intelligentsia in the following way: 'More attention is paid to the needs and rights of the individual detached from obligations to the collectivity

and relieved of the heavy burden of a history for which he or she would have been fully responsible. While the link between philosophical thought and civic engagement generally remains and indeed, in some cases, becomes radicalized to the point of transforming theoretical reflection into mere militancy, in others it looks different or even disappears' (Bodei 1998: 115).

5 Tronti describes this journal in an interview: '*Laboratorio Politico* ... was a completely different experience, also very different from *Contropiano*, because it really was completely a journal of intellectuals ... we theorized the need to unite various experts, including notable intellectual figures, and it also had a certain following, with good international contacts and collaborations. Today I see it as an attempt to provide the left (we were already talking less about the workers' movement and more about the left) with slightly more refined tools for the analysis and knowledge of things, and it certainly fulfilled this function' (Borio, Pozzi and Roggero 2005: 303–4).

6 This was the case with Cacciari and de Giovanni, who in different ways both developed a philosophical thought of Europe. See Cacciari, M. (1994), *Geofilosofia dell'Europa*, Milano: Adelphi and Cacciari, M. (1997), *L'Arcipelago*, Milano: Adelphi; de Giovanni, B. (2002), *L'ambigua potenza dell'Europa*, Napoli: Guida and de Giovanni, B. (2004), *La filosofia e l'Europa moderna*, Bologna: il Mulino.

7 For an interpretation of the divergent paths taken, beginning from the 1980s and the crisis of that Marxism which had previously been dominant in the Italian left intelligentsia, see Fistetti, F. (2006), *La crisi del marxismo in Italia. Cronache di filosofia politica (1980–2005). Un abbozzo di storia degli intellettuali*, Genova: il nuovo melangolo.

8 Weak thought found fertile ground both in Europe with the hermeneutic and communicative theories of Gadamer, Jürgen Habermas and Karl-Otto Apel, as well as with Jacques Derrida's deconstruction, and in the United States, where it found affinities with those philosophies sensitive to the European tradition, such as that of Richard Rorty. See, amongst others, Benso, S. and B. Schroeder, eds (2010), *Between Nihilism and Politics. The Hermeneutics of Gianni Vattimo*, New York: SUNY Press and Zabala, S., ed. (2007), *Weakening Philosophy. Essays in Honour of Gianni Vattimo*, Montreal: McGill-Queen's University Press.

9 Benjamin's thought has been widely studied in Italy since the 1970s/1980s, and many Italian interpretations of Benjamin have gained international prominence. Amongst the first and most important books on Benjaminian thought, see Desideri, F. (1980), *Walter Benjamin. Il tempo e le forme*, Roma: Editori Riuniti; Moroncini, B. (1984), *Walter Benjamin e la moralità del moderno*, Napoli: Guida. A key text on Bloch is Bodei, R. (1983), *Multiversum. Tempo e storia in Ernst Bloch*, Napoli: Istituto Italiano per gli Studi Filosofici.

10 See Rovatti, P. A. (2009), 'Foucault *docet*', L. Chiesa and A. Toscano (eds), *The Italian Difference*, 25–9. In this text, Rovatti uses Foucault to respond to the attack that Negri made on weak thought in *The Italian Difference.*

11 See Dal Lago, A. and P. A. Rovatti (1989), *Elogio del pudore. Per un pensiero debole*, Milano: Feltrinelli. The first chapter of the book 'Effetti del pensiero debole' (Effects of weak thought) is a critical account of the controversy arising from the publication of *Weak Thought.*

12 While fundamental to the development of Vattimo's thought, *Il soggetto e la maschera: Nietzsche e il problema della liberazione* (1974) interprets Nietzsche within the context of a dialectic of overcoming and liberation, as the author himself said in an interview: 'The book on Nietzsche was written in the wake of 1968; and while I still think that the sections on textual analysis, explicating key concepts of Nietzsche's philosophy are valid, I now realize that the book, especially in the final section, was too much under the sway of dialectics. . . . Rereading Nietzsche and, if you will, also living through the experiences of the movement in these past few years, I now think that the definition of the Nietzschean overman and his ideal of freedom must be more strictly distinguished from any dialectical perspective' (Vattimo 2019). On the differing interpretations that, over the years, Vattimo made of Nietzschean thought, see Azzarà, S. G. (2011), *Un Nietzsche italiano. Gianni Vattimo e le avventure dell'oltreuomo rivoluzionario*, Roma: manifestolibri.

13 See Vattimo, G. (1994), 'La vocazione nichilistica dell'ermeneutica', in *Oltre l'interpretazione. Il significato dell'ermeneutica per la filosofia*, 3–19, Roma-Bari: Laterza. Over time, Vattimo increasingly stressed the correspondence between nihilism and hermeneutics, understanding it also in a political and religious sense. See Vattimo, G. (2009), 'Nihilism as Emancipation', in L. Chiesa and A. Toscano (eds), *The Italian Difference*, 31–5. He also ultimately understood the idea of communism itself in a hermeneutic sense, see Vattimo, G. and S. Zabala (2011), *Hermeneutic Communism: From Heidegger to Marx*, New York: Columbia University Press. For an examination of the development of the idea of a connection between nihilism and postmodernism, see Ferraris, M. (2006), *Tracce. Nichilismo Moderno Postmoderno*, Milano-Udine: Mimesis. Ferraris then distanced himself from postmodern and hermeneutic philosophies, as shown, for example, in the Afterword to the new edition of *Tracce*, 'Postmoderno vent'anni dopo', in Ferraris, *Tracce*, 165–71.

14 In *The Will to Power as Art*, Vattimo argues that the Heideggerian interpretation of Nietzsche is misleading when comparing Nietzsche and Heidegger, thus challenging Cacciari's reading: 'neither Heidegger . . . nor even his left-wing followers seem to have paid sufficient attention to the aesthetic model which in reality underlies the will to power, and which prevents us from identifying it *tout court* with the will to a total technocratic organization of the world' (Vattimo 1993a: 88).

15 See Rorty, R. M. ed (1992), *The Linguistic Turn: Essays in Philosophical Method*, Chicago: University of Chicago Press. The text that first identifies aspects of the postmodern in philosophy is Lyotard's *The Postmodern Condition*: 'I define *postmodern* as incredulity toward metanarratives . . . To the obsolescence of the metanarrative apparatus of legitimation corresponds, most notably, the crisis of metaphysical philosophy [. . .]. The narrative function is losing its functors, its great hero, its great dangers, its great voyages, its great goal. It is being dispersed in clouds of narrative language elements—narrative, but also denotative, prescriptive, descriptive, and so on' (Lyotard 1984: xxiv).

16 Among others, see, in particular Viano, C. A. (1995), *Va' pensiero. Il carattere della filosofia italiana contemporanea*, Torino: Einaudi.

17 On the interpretation of subjectivity in Foucault, which Rovatti continued to explore, see Rovatti, P. A. (2008), 'Il soggetto che non c'è', in M. Galzigna (ed.), *Foucault, oggi*, 216–25, Milano: Feltrinelli. In this essay, Rovatti prefers to speak of practices of de-subjectification.

18 It is interesting that Alessandro Dal Lago, when describing the 'place of weakness', stresses its ethical connotation. See Dal Lago, A. (1984), 'Il luogo della debolezza', *aut aut*, 202–203: 15–22.

19 It is important to remember that there was also a critical, Marxist, even operaist, branch of feminism in Italy (interested in production, social reproduction and the refusal of labour), which is found, for instance, in the Lotta Femminista group and figures such as Mariarosa Dalla Costa, Leopoldina Fortunati, Silvia Federici and Alisa Del Re.

20 Luce Irigaray developed the first philosophical approach to the thought of sexual difference: 'Sexual difference is one of the major philosophical issues, if not the issue, of our age. According to Heidegger, each age has one issue to think through, and one only. Sexual difference is probably the issue in our time' (Irigaray 1993: 5).

21 The philosopher most representative of queer theory, which is one of the most important strands of Anglo-American feminist thought, is Judith Butler, whose works on this theme include *Gender Trouble*. See Butler, J. (1990), *Gender Trouble: Feminism and the Subversion of Identity*, New York-London: Routledge.

22 For a philosophical account that is particularly interested in the postmodern conception of difference, which can be found across diverse feminist theories, and which pays particular attention to the idea of the subject, see Braidotti, R. (1991), *Patterns of Dissonance: A Study of Women and Contemporary Philosophy*, New York-London: Routledge.

23 'Luce Irigaray wrote that sexual difference is one of the issues, or *the* issue, to think about today. Without abandoning this task, on the contrary, while remaining faithful to it, we wanted to look at another difference, that between the thought of thought and the thought of experience . . . The thought of experience is a figure that is "out of joint", a non-alignment' (Buttarelli and Giardini 2008: 10–1).

24 See Libreria delle donne di Milano (1987), *Non credere di avere diritti. La generazione della libertà femminile nell'idea e nelle vicende di un gruppo di donne*, Torino: Rosenberg & Sellier.

25 'The (female) part separating itself from the whole, and not for some particular interest of its own but to defend the true and the just, seemed to lack logical status. But in fact, by separating itself, it did nothing but expose the partiality and privilege hiding under universal forms' (Fischer et al. 1987: 20).

26 See Irigaray, L. (1985), *Speculum of the Other Woman*, Ithaca, NY: Cornell University Press.

27 See Diotima (1990), *Mettere al mondo il mondo. Oggetto e oggettività alla luce della differenza sessuale*, Milano: La Tartaruga.

28 See A. Cavarero, *Stately Bodies: Literature, Philosophy, and the Question of Gender*, trans. R. de Lucca and D. Shemek, Ann Arbor: University of Michigan Press, 2002.

29 See Muraro, L. (2018), 'To Knit or to Crochet: A Political-Linguistic Tale on the Enmity between Metaphor and Metonymy', in C. Casarino and A. Righi (eds), *Another Mother: Diotima and the Symbolic Order of Italian Feminism*, 67–119, Minneapolis-London: University of Minnesota Press. As well as Muraro's contribution, this book contains other important articles on the symbolic order of the mother written by members of the Diotima community (for instance, Ida Dominijanni, Chiara Zamboni and Diana Sartori).

30 'The "choice" between authority and power depends on this scenario, and is supported by practice: it is on the side of authority that the space of female symbolic productivity opens up, whereas on the side of power only a mimetic dynamic of rituality and male competition is repeated . . . Finally, the historically sedimented asymmetry between the two terms demands their asymmetrical, and conflicting, re-definition: no longer, as Hannah Arendt understood it, authority as the source of legitimation of a communicative and relational power, but authority versus power – that is, against a power reduced to pure dispositifs for the control and self-control of the crisis of masculine identity' (Dominijanni 2001: 81).

31 On the wider political thought of Cavarero, see Landerreche Cardillo, P. and R. Silverbloom, eds (2024), *Political Bodies: Writings on Adriana Cavarero's Political Thought*, Albany, NY: SUNY.

32 On the conception of a politics that is symbolically independent from power, as well as the already cited *Introduzione di un'idea*, see also Muraro, L. (2009), *Al mercato della felicità. La forza irrinunciabile del desiderio*, Milano: Mondadori.

33 As an example of that practice, Muraro points to Paul the Apostle's advice to the first Christian communities in his *Epistles*.

34 In *The Italian Difference*, Negri places Tronti and Muraro side by side under the common denominator of 'difference': the difference of the

worker and sexual difference. Yet, in *The Twilight of Politics*, while recognizing the importance of the contribution to the critique of dialectical synthesis made by the thought of sexual difference, Tronti points to its political limits due to its arriving too late for the era in which conflict was possible as the liberation of the oppressed part (Tronti 2025).

35 In particular, on the genealogy of the concept of secularization, see Marramao, G. (1994), *Cielo e terra. Genealogia della secolarizzazione*, Roma-Bari: Laterza.

36 See, amongst others, Löwith, K. (1949), *Meaning in History: The Theological Implications of the Philosophy of History*, Chicago: University of Chicago Press.

37 See Koselleck, R. (2004), *Futures Past: On the Semantics of Historical Time*, New York: Columbia University Press.

38 See Marramao, G. (2008), 'Messianismo. Walter Benjamin e noi', in *La passione del presente. Breve lessico della modernità-mondo*, 108–30, Torino: Bollati Boringhieri.

39 Marramao argues that his conception of hypermodernity has less in common with Anthony Giddens's conception of hypermodernity or radical modernity or Ulrich Beck's second modernity – all of which come from sociology – than with the notion of *surmodernité* proposed by Augé, M. (2023), *Non-Places: An Introduction to Supermodernity*.

40 On the critique of the postmodern, see also Marramao, G. (2000), '"Idola" del postmoderno: secolarizzazione, esodo, politeismo', in *Dopo il Leviatano. Individuo e comunità*, 369–86, Torino: Bollati Boringhieri.

41 Vattimo's position here is inspired in particular by Girard, R. (1979), *Violence and the Sacred*, trans. P. Gregory, Baltimore: John Hopkins University Press.

42 For a critical examination of Vattimo's conception of secularization in comparison with that of Augusto Del Noce, see Esposito (2012a: 241–7).

43 'What is our present? What is the present field of possible experiences? This is not an analytics of truth; it will concern what might be called an ontology of the present, an ontology of ourselves, and it seems to me that the philosophical choice confronting us today is this: one may opt for a critical philosophy that will present itself as an analytic philosophy of truth in general, or one may opt for a critical thought that will take the form of an ontology of ourselves, an ontology of the present' (Foucault 1990: 95). On Vattimo's proposal for an 'ontology of actuality' (a translation adhering more closely to Foucault's original French than 'ontology of the present'), see Vattimo, G. (2011), *A Farewell to Truth*, 36–46, New York: Columbia University Press. Marramao prefers instead to elaborate on Foucault's ontology of actuality as an ontology of the contingent; see Marramao, G. (2007), 'Which Ontology after Metaphysics? Conversations with Gianni Vattimo and Richard Rorty', in S. Zabala (ed.), *Weakening Philosophy*, 77–86.

44 Marramao reworks Deleuze's category of 'disjunctive synthesis': 'The reconstructive principle of the universal can thus be understood only in terms of a *disjunctive synthesis*: beginning from the premise of the inalienable and inappropriable specific difference of each individual. In my concept of the universal the relation is only truly thinkable *between irreducible and mutually unassimilable singularities*: the precise opposite of the conception of a social link understood as belonging to a common identity-substance (the Community, the State, but also Reason, Humanity, and Language)' (Marramao 2008: 37).

45 For a genealogy of the category of 'political representation', the work of Giuseppe Duso is fundamental. See, amongst others, Duso, G. (2003), *La rappresentanza politica. Genesi e critica del concetto*, FrancoAngeli: Milano.

46 'But it may, instead, be that this caging of historical time has exhausted its trajectory and is destined to increasingly reveal its impotence and to further reduce the dangerously small margin in which the "gnostic pearl" of the moderns has been preserved. Perhaps this margin of will for redemption that is not tied to a project is less narrow than we believe' (Marramao 1984: 66).

47 In addition to Nietzsche, already referenced by Cacciari, the authors that Esposito identifies as contributing to the thought of the impolitical in different ways are Arendt, in her later works, and Karl Barth, Georges Bataille, Maurice Blanchot, Hermann Broch, Elias Canetti, Jan Patočka, Romano Guardini, and Simone Weil, all of which Esposito takes significant passages from for his anthology of the impolitical. See Esposito, R., ed. (1996), *Oltre la politica. Antologia del pensiero 'impolitico'*, Milano: Bruno Mondadori.

48 For a contextualization of the impolitical in light of later developments in his thought, see the preface to Esposito, R. (2011), *Dieci pensieri sulla politica*, 7–27, Bologna: il Mulino; Esposito, R. (2010), 'Vom Unpolitischen zur Biopolitik', in T. Bedorf and K. Röttgers (eds), *Das Politische und die Politik*, 89–101, Frankfurt a. M.: Suhrkamp; Esposito, R. and R. Ciccarelli (2008), 'La politica al presente', in L. Bazzicalupo (ed.), *Impersonale. In dialogo con Roberto Esposito*, 13–37, Milano-Udine: Mimesis.

49 'The unpolitical is the work of deconstruction of this totality. Not in the superficial sense of the term 'critique of ideology', whereby this totality is said to be 'false'—but in the sense that this totality is historically marked and produces the forces of its own crisis . . . Naming the multiplicity of forces that make up the crisis of that totality, the unpolitical represents the critique of values on whose bases alone such totality is conceivable' (Cacciari 2009a).

50 An examination of the question of the impolitical responding to the debate raised by the publication of *Categories of the Impolitical* is made in the preface to its second Italian edition (Esposito 2015a: xi–xxx).

51 Esposito dedicated a number of his early works to Machiavelli, who has remained a constant reference in his thinking to this day, as demonstrated in the collected edition of his writings on Machiavelli: Esposito (2025), *Machiavelli*, ed. Del Lucchese, F. and E. Zaru, Bologna: DeriveApprodi. On Esposito's interpretation of Machiavelli, see Serratore, C. (2018), '*Differenza italiana*: la política como sujeto. Machiavelli en la lectura de Roberto Esposito', *Revista Diálogos Mediterrânicos*, 14: 175–95.

52 See, amongst others, Blanchot, M. (1988), *The Unavowable Community*, trans. P. Joris, New York: Station Hill Press and Nancy, J.-L. (1991), *Inoperative Community*, ed. P. Connor, Minneapolis: University of Minnesota Press.

53 'The impolitical perspective has known intimately, from the very beginning, that community can never coincide with itself: and can never appear historically without being distorted. This is community's constitutive conflict, and it cannot be resolved except by falling into political theology, or, to the contrary, being neutralized along the more dominant lines of the modern project. But l would like to insist that it is now necessary that this originary void [*vuoto*] not be inflected only negatively, nor in a simply deconstructive sense' (Esposito 2015a: xxix–xxx).

Chapter 4

1 For an analysis and comparison, beginning from the Foucauldian paradigm, of the various elaborations of biopolitics by Agamben, Negri and Esposito see Bazzicalupo, L. (2010), *Biopolitica: Una mappa concettuale*, Roma: Carocci. For an explicit exploration of biopolitics in contemporary Italian politics, see the special issue of *Angelaki*, 'Biopolitics in Early Twenty-First-Century Italian Theory' (2011), ed. L. Chiesa, 16 (3); Righi, A. (2011), *Biopolitics and Social Change in Italy: From Gramsci to Pasolini to Negri*, London: Palgrave Macmillan; Vatter, M. E. (2016), 'Community, Life, and Subjectivity in Italian Biopolitics', in S. Prozorov and S. Rentea (eds), *The Routledge Handbook of Biopolitics*, 123–39, New York: Routledge Taylor & Francis.

2 See Derrida, J. (1997), *Of Grammatology*, trans. G. C. Spivak, Baltimore-London: John Hopkins University Press.

3 In various significant points in his work – for example in *Homo Sacer* and in *State of Exception* and in the essay 'The Messiah and the Sovereign: The Problem of Law in Walter Benjamin' – Agamben cites the following passage from a letter written by Benjamin to Gershom Scholem on Kafka, where Benjamin suggests that writing 'without the key' – that is, a language that is not founded on the removal of the voice – is life, such as that found in 'the village' in Kafka's *The Castle*, where it does not matter

whether the messages coming from the castle are deciphered or not: 'Whether the pupils have lost it or whether they are unable to decipher it comes down to the same thing, because, without the key that belongs to it, the Scripture is not Scripture, but life. Life as it is lived in the village at the foot of the hill on which the castle is built' (Scholem, G. and T. W. Adorno, eds (1994), *The Correspondence of Walter Benjamin, 1910–1940*, trans. M. R. Jacobson and E. M. Jacobson, 453, Chicago-London: The University of Chicago Press).

4 For an analysis of the connections between French philosophy and Italian philosophy, see G. Bird (2016), *Containing Community: From Political Economy to Ontology in Agamben, Esposito, and Nancy*, New York: SUNY Press.

5 For an interpretation of Agamben's thought that begins from the question of 'indifference', see Watkin, W. (2014), *Agamben and Indifference: A Critical Overview*, London-New York: Rowman and Littlefield.

6 'Ease is the proper name of this unrepresentable space. The term "ease" in fact designates, according to its etymology, the space adjacent (*ad-jacens, adjacentia*), the empty place where each can move freely, in a semantic constellation where spatial proximity borders on opportune time (*ad-agio*, moving at ease) and convenience borders on the correct relation . . . [E]ase names perfectly that "free use of the proper."' (Agamben 2007: 24).

7 See, amongst others, Norris, A., ed. (2005), *Politics, Metaphysics, and Death. Essays on Giorgio Agamben's Homo Sacer*, Durham-London: Duke University Press and Calarco, M. and S. DeCaroli, eds (2007), *Giorgio Agamben. Sovereignty & Life*, Stanford, CA: Stanford University Press.

8 In his most recent works after the *Homo Sacer* project was completed, Agamben returned to an explicit examination of language; see, for example, Agamben, G. (2024), *La lingua che resta. Il tempo, la storia, il linguaggio*, Torino: Einaudi.

9 In fact, the figure of *homo sacer* is also present in *The Coming Community* (Agamben 2007: 85–6).

10 On Schmitt's thought in general and on his reception in Italy, see Galli, C. (2010), *Genealogia della politica. Carl Schmitt e la crisi del pensiero politico moderno*, Bologna: il Mulino.

11 'It is clear that the city-state is a natural growth, and that man is by nature a political animal, and a man that is by nature and not merely by fortune citiless is either low in the scale of humanity or above it' (Aristotle 2005: 9).

12 Derrida's critique of Agamben's biopolitical paradigm and the distinction that he poses between *bios* and *zoe* begins from the latter's 'correction' of Foucault. See Derrida, J. (2010), *The Beast and the Sovereign, Volume I*, trans. G. Bennington, Chicago: University of Chicago Press.

13 Agamben analyses the dispositif of exception, particularly highlighting its political-juridical implications in Agamben, G. (2004), *State of Exception (Homo Sacer, II, 1)*, Chicago: University of Chicago Press.
14 'It might be well worthwhile to track down the origin of the dogma of the sacredness of life. Perhaps, indeed probably, it is relatively recent, the last mistaken attempt of the weakened Western tradition to seek the saint it has lost in cosmological impenetrability . . . Finally, this idea of man's sacredness gives grounds for reflection that what is here pronounced sacred was, according to ancient mythic thought, the marked bearer of guilt: life itself' (Benjamin 1996: 251).
15 'Propagation, births and mortality, the level of health, life expectancy and longevity, with all the conditions that can cause these to vary. Their supervision was effected through an entire series of interventions and *regulatory controls: a bio-politics of the population*' (Foucault 1978: 139). See also Foucault, M. (2007), *Security, Territory and Population: Lectures at the College De France, 1977–78*, trans. G. Burchell, London: Palgrave Macmillan.
16 In an interview centred on this 'new politics', Agamben describes it, with a Deleuzian echo, as 'a minor biopolitics'. See Grelet, S. and M. Potte-Bonneville (2002), 'Una biopolitica minore. Intervista a Giorgio Agamben', in P. Perticari (ed.), *Biopolitica minore*, 191–204, Roma: manifestolibri.
17 Politics as 'inoperativity' is a recurrent theme in Agamben, but gains particular prominence in his treatment of glory within the genealogy of power as government and *oikonomia* in *The Kingdom and the Glory*: 'The political is neither a *bios* nor a zoē, but the dimension that the inoperativity of contemplation, by deactivating linguistic and corporeal, material and immaterial praxes, ceaselessly opens and assigns to the living' (Agamben 2011: 251).
18 See Agamben, G. (2010), *The Sacrament of Language: An Archaeology of the Oath*, trans. A. Kotsko, Stanford, CA: Stanford University Press.
19 In *The Time that Remains*, the remainder or remnant – a messianic theme that, together with 'inoperativity', emerges from Agamben's commentary on Paul the Apostle's *Epistle to the Romans* – is what is left over from the suspension of the election of the part as 'the all': '[The remnant] is therefore neither the all, nor a part of the all, but the impossibility for the part and the all to coincide with themselves or with each other. *At a decisive instant, the elected people, every people, will necessarily situate itself as a remnant, as not-all*' (Agamben 2005: 55).
20 'From the perspective of our study, we must . . . investigate not the metaphysical mystery of conjunction but the practical and political one of their disjunction' (Agamben 2016: 272).
21 Twenty years after *Fabbriche del soggetto*, Negri continued to show interest in Agamben, although above all in the Agamben of *Language and Death*, rather than in his later elaboration of biopolitics, which he argued ends

up reducing biopolitics to the negative of the crisis: 'For a long phase of his philosophical apprenticeship, Agamben, in contrast to Deleuze, to whom he is in other respects very close, exalted the negative aspect of being in contrast to desire and to the constructive movement of *conatus*, and arranged the determinations of life within this sundered horizon. This will become increasingly difficult – frankly impossible – once Agamben enters the field of biopolitics. *Homo Sacer* marks this point . . . The reason for Agamben's decision to test himself on the biopolitical terrain stems from contradictions within his thought, that is, from his irresoluteness in considering the dimensions and (positive) powers of being. In Agamben, the translation of the idea of being into that of biopolitics occurs within the framework of an operation of *neutralization* of the biopolitical itself' (Negri 2007b: 119–20). And so 'the later Agamben constitutes a regression when compared to the Agamben of *Language and Death*' (Negri 2007b: 123).

22 Negri traces the 'cursed line' of modern thought in the first Italian edition of *The Savage Anomaly: The Power of Spinoza's Metaphysics and Politics* (1999), when discussing the history of the political found in *Il Politico: Da Machiavelli a Cromwell*, the two volume anthology edited by Tronti: 'it seems to me that between the seventeenth and the early nineteenth centuries there are, in the field of the metaphysics of power, at least two antagonistic lines: the first blessed line that goes from Hobbes to Rousseau to Kant to Hegel; the other cursed line that goes from Machiavelli to Spinoza to Marx; the one constructs the theoretical basis of bourgeois domination and its law (the transcendence of normativity), the other raises the concept of the productive force from republicanism to constitutionalism and to class struggle. This historical alternative is certainly not linear' (Negri 1981: 289). It is not surprising that these notes are in Negri's book on Spinoza, who affirmed *potenza* as such in metaphysical thought. Negri had also previously defined bourgeois ideology in *Political Descartes* as the limitation of the infinite productive power (*potenza*) of the subject. See Negri, A. (2007), *Political Descartes: Reason, Ideology and the Bourgeois Project*, trans. M. Mandarini e A. Toscano, London-New York: Verso.

23 See Zaru, E. (2020), *La postmodernità di 'Empire'. Antonio Negri e Michael Hardt nel dibattito internazionale (2000–2018)*, Milano-Udine: Mimesis.

24 In *The Porcelain Workshop* and then in *Commonwealth* (2009), Negri defines the current epoch as 'altermodernity' rather than 'postmodernity', in order to emphasize the connotations of rupture and discontinuity with respect to the modern. See Negri, A. (2008), *The Porcelain Workshop: For a New Grammar of Politics*, Los Angeles: Semiotext(e).

25 'The multiplicity of singularities that produce and are produced in the biopolitical field of the common do not spontaneously accomplish exodus and construct their autonomy. Political organization is needed

to cross the threshold and generate political events' (Hardt and Negri 2009: 165). Negri and Hardt particularly insist on the question of political organization in the last of the four books. See Hardt and Negri (2016).

26 In his analysis of immaterial labour, Maurizio Lazzarato considers biopolitics as intrinsically connected to the transformations in the production process of the information economy: 'it seems to me that what is, for convenience, defined "bio-political", can, on the one hand, impact the tendency of capitalist development on its own terrain, and, on the other, "express" the multiplicity of forms of life, of production and of subjectivity of the global proletariat' (Lazzarato 1997: 21).

27 Hardt and Negri discuss the positions of Virno and others on the concept of the 'multitude' in Hardt and Negri (2009: 165–78).

28 First published in Italian as 'Il cosiddetto "male" e la critica dello Stato' in *Forme di vita* (2005, n. 4). The latter was an Italian philosophical journal that largely followed in the footsteps of the journals from the 1960s, 1970s and 1980s that we referred to earlier.

29 'The community is and needs to remain constitutively unpolitical in the sense that we can correspond to our being in common only to the degree in which we keep it away from every demand for historical-empirical actualization, that is, if we do not take on for ourselves the roles of subjects: the community cannot have "subjects" because it is the community itself that constitutes – that deconstructs – subjectivity in the form of its alteration' (Esposito 2010: 97).

30 Translation slightly modified to remove question mark on third sentence.

31 In *Bíos*, this agreement with Foucault becomes clearer, going beyond any Foucauldian hesitation to stress an intrinsic link between biopolitics and modernity. Biopolitics does not arise out of the crisis of the modern political, but within the immune paradigm that has constituted the modern political from the beginning: 'the element that quickly needs to be established is the peculiar knot that immunization posits between biopolitics and modernity. I say quickly because it restores the missing link of Foucault's argumentation. What I want to say is that only when biopolitics is linked conceptually to the immunitary dynamic of the negative protection of life does biopolitics reveal its specifically modern genesis. This is not because its roots are missing in other preceding epochs (they aren't), but because only modernity makes of individual self-preservation the presupposition of all other political categories, from sovereignty to liberty' (Esposito 2008: 9). Developing another Foucauldian suggestion, taken from *The Order of Things* (1966) and therefore prior to his definition of biopolitics, Davide Tarizzo shows how the category of life is typically modern and appears in conjunction with the establishment of biology as a science. See Tarizzo, D. (2017), *Life: A Modern Invention*, trans. M. W. Epstein, Minneapolis: University of Minnesota Press.

32 See, for example, the special issue Campbell, T., ed. (2006), '"Bios," Immunity, Life: The Thought of Roberto Esposito', *Diacritics*, 36 (2): 2–22.
33 Esposito's conception of origin was inspired by Machiavelli, see Esposito (2012a: 45–103).
34 On the concept of immanence, see Ciccarelli, R. (2018), 'Inhabiting Immanence: The Logic, History, and Politics of an Italian Thought's Concept', in D. Gentili, E. Stimilli and G. Garelli (eds), *Italian Critical Thought*, 113–27.

Chapter 5

1 'When faced with the impossibility of reconciling immanence and conflict, Tronti chose conflict; Negri, by contrast, chose immanence, sacrificing the political form of conflict in favor of the social being. What separates them, despite their shared rejection of legal formalism, is the very definition of ontology—intended by Negri in a fully immanent sense, but pushed increasingly in a transcendental direction by Tronti' (Esposito 2012a: 233).
2 See, amongst others: Badiou, A. (1997), *Saint Paul: The Foundation of Universalism*, trans. R. Brassler, Stanford: Stanford University Press; Žižek, S., J. Milbank and C. Davis (2010), *Paul's New Moment: Continental Philosophy and the Future of Christian Theology*, Grand Rapids, MI: Brazos; Eagleton, T. (2010), *On Evil*, New Haven-London: Yale University Press; Zizek, S. (2011), *Living in the End Times*, London-New York: Verso; Mendieta, E. and J. Vanantwerpen, eds (2011), *The Power of Religion in the Public Sphere*, New York: Columbia University Press (with essays by Judith Butler, Jürgen Habermas, Charles Taylor and Cornel West); Critchley, S. (2012), *The Faith of the Faithless: Experiments in Political Theology*, London-New York: Verso; Sloterdijk, P. (2015), *God's Zeal: The Battle of the Three Monotheisms*, Cambridge: Polity Press.
3 On the debate around the issue of debt, see: Stimilli, E. (2017). *The Debt of the Living: Ascesis and Capitalism*, trans. A. Bove, New York: SUNY Press; Stimilli, E. (2018), *Debt and Guilt: A Political Philosophy*, trans. S. Porcelli, London: Bloomsbury.
4 Tronti uses the political-theological motifs of the *éschaton* and the *katéchon* to characterize his position with respect to late operaismo, and in order to stress the main difference between him and Negri: 'The difference between me and Toni Negri isn't necessarily traceable back to Spinoza or Hobbes; it is of a different type. Toni maintains an eschatological paradigm; I, instead, assume a katechontic one' (Tronti 2009: 111).
5 On the connection in Tronti's work between the conception of the 'autonomy of the political' and political theology as a critique of the

politics of immanence, see Mandarini, M. (2010), 'Critical Thoughts on the Politics of Immanence', *Historical Materialism*, 18 (3): 175–85.

6 For a comparison between Tronti's and Cacciari's political-theological approach, see: Cacciari, M. and M. Tronti (2007), *Teologia e politica al crocevia della storia*, ed. M. Gasparri, Milano: AlboVersorio.

7 In *Stasis*, Agamben controversially argues that even Hobbes's Leviathan does not have the katechontic function traditionally attributed to it by modern political theory, in a long tradition culminating in Carl Schmitt. He instead claims that the Leviathan has an eschatological function, and so will disappear with the realization of God's Kingdom on Earth, which Hobbes understands as having a concretely political role (Agamben 2015: 33–77).

8 Late operaist thought in particular has reflected on the notion of 'biocapitalism'. See for instance: Marazzi, C. (2010), *Il comunismo del capitale: Finanziarizzazione, biopolitiche del lavoro e crisi globale*, Verona: ombre corte.

9 For a broader and more detailed discussion of the relationship between neoliberal crisis, biopolitics and political movements, see Hardt M. and T. Negri (2012), *Declaration*, Argo Navis (self-published).

10 'What socialism lacks is not so much a theory of the state as a governmental reason, the definition of what a governmental rationality would be in socialism, that is to say, a reasonable and calculable measure of the extent, modes, and objectives of governmental action . . . But I do not think that there is an autonomous socialist governmentality. There is no governmental rationality of socialism' (Foucault 2008: 91–2).

11 On Esposito's institutionalism in relation to Foucault, see Castro, E. M. (2024), 'La lectura de Michel Foucault en el pensamiento instituyente de Roberto Esposito', *Idea y Valores*, 73 (186): 47–73.

12 On the notion of hegemony and its different formulations within Gramsci's thought, see Cospito, G. (2023), 'Dizionario gramsciano / Gramsci dictionary: Hegemony', *International Gramsci Journal*, 3 (1), https://doi.org/10.14276/igj.v3i1.4024

REFERENCES

Adorno, T. W. (2004), *Negative Dialectics*, trans. E. B. Ashton, London-New York: Routledge.

Agamben, G. (1993), *Infancy & History: Essays on the Destruction of Experience*, London-New York: Verso.

Agamben, G. (1998), *Homo Sacer: Sovereign Power and Bare Life*, trans. D. Heller-Roazen, Stanford, CA: Stanford University Press.

Agamben, G. (1999a), 'Tradition of the Immemorial', in D. Heller-Roazen (ed.), *Potentialities: Collected Essays in Philosophy*, 104–15, Stanford, CA: Stanford University Press.

Agamben, G. (1999b), *Remnants of Auschwitz: The Witness and the Archive (Homo Sacer III)*, trans. D. Heller-Roazen, New York: Zone Books.

Agamben, G. (2004), *The Open: Man and Animal*, trans. K. Attell, Stanford, CA: Stanford University Press.

Agamben, G. (2005), *The Time That Remains: A Commentary on the Letter to the Romans*, trans. P. Dailey, Stanford, CA: Stanford University Press.

Agamben, G. (2006), *Language and Death: The Place of Negativity*, trans. K. E. Pinkus and M. Hardt, Minneapolis-Oxford: University of Minnesota Press.

Agamben, G. (2007), *The Coming Community*, trans. M. Hardt, Minneapolis-London: University of Minnesota Press.

Agamben, G. (2011), *The Kingdom and the Glory: For a Theological Genealogy of Economy and Government (Homo Sacer, II, 2)*, trans. L. Chiesa with M. Mandarini, Stanford, CA: Stanford University Press.

Agamben, G. (2013), 'The Endless Crisis as an Instrument of Power: In conversation with Giorgio Agamben', *Verso Blog Post*, 4 June 2013. Available online: https://www.versobooks.com/blogs/news/1318-the-endless-crisis-as-an-instrument-of-power-in-conversation-with-giorgio-agamben?srsltid=AfmBOoo83Fv0K1Ju9eNs0eIcICYiEiXAnznuv1s_gHHbyH-nU9n8tbPk (accessed 21 July 2025).

Agamben, G. (2015), *Stasis: Civil War as a Political Paradigm*, trans. N. Heron, Edinburgh: Edinburgh University Press.

Agamben, G. (2016), *The Use of Bodies (Homo Sacer IV,2)*, trans. A. Kotsko, Stanford, CA: Stanford University Press.

Agamben, G. (2017), *The Mystery of Evil: Benedict XVI and the End of Days*, trans. A. Kotsko, Stanford, CA: Stanford University Press.

Aristotle (2005), *Politics*, ed. J. Henderson, Cambridge, MA: Harvard University Press.

Asor Rosa, A. (1962), 'Il punto di vista operaio e la cultura socialista', *Quaderni rossi*, 2: 117–30.

Badiou, A. (2022), *The Adventure of French Philosophy*, ed. B. Bosteels, London-New York: Verso.

Benjamin, W. (1996), 'Critique of Violence', in M. Bullock and M. W. Jennings (eds), *Selected Writings. Volume 1: 1913–1926*, Cambridge, MA and London: The Belknap Press of Harvard University Press.

Benjamin, W. (2006), 'On the Concept of History', in H. Eiland and M. W. Jennings (eds), *Selected Writings. Volume 4, 1938–1939*, 389–400, Cambridge, MA: Harvard University Press.

Bobbio, N. (1968), '*Introduzione*', in R. Mondolfo, *Umanismo di Marx. Studi filosofici 1908–1966*, XI–XLVIII, Torino: Einaudi.

Bobbio, N. (1990), *Saggi su Gramsci*, Milano: Feltrinelli.

Bodei, R. (1998), *Il noi diviso. Ethos e idee dell'Italia repubblicana*, Torino: Einaudi.

Borio, G., F. Pozzi and G. Roggero, eds (2005), *Gli operaisti. Autobiografie di cattivi maestri*, Roma: DeriveApprodi.

Buttarelli, A. and F. Giardini (2008), 'Introduzione: La cosa da pensare', in A. Buttarelli and F. Giardini (eds), *Il pensiero dell'esperienza*, 9–15, Milano: Baldini Castoldi.

Cacciari, M. (1969), 'Sulla genesi del pensiero negativo', *Contropiano*, 1: 131–200.

Cacciari, M. (1971), 'Entsagung', *Contropiano*, 2: 411–40.

Cacciari, M. (1975), 'Lavoro, valorizzazione, "cervello sociale"', *aut aut*, 145–146: 3–40.

Cacciari, M. (1976), *Krisis. Saggio sulla crisi del pensiero negativo da Nietzsche a Wittgenstein*, Milano: Feltrinelli.

Cacciari, M. (1977), *Pensiero negativo e razionalizzazione*, Venezia: Marsilio.

Cacciari, M. (1978a), *Dialettica e critica del Politico. Saggio su Hegel*, Milano: Feltrinelli.

Cacciari, M. (1978b), 'Critica della "autonomia" e problema del politico', in V. Finzi Ghisi (ed.), *Crisi del sapere e nuova razionalità. Psicanalisi linguistica economia: sulla transizione*, 123–35, Bari: De Donato.

Cacciari, M. (1982), 'Sinisteritas', in VV. AA., *Il concetto di sinistra*, 7–19, Milano: Bompiani.

Cacciari, M. (1986), 'Sul presupposto. Schelling e Rosenzweig', *aut aut*, 211–212: 43–65.

Cacciari, M. (1996), *Posthumous People: Vienna at the Turning Point*, trans. R. Friedman, Stanford, CA: Stanford University Press.

Cacciari, M. (2009a), 'Nietzsche and the Unpolitical', in A. Carrera (ed.), *The Unpolitical: On the Radical Critique of Political Reason*, trans. M. Verdicchio, New York: Fordham University Press [ebook].

Cacciari, M. (2009b), 'Project', in A. Carrera (ed.), *The Unpolitical: On the Radical Critique of Political Reason*, trans. M. Verdicchio, New York: Fordham University Press [ebook].

Cacciari, M. (2009c), 'Law and Justice: On the Theological and Mystical Dimensions of the Modern Political', in A. Carrera (ed.), *The Unpolitical: On the Radical Critique of Political Reason*, trans. M. Verdicchio, New York: Fordham University Press [ebook].

Cacciari, M. (2018), *The Withholding Power: An Essay on Political Theology*, trans. E. Pucci, London: Bloomsbury.

Cacciari, M. and R. Esposito (1988), 'Pensiero e politica', *Leggere*, 7: 15–9.

Cacciari, M. and R. Esposito (2014), 'Dialogo sulla teologia politica', ed. A. Ardovino, *MicroMega*, 2: 3–25.

Cavarero, A. (1987), 'Per una teoria della differenza sessuale', in Diotima, *Il pensiero della differenza sessuale*, 43–79, Milano: La Tartaruga.

Cavarero, A. (1995), *In Spite of Plato: A Feminist Rewriting of Ancient Philosophy*, trans. S. Anderlini-D'Onofrio and A. O'Healy, New York: Routledge.

Cavarero, A. (2002), 'Il pensiero femminista. Un approccio teoretico', in A. Cavarero and F. Restaino (eds), *Le filosofie femministe. Due secoli di battaglie teoriche e pratiche*, 78–115, Milano: Bruno Mondadori.

Colletti, L. (1975), *Intervista politico-filosofica*, Roma-Bari: Laterza.

Colletti, L. (1986), *Tramonto dell'ideologia*, Roma-Bari: Laterza.

Cusset, F. (2008), *French Theory: How Foucault, Derrida, Deleuze, & Co. Transformed the Intellectual Life of the United States*, trans. J. Fort, Minneapolis: University of Minnesota Press.

de Giovanni, B. (1976), *La teoria politica delle classi nel 'Capitale'*', Bari: De Donato.

de Giovanni, B. (1986), 'Apologia del moderno contro il pensiero debole', *il Centauro*, 17–18: 48–70.

Della Volpe, G. (1949), *Per la teoria di un umanismo positivo. Studi e documenti sulla dialettica materialistica*, Bologna: Zuffi.

Della Volpe, G. (1980), *Logic as a Positive Science*, trans. J. Rothschild, London: NLB [ebook].

Dominijanni, I. (2001), 'L'eccedenza della libertà femminile', in I. Dominijanni (ed.), *Motivi della libertà*, 47–88, Milano: FrancoAngeli.

Esposito, R. (1993), *Nove pensieri sulla politica*, Bologna: il Mulino.

Esposito, R. (2008), *Bios: Biopolitics and Philosophy*, trans. T. Campbell, Minneapolis: University of Minnesota Press.

Esposito, R. (2010), *Communitas: The Origin and Destiny of Community*, trans. T. Campbell, Stanford, CA: Stanford University Press.

Esposito, R. (2011), *Immunitas: The Protection and Negation of Life*, trans. Z. Hanafi, Cambridge: Polity Press.

Esposito, R. (2012a), *Living Thought: The Origin and Actuality of Italian Philosophy*, trans. Z. Hanafi, Stanford, CA: Stanford University Press.

Esposito, R. (2012b), *Third Person: Politics of Life and Philosophy of the Impersonal*, trans. Z. Hanafi, Cambridge and Malden: Polity Press.

Esposito, R. (2015a), *Categories of the Impolitical*, trans. C. Parsley, New York: Fordham University Press.

Esposito, R. (2015b), *Two: The Machine of Political Theology and the Place of Thought*, trans. Z. Hanafi, New York: Fordham University Press.

Esposito, R. (2019), *Politics and Negation: Towards an Affirmative Philosophy*, trans. Z. Hanafi, Cambridge-Medford, MA: Polity Press.

Esposito, R. (2022), *Institution*, trans. Z. Hanafi, Cambridge-Medford, MA: Polity Press.

Esposito, R. (2023), *Common Immunity: Biopolitics in the Age of the Pandemics*, trans. Z. Hanafi, Cambridge-Medford, MA: Polity Press.

Fischer, C., E. Franco, G. Longobardi, V. Mariaux, L. Muraro, A. Sanvitto, B. Zamarchi, C. Zamboni e G. Zanardo (1987), 'La differenza sessuale: da scoprire e da produrre', in Diotima, *Il pensiero della differenza sessuale*, 7–39, Milano: La Tartaruga.

Foucault, M. (1978), *The History of Sexuality. Volume I: An Introduction*, trans. P. Hurley, New York: Pantheon Books.

Foucault, M. (1990), '*The Art of Telling the Truth*', in L. D. Kritzman (ed.), *Politics, Philosophy, Culture: Interviews and Other Writings 1977–1984*, 86–95, New York: Routledge.

Foucault, M. (2008), *The Birth of Biopolitics: Lectures at the Collège de France, 1978–79*, ed. M. Senellart, trans. G. Burchell, New York: Palgrave Macmillan.

Garin, E. (1997), *Intervista sull'intellettuale*, ed. M. Ajello, Roma-Bari: Laterza.

Gentili, D., ed (2007), *La crisi del politico. Antologia de "il Centauro"*, Napoli: Guida.

Gramsci, A. (1971), *Selections from the Prison Notebooks*, ed. Q. Hoare and G. Nowell Smith, New York: International Publishers.

Gramsci, A. (1975), *Quaderni del carcere*, 4 vols., ed. V. Gerratana, Torino: Einaudi.

Gramsci, A. (1995), *Further Selections from the Prison Notebooks*, ed. D. Boothman, Minneapolis: Minnesota University Press.

Gramsci, A. (2000), 'The Revolution Against *Capital*', in D. Forgacs (ed.), *The Gramsci Reader: Selected Writings 1916–1935*, 32–6, New York: New York University Press.

Guattari, F. and A. Negri (2010), *New Lines of Alliance, New Spaces of Liberty*, New York: Autonomedia.

Hardt, M. and A. Negri (2000), *Empire*, Cambridge, MA and London: Harvard University Press.

Hardt, M. and A. Negri (2004), *Multitude. War and Democracy in the Age of Empire*, New York: The Penguin Press.

Hardt, M. and A. Negri (2009), *Commonwealth*, Cambridge, MA: The Belknap Press of Harvard University Press.

Hardt, M. and A. Negri (2016), *Assembly*, New York: Oxford University Press.

Hayek, F. A. (1967), 'The Principles of a Liberal Social Order', in *Studies in Philosophy, Politics and Economics*, 160–77, Chicago: University of Chicago Press.

Heidegger, M. (1993), 'Letter on Humanism', in D. Farrell Krell (ed.), *Basic Writings: Basic writings from Being and Time to The Task of Thinking*, 213–65, San Francisco: HarperOne.

Irigaray, L. (1993), *An Ethics of Sexual Difference*, trans. C. Burke and G. Gill, Ithaca, NY: Cornell University Press.

Lazzarato, M. (1997), *Lavoro immateriale. Forme di vita e produzione di soggettività*, Verona: ombre corte.

Lonzi, C. (1970), *Sputiamo su Hegel*, Roma: Scritti di Rivolta Femminile.

Lyotard, J.-F. (1984), *The Postmodern Condition. Report on Knowledge*, trans. G. Bennington and B. Massumi, Minneapolis: University of Minnesota Press.

Marramao, G. (1979), *Il Politico e le trasformazioni. Critica del capitalismo e ideologie della crisi tra anni Venti e Trenta*, Bari: De Donato.

Marramao, G. (1983), 'Metapolitica', *Laboratorio Politico*, III (1): 95–121.

Marramao, G. (1984), *Potere e secolarizzazione. Le categorie del tempo*, Roma: Editori Riuniti.

Marramao, G. (2008), *La passione del presente. Breve lessico della modernità-mondo*, Torino: Bollati Boringhieri.

Marramao, G. (2012), *The Passage West: Philosophy After the Age of the Nation State*, London-New York: Verso [ebook].

Marramao, G. (2024), *Kairós: In Defence of 'Due Time'*, trans. P. Larrey and S. Cattaneo, London- New York: Bloomsbury.

Marx, K. (2010), 'The Eighteenth Brumaire of Louis Bonaparte', in *The Collected Works of Karl Marx and Frederick Engels*, vol. 11, 99–197, London: Lawrence & Wishart.

Marx, K. (2015), *Grundrisse: Foundations of the Critique of Political Economy*, trans. M. Nicolaus, London: Penguin.

Matheron, F. (1999), *Operaïsme*, in *Dictionnaire critique du marxisme*, 816, Paris: Quadrige/PUF.

Muraro, L. (2009a), 'Introduzione di un'idea', in Diotima, *Potere e politica non sono la stessa cosa*, 5–13, Napoli: Liguori.

Muraro, L. (2009b), 'The Symbolic Independence from Power', in L. Chiesa and A. Toscano (eds), *The Italian Difference. Between Nihilism and Biopolitics*, 81–94, Melbourne: re.press.

Muraro, L. (2018), *The Symbolic Order of the Mother*, ed. T. S. Murphy, trans. F. Novello, New York: Suny Press.

Negri, A. (1976), 'Simplex sigillum veri. Per la discussione di "Krisis" e di "Bisogni e teoria marxista"', *aut aut*, 152–153: 180–95.

Negri, A. (1981), *L'anomalia selvaggia. Potere e potenza in Baruch Spinoza*, Milano: Feltrinelli.

Negri, A. (1987), *Fabbriche del soggetto. Profili, protesi, transiti, macchine, paradossi, passaggi, sovversioni, sistemi, potenze: appunti per un dispositivo ontologico*, Livorno: XXI secolo.

Negri, A. (1988), '*Marx on Cycle and Crisis*', in *Revolution Retrieved: Writings on Marx, Keynes, Capitalist Crisis and New Social Subjects (1967–83)*, 43–90, London: Red Notes.

Negri, A. (1991), *Marx Beyond Marx: Lessons on the* Grundrisse, New York-London: Autonomedia/Pluto.

Negri, A. (1999), *Insurgencies: Constituent Power and the Modern State*, trans. M. Boscagli, Minneapolis-London: University of Minnesota Press.

Negri, A. (2005a), 'Proletarians and the State: Toward a Discussion of Worker's Autonomy and the Historic Compromise', in *Books for Burning: Between Civil War and Democracy in 1970s Italy*, trans. A. Bove, E. Emery, T. S. Murphy and F. Novello, 118–79, London-New York: Verso.

Negri, A. (2005b), 'Preface to the Italian Edition: 1997 – Twenty Years Later', in *Books for Burning: Between Civil War and Democracy in 1970s Italy*, trans. A. Bove, E. Emery, T. S. Murphy and F. Novello, xxxviii–li, London-New York: Verso.

Negri, A. (2005c), 'Domination and Sabotage: On the Marxist Method of Social Transformation', in *Books for Burning: Between Civil War and Democracy in 1970s Italy*, trans. A. Bove, E. Emery, T. S. Murphy and F. Novello, 231–90, London-New York: Verso.

Negri, A. (2007a), *Dall'operaio massa all'operaio sociale. Intervista sull'operaismo*, ed. P. Pozzi and R. Tomassini, Verona: ombre corte.

Negri, A. (2007b), 'Giorgio Agamben. The Discreet Taste of the Dialectic', in M. Calarco and S. DeCaroli (eds), *Giorgio Agamben. Sovereignty & Life*, 109–25, Stanford, CA: Stanford University Press.

Negri, A. (2009), 'The Italian Difference', in L. Chiesa and A. Toscano (eds), *The Italian Difference. Between Nihilism and Biopolitics*, 13–23, Melbourne: re.press.

Negri, A. (2013), 'From the End of National Lefts to Subversive Movements for Europe', *Radical Philosophy*, 181: 26–32.

Rovatti, P. A. (1992), *Trasformazioni del soggetto: un itinerario filosofico*, Padova: il poligrafo.

Togliatti, P. (1956), *La via italiana al socialismo*, Roma: Editori Riuniti.

Togliatti, P. (1967), *Gramsci*, ed. E. Ragionieri, Roma: Editori Riuniti.

Tosel, A. (2009), *Le marxisme du 20e siècle*, Paris: Syllepse.

Tronti, M. (1961), 'Studi recenti sulla logica del *Capitale*', *Società: rivista trimestrale*, XVII (6): 881–903.

Tronti, M. (1981), 'Sinistra', *Laboratorio Politico*, I (3): 132–47.

Tronti, M. (1992), *Con le spalle al futuro. Per un altro dizionario politico*, Roma: Editori Riuniti.

Tronti, M. (2006), *Politica e Destino*, Roma: Sossella.

Tronti, M. (2009), *Noi operaisti*, Roma: DeriveApprodi.

Tronti, M. (2011), *Dall'estremo possibile*, Roma: Ediesse.

Tronti, M. (2013), *Per la critica del presente*, Roma: Ediesse.

Tronti, M. (2016a), 'Between Dialectical Materialism and Philosophy of Praxis: Gramsci and Labriola (1959)', *Viewpoint Magazine*, 3 October 2016. Available online: https://viewpointmag.com/2016/10/03/between-dialectical-materialism-and-philosophy-of-praxis-gramsci-and-labriola-1959/ (accessed 16 July 2025).

Tronti M. (2016b), 'Some Questions around Gramsci's Marxism (1958)', *Viewpoint Magazine*, 3 October 2016. Available online: https://viewpointmag.com/2016/10/03/some-questions-around-gramscis-marxism-1958/ (accessed 16 July 2025).

Tronti, M. (2019), *Workers and Capital*, trans. D. Broder, London–New York: Verso.

Tronti, M. (2020), 'The Autonomy of the Political (1972)', *Viewpoint Magazine*, 26 February 2020. Available online: https://viewpointmag.com/2020/02/26/the-autonomy-of-the-political/ (accessed 16 July 2025).

Tronti, M. (2025), *Twilight of Politics*, trans. M. Mandarini, Kolkata: Seagull Books.

Trotta, G. and F. Milana, eds (2008), *L'operaismo degli anni Sessanta. Da «Quaderni rossi» a «classe operaia»*, Roma: DeriveApprodi.

Vattimo, G. (1982), 'La "parte maledetta". Sinistra e Nichilismo', in VV. AA., *Il concetto di sinistra*, 77–86, Milano: Bompiani.

Vattimo, G. (1984), 'La filosofia del mattino', *aut aut*, 1984, 202: 2–14.

Vattimo, G. (1988a), 'Hermeneutics and Anthropology', in *The End of Modernity: Nihilism and Hermeneutics in Postmodern Culture*, trans. J. R. Snyder, 145–63, Baltimore: The Johns Hopkins University Press.

Vattimo, G. (1988b), 'Nihilism and the Post-modern in Philosophy', in *The End of Modernity: Nihilism and Hermeneutics in Postmodern Culture*, trans. J. R. Snyder, 164–81, Baltimore: The Johns Hopkins University Press.

Vattimo, G. (1988c), 'Metaphysics, Violence, and Secularization', in G. Borradori (ed.), *Recoding Metaphysics: The New Italian Philosophy*, 45–61, Evanston: Northwestern University Press.

Vattimo, G. (1993a), 'The Will to Power as Art', in *The Adventure of Difference: Philosophy after Nietzsche and Heidegger*, trans. C. Blamires, 85–109, Baltimore: The Johns Hopkins University Press.

Vattimo, G. (1993b), 'The Adventure of Difference', in *The Adventure of Difference: Philosophy after Nietzsche and Heidegger*, trans. C. Blamires, 137–57, Baltimore: The Johns Hopkins University Press.

Vattimo, G. (1993c), 'Introduction', in *The Adventure of Difference: Philosophy after Nietzsche and Heidegger*, trans. C. Blamires, 1–7, Baltimore: The Johns Hopkins University Press.

Vattimo, G. (1999), *Belief*, trans. L. D'Isanto and D. Webb, Stanford, CA: Stanford University Press.

Vattimo, G. (2012), 'Dialectics, Difference, Weak Thought', in G. Vattimo and P. A. Rovatti (eds), *Weak Thought*, trans. P. Carravetta, 39–52, Albany, NY: SUNY Press.

Vattimo, G. (2019), 'The Bottle, the Net, the Revolution, and the Tasks of Philosophy: A Dialogue with *Lotta Continua*', in P. Carravetta (ed.), *Beyond the Subject: Nietzsche, Heidegger, and Hermeneutics*, Albany: SUNY Press [ebook].

Vattimo, G. and P. A. Rovatti, eds (2010), 'Premessa', in *Il pensiero debole*, 7–11, Milano: Feltrinelli.

Virno, P. (2002), 'Citazioni di fronte al pericolo', in *Esercizi di esodo. Linguaggio e azione politica*, 159–64, Verona: ombre corte.

Virno, P. (2004), *A Grammar of the Multitude: For an Analysis of Contemporary Forms of Life*, trans. I. Bertoletti, J. Cascaito and A. Casson, Los Angeles: Semiotext(e).

Virno, P. (2007), 'So-Called "Evil" and Criticism of the State', in *Multitude: Between Innovation and Negation*, trans. I. Bertoletti, J. Cascaito and A. Casson, 11–65, Los Angeles: Semiotext(e).

Virno, P. and M. Hardt, eds (1997), *Radical Thought in Italy. A Potential Politics*, Minneapolis-London: University of Minnesota Press.

Wittgenstein, L. (2001), *Tractatus Logico-Philosophicus*, trans. F. Pears and B. F. McGuinness, London-New York: Routledge.

INDEX